W9-DBM-502

NOBLE
REFLECTIONS

Esther Kamali Prabhakar
June 14 'Never postpone to kindness'

To

_____

From

_____

For

_____

Date

_____

NOBLE
REFLECTIONS
ABIDING IN THE VINE DAY BY DAY

ESTHER PRABHAKAR

Copyright © 2012 by Esther Prabhakar.

Library of Congress Control Number:		2012902485
ISBN:	Hardcover	978-1-4691-6453-3
	Softcover	978-1-4691-6452-6
	Ebook	978-1-4691-6454-0

All rights reserved. No part of this book may be reproduced or transmitted in any form or by any means, electronic or mechanical, including photocopying, recording, or by any information storage and retrieval system, without permission in writing from the copyright owner.

This book was printed in the United States of America.

To order additional copies of this book, contact:
Xlibris Corporation
1-888-795-4274
www.Xlibris.com
Orders@Xlibris.com
110061

Contents

Photos

Dedication

To my beloved parents
**Ganugapati Noble Kantayya and Mary Kamalam
(nee Samuel)
whose daily devotion to God was reflected in their
daily Christian living**

In the world's broad field of battle
In the bivouac of Life
Be not like dumb, driven cattle!
Be a hero in the strife!
Trust no Future, howe'er pleasant
Let the dead Past bury its dead!
Act, act in the glorious Present!
Heart within and God o'erhead!
Lives of great men all remind us
We can make our lives sublime,
And, departing, leave behind us . . .
Foot prints on the sands of time.
—Henry Wadsworth Longfellow

Foreword

Through the release of this devotional book, we are honoring our father, Rev. Dr. G. Noble Kantayya, a noble servant of God whom six of us including our precious brother Jayasurya (now in Heaven) were privileged to call "*Appa.*" Although he was both a Physician and a Priest he wore only one hat . . . God's servant.

Father would often quote the adage which said one should always try to "catch time by its forelock." That is exactly what he did every day. He got up when our rooster got up in our backyard! By the way, he could imitate the rooster's call very well too! New and creative ideas popped out of his head almost every day, and he would run with it and get things done. In other words, he was a Go Getter! He did God's work with great zeal and his medical work with genuine compassion. At the same time, he made sure we were all well taken care of at home, and he would bring us delicious sweets from the famous *Lala Kadai* from time to time as a token of his love for us.

I strongly believe that whatever my father was able to accomplish in a day was the direct result of the time he spent in God's presence that morning. Our mother Mary who had a meek and quiet spirit understood her husband's calling and faithfully supported him in all his undertakings throughout his lifetime.

Before I proceed further, let me share with you a personal story. For my twelfth birthday, my father gave me a unique gift—a little book called the "The Daily Light" containing related Bible verses grouped together for daily reading from January 1 through December 31. That book has been with me ever since, and God's Word from that book has ministered to me time and time again. He did this with all his children. He also set aside for us a small room which we called "*Jeba Arai*" or Prayer Room close to our dormitory-style bedroom upstairs where one could privately meditate on God's Word and pray . . . the beginning of a good habit that has stuck with us for a lifetime.

Ever since he committed his life to Christ as a young lad, my father has been passionate about reading God's Word and having a daily time of prayer before starting the day's activities. He wrote English fluently and flawlessly and kept a small diary each year when he was a young man. He always started off the day's writing with one or two Scripture verses that spoke to him that day and then wrote down some of the activities and events of the day. His 1924 journal, however, is different from the other diaries in the sense that it is purely a record of his devotional experience for the day. Father started this journal in Masulipatinam and continued it in Madras from June onward after joining the BA degree course at Madras Christian College.

Whenever God-allowed suffering came into father's life, whether it was in his youth or midlife or old age, the diaries he had kept during most of his life reveal that he always stayed connected to God no matter what the situation in his life was like. The same God who helped him bear fruit for His Kingdom during his good times faithfully and lovingly carried him through his difficult times.

May God help us to stay connected to JESUS all the time because He has told us, "I am the vine, you are the branches. He who abides in Me, and I in him, bears much fruit; for without Me you can do nothing" (John 15:5). Praise be to God!

*Samuel *Nirmalkumar Kantayya*
Eldest Son.

---

*   "Nirmal" was the Indian name my father called himself during the Indian Nationalistic Movement days.

Editor's Reflections: My Own Dead Sea Scrolls

'Tis opportune to look back upon old times, and contemplate our forefathers. Sir Thomas Browne: *Hydriotaphia*.

Is it possible to understand people more fully after they are gone from us and appreciate them more when they are no more? Is it true that legacies left behind speak louder and bring deeper understanding to the next generation? In my case, it is "yes" to all of the above questions. My father Rev. Dr. Ganugapati Noble Kantayya was an ordinary man who accomplished extraordinary things by the grace of God. He bloomed in the new community of Palayamkottai in Southern India where he was transplanted after marriage.

After our parents Noble and Mary Kantayya went to their heavenly home, their earthly home was dismantled. All the children took a little bit of heirlooms and childhood memories with them. One such treasure I discovered in 2010 was the devotional journal of my father for the year 1924 written in his own stylish penmanship. As I read through the little, brown, frayed eighty-eight-year-old antique book of writings, I was overwhelmed by a Dead Sea Scroll discovery-like emotions. As a nineteen-year-old, *Appa* (Dad in Tamil—pronounced *up-paw*.) had the discipline and devotion to write these spiritual reflections every day.

A deep desire to preserve these and thus leave a positive path for posterity to follow in the sands of time rose in my heart. So my husband and I decided to publish *Appa*'s works, as an act of reverence and thanksgiving to honor *Appa* while serving as an inspiration to readers, young and old. The first page of each month is a scanned copy of the original, except for December where *Jehovah Nissi*—"The LORD our banner" is added by us. The rest of the devotional has been typed for easy reading. Lost or torn pages are substituted from the 1925 devotional except for December 31. One of *Appa*'s letters is inserted there. The English spelling and King James Bible language used by *Appa* is not altered. Words added by me are in italics. I penned questions or thoughts at the end of each day to kindle our own reflections. It is connected to the bold print sentence in that page.

Appa's devotional is a combination of Bible verses, poems, his own interpretation and reflections that flowed from it. He did not write this for someone else. He wrote these to set a gold standard for himself, to do good, to serve God and God's people. Writing the date of birth of loved ones in a devotional book is a custom his children follow unto this day!

What kind of world was it in 1924 when *Appa* wrote this? India was still under the rule of the British, the Governor General of India being Daniel Rufus Isaacs. The freedom movement in India was gaining momentum under charismatic leaders like Gandhi, Nehru, and Jinnah. *Appa* wore Indian outfits often in that period to identify with the movement. Elsewhere in the world, in Russia, Lenin died and Stalin took over. The Ottoman Empire founded in 1290 dissolved when Turkish President Mustafa Kemal Pasha ended the Caliphate. Calvin Coolidge was the president of USA and Walt Disney created his first cartoon—*Alice's Wonderland*. Macy's held the first Thanksgiving Parade in New York.

While the world was fast changing, all the discipline and values taught in the Kantayya household remained intact in *Appa*'s young mind. His father and mother were a God-fearing couple who passed on the unselfish, giving lifestyle to all their five children. What amazes me is the conviction with which this nineteen-year-old wrote, especially when compared to the values and interests of young people of his age!

As we take a look at *Appa*'s later life, we realize how well he carried out his convictions and passed on his values. All of us, *Appa*'s children, are active in our churches even though we belong to five different denominations. *Appa* impacted my life more than I care to admit! His emphasis on daily quiet time with God and creating the upper prayer room in our home *Shanti Alaya,* later motivated me to publish my *Pictorial Prayer Book.* His love of celebrating birthdays, organizing events, recording them, good correspondence skills, welcoming newcomers, keeping up friendships, collecting for worthy causes etc. rubbed off on me too.

Appa served God as an honorary pastor of the Church of South India. He also served the community through Red Cross, YMCA, Boys Home, Toc H, Medical Society, and Rotary Club besides educating countless poor students and relatives and finding jobs for them. He even took in two orphaned nephews and we shared our home with them!

My mother whom we call *Amma* was his perfect helpmate. She personified the Bible verse, "In quietness and confidence shall be your strength" (Isaiah 30:15).

Appa faced tough challenges physically and mentally in his later years. Yet his abiding in the vine daily gave him the strength to face the issues courageously. He wrote on December 30, 1924, "Fight the good fight of faith. Fear not death for it is the gateway to the visible presence of God." With God's help, he lived up to his high ideals of service and fought a good fight till July 26, 1981, when he was transported to the visible presence of God for his eternal rest and rewards.

Prayer and countless hours of hard work of many resulted in this book of *Noble Reflections*. We chose this title for two reasons. *Appa*'s name "Noble" was the perfect description of his "Reflections." Secondly, like my dear sister Pritha pointed out, "That is what *Appa* tried to do, reflecting on good and noble things daily, through this journal." It flows from the Bible verse from Philippians 4:8. "Whatever is true, whatever is **noble**, whatever is right . . . think about these things." The Scripture verse John 15:5, quoted by my beloved brother Sam in his Foreword supplies the Sub-Title of this book.

I pray that this reflective devotional by my father will encourage parents, teenagers, teachers, and caregivers to continue to pass on visions and values to the next generation.

"Instruct the young in the way they should go; when they are old, they may not depart from it" Proverbs 22:6.

Proud to be the fourth child in the birth order
Just like my *Amma* and *Appa*.
Esther Kamali

Esther Kamali Prabhakar.
Rochelle, IL 61068. USA.
E-mail: *esther@prabhakar.net*.

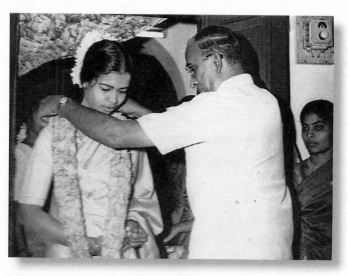

Appa garlanding Kamali on her engagement to Prabhu
on 26 December 1964

Photos of Noble's Family

Johanna & Ganugapati Krishnayya, Grandparents
of Noble

Rev. G. Krishnayya, Grandfather and Rev. G. Kantayya,
Father of Noble

The Kantayya Family 1920
Standing. Anandrao, Stephen, Nesamma, Noble
Sitting. Mary Doraichi, Sundaramma, Rev.G. Kantayya

The Family December 1928, Masulipatnam.
Standing. Dr. G.S. Krishnayya, A.G. Kantayya, Dr. G.
Noble Kantayya
Sitting. Dr. Nesamma Kantayya, Rev. G. Kantayya, Mary
Doraichi Kantayya, Sundaramma Kantayya

Ellore Parsonage, Home of the Kantayyas.

Photos of Madras Christian College Days

ICC Lodge Hostel where Noble stayed while
attending College

Noble's room and desk in ICC Lodge from where he
probably wrote this devotional journal.

MCC in the 1920's in Georgetown, Madras, where Noble
graduated with a Bachelor of Arts Degree

The graduate with three gold medals—Scripture, General
proficiency and most distinguished in the graduating class

Nirmal visited MCC in 2011. Pritha and Lavanya studied
for their Master's degree in MCC also much later

MAGDIEL

Preciousness of God,
The Mighty Tower

January

First Day in the Month of January 1924. Tuesday

Pappa Aunty's Birthday

So run that ye may obtain.
He which hath begun a good work in you will perform it until
the Day of Jesus Christ. *Philippians 1:6.*

Whether therefore ye eat or drink, or whatsoever ye do, do all
to the glory of God. Let your heart be perfect with the Lord thy
God. *I Corinthians 10:31.*

Lay aside every weight and run forward looking unto Jesus.
Dedicate the year unto the Lord and it shall be blessed indeed.
Sanctify your life every moment.

Holy life is very eloquent.

The Word of the Lord will never fail. He is merciful and will not
utterly destroy. Worship the Lord your God. He is your God and
King. Tempt Him not.

The Lord He it is that doth go before you. He will not leave
you nor forsake you. The Lord orders all things for you. He is
continually with you. Nothing can separate you from the love of
God. Be earnest and persevering in running the race that is set
before you. Look to Jesus. He is your Lord.

*"Eloquent Holy life" means your everyday life speaks for itself
by your righteous conduct and character. Would you like that
as your goal this year?*

————◄❖►————

2nd Jan '24 Wednesday

*B*e strong and of a good courage, be not afraid, neither be thou dismayed, for the Lord thy God is with thee whithersoever thou goest. *Joshua 1:9.*
Put ye on the Lord Jesus Christ and make not provision for the flesh, to fulfill the lust thereof. *Romans 13:14.*

Rejoice in the Lord. Rise out of your sleep and put on the armor of Christ. Give yourself up to the Master. Be just and true. Find out good qualities and be silent about imperfections in others. See that all things are done in and by love. That is the supreme panacea for all ills. The Word of the Lord will surely come to pass. Be filled with the Spirit of the Lord.

Pray without ceasing. The Lord will surely hear your cry and not turn a deaf ear. Abide in the love of Christ. He is able to subdue all things. Consecrate yourself to the Master for His service.

You can, with God's help, rule by Love.

It is not impossible with Him. With brotherly kindness rebuke one another.

Are you willing to let God "rule by love" in your life?

———⋅❸⋅❿⋅———

3rd Jan '24 Thursday

*E*ven to your old age am I He, and even to hoar hairs will I carry you. I have made and I will bear, even I will carry and will deliver you. *Isaiah 46:4.*

The Lord shall guide thee continually.

The Lord knoweth the way He is leading you by. Fear not, He keeps you like the apple of His eye. He is your God.

Bring your heart to Jesus and He will look after it.

Yield to it. Remember that your life is a consecrated one. All that the Lord says will come to pass. He is able to do great things. At His word, diseases fly. Many things can be done in love.

Cooperation pays. People united together can work for the good of mankind as a whole. Disobedience to the Word of the Lord will always end in dismissal from His presence. Spend much time in secret with Jesus alone. See the Lord at all times. You are God's Holy temple. Strive to do God's will. Ask that your eyes be opened. The Lord is great. The Lord will teach you what to do if you lean on Him.

What does "bring your heart to Jesus" mean to you?

————⊰⊱————

4ᵗʰ Jan '24 Friday

*T*here remaineth therefore a rest to the people of God.
Set your affection on things above, not on things on the earth.
Colossians 3:2.

I'll come to Thee, O Jesus Christ!
I'll Thy disciple be;
Not tears, not deeds, but self I'll bring,
Because Thou callest me—B. Waugh

The rest which the Lord gives is enviable. He will wipe away all
tears from your eyes. Ask and plead for God's Presence always.
Live well in your own place. Fight well your battles.

**Look for all that's good and strong in all you meet. Imitate
it.**

Strive after righteousness. Cooperation requires many virtues.
Individual service is easier. Cleave unto the Lord your God. He
will order all things for you. The Lord can make you a fisher of
men. Trust Him.

Wherever you are and whatever you be, God is with you. He
orders and overrules all things and He will never forsake you.
Everyone who trusts in Him is under His loving care and so is
safe.

Take an inventory of all that is good in your family

————◦❀◦————

5th Jan '24 Saturday

*F*ather, whatever of earthly bliss
Thy sovereign will denies,
Accepted at Thy throne of grace
Let this petition rise.
Give me a calm and thankful heart,
From every murmur free:
The blessings of Thy grace impart,
And make me live to Thee.

Before you begin, consider; and When you have considered, act.—Cicero

Come unto me, all ye that labour and are heavy laden, and I will give you rest. *Matthew 11:28.*

Ask the Lord to keep a watch on your lips. Put off anger and all filthy communication.

The Lord wills your sanctification.

Be harmless and blameless.

Look up the word "sanctification."

———◈◆◈———

6th Jan '24 Sunday

*C*ourage, brothers! Do not stumble,
Though thy path be dark as night;
There's a star to guide the humble;
"Trust in God, and do the right."
Though the road be long and dreary,
And its ending out of sight,
Foot it bravely—strong or weary;
"Trust in God and do the right."—N. Macleod.

Full of joyful hope, patient under persecution, earnest and persistent in prayer.—*Romans 12:12.*

Fear the Lord and walk in His paths. Commit your ways unto Him. Work out your salvation with fear and trembling. Christ sticks close to you.

You are Christ's friend.

Ask for guidance. Courage! Do not stumble. Trust in God and do the right. Be joyful and persistent in prayer. Raise the standard of Christ high.

Do you consider yourself as Christ's friend? Explain.

7ᵗʰ Jan '24 Monday

*W*ho like Thyself my guide and Stay can be?
Through cloud and sunshine, Lord, abide with me!
Oh how we need from day to day
A guiding hand for all the way;
Oh how we need from hour to hour
That faithful ever present power!

Hold fast the Lord's hand and all will be safe. He will shield you from suffering and lead you on. Seek the Lord in your faith. The Lord will keep His Word. The Lord will at all times seek to do you good. You have but to submit. He will bless you.

The Lord is your Guide. You live by faith. The Lord will never forsake you.

The Lord is always mindful of you.

He will save you. The Lord will perform mighty things. He is a zealous God and will not leave alone those that trust in Him. He is your God and He will bless you. Only trust in Him.

How can you remind yourself of God's presence at all times?

————⟨⊰⊱⟩————

8ᵗʰ Jan '24 Tuesday

I will trust and not be afraid: for the Lord Jehovah is my strength and my song: He also is become my salvation. *Psalm 118:14.*

More of Thy presence, Lord, impart,
More of Thine image let me bear:
Erect Thy Throne within my heart,
And reign without a rival there.

The Lord your God is a strong tower. He will not forsake you. He is your Helper. Do what the Lord bids you to. Do everything in the best way possible. Remember at all times to humble yourself. The Word and dealings of the Lord are always good.

All power is given to the Son of man.

Have faith in God and He will work wonders before you.

The Lord is able to keep you blameless and spotless, if only you submit yourself to His will. Look unto Jesus. Be true and loving. Evildoers bring ruin upon *those* connected with them. Follow the Lord. He calls you.

Give examples of the power of God.

9th Jan '24 Wednesday

*W*e are more than conquerors through Him that loved us. *Romans 8:37.*

Be strong in the Lord—Valiant for the truth—fighting the Lord's battles.
Be strong and work—fear ye not.

Rejoice in the Lord who is your strength. Be brave for the Lord is with you. The Lord goes before you. Love God with all your heart.

Brighten darkened lives, soften the road for others.

Be loving. Be gentle. Let Christ's Image grow in you. Do that which is right in God's sight and He will send for peace on all sides. Feel His Presence.

Desire earnestly communion with God. The Lord, He is your God. Give to others freely and the Lord will bless you. Take and give pleasure. Do gentle deeds. Make the world better for your living in it. Continue often and long in prayer. Do good to all. Seek to promote the fear of the Lord. Fear not to do what is right for God strengthens you.

Whose dark road are you going to brighten today?

10ᵗʰ Jan '24 Thursday

*B*elieving that Jesus died—will save nobody—is simply a matter of history.
Believing that Jesus died for me—will save anybody—this is an act of faith.

He loved me and gave Himself for me.
Let the peace of God rule your mind and heart. *Philippians 4:7.* and you shall never be troubled. Worries may prove stepping stones. Brighten other's lives.

Make the best of life while you do live.

Seek the Lord. Many are so closely connected with you that your actions, good or bad, tell upon them. Let the Spirit of the Lord be upon you.

Never be troubled but at all times rest in the Lord. Live each day well.

Your body is the temple of the Holy Ghost. *I Corinthians 6:19.* The Lord God, most Holy will dwell there in. Keep it worthy for Him.

If this is the last day of your life, how will you live differently?

———— ⸰❀⸰ ————

11ᵗʰ Jan '24 Friday

*J*udge not, that thou be not judged. *Matthew 7:1.*

Let us be silent about others' weakness whoso offereth praise glorifieth me and to Him that ordereth His conversation aright will I show the salvation of God.

Be not hasty in faultfinding. Be not anxious. Give others their due. Praise the Lord at all times. The Lord is your God and Father.

The Lord punishes evil. He gives many chances. Beware! Rejoice and be glad when you suffer for Christ.
Submit yourself to the Lord your God.

Be at peace with all men.

Control yourself. Humble yourself before all. Be cheerful and serve the Lord. Let your acquaintance be for good to all.

What can you do today to be at peace with all?

———•❖•———

12th Jan '24 Saturday

*L*et us then be what we are, and speak what we think, and in all things keep ourselves loyal to the truth.—Longfellow.

Acquaint now yourself with Him and be at peace.
Sacrifice yourself and then alone will you be of any use to others.

Don't look for faults and flaws. Make the best of life.

Be good natured. Be wise spiritually. Ask earnestly of the Lord.

Love your enemies and do good to them. Return not evil for evil. Pray for all. Serve the Lord.

It is more blessed to give than to receive. *Acts 20:35.*

Seek the Lord while He may be found. *Isaiah 55:6.*

He has a place prepared for you. Be not troubled. Be a child of light and of God. Do to all men as you would they should do to you. Love all men. Do good never asking for a return.

What did you do this past Christmas to prove that it is, "blessed to give than to receive"?

———·✥·———

13ᵗʰ Jan '24 Sunday

*B*eware of two enemies—
The Devil and yourself.

Guide me, O Thou Great Redeemer
Pilgrim through this barren land
I am weak, but Thou art mighty,
Hold me with Thy powerful hand.

We never have more than we can bear. The present hour we are always able to endure.

As our day, so is our strength.

Forgive others even as you hope to be forgiven. Hear not nor give thought to evil reports about others. Trust in the Lord and be at peace. Be not anxious.

Le not your heart be troubled. *John 14:1.*

The peace of God will keep your heart and mind.
Cherish Christian love. Help others onward.

Be angry and sin not. *Ephesians 4:26.*

Forgive as Christ forgives. Evil is surely punished. The Lord will be gracious if you repent.

Ask God for strength enough for today, January 13.

14th Jan '24 Monday

Appa's Birthday

The blessing of the Lord it maketh rich and He addeth no sorrow there to. *Proverbs 10:22.*

Holiness unto the Lord. *Exodus 28:36.*

I, even I, am He that comforteth you. *Isaiah 51:12.*

The Lord your God is very merciful. He has spared you and blessed you richly. Be merciful to others as the Father has been merciful to you. Do good, hoping for no reward. With what measure you mete with the same shall it be measured to you again. You are your Father's child. Keep His commandments and abide in His Love.

Trust in the Lord to order all things for you. One step is enough for you.

Make the best use of all things put within your reach. Be grateful for all you receive at His hands. The Lord suffered for you, leaving you an example.

All power is given to your Saviour. Fear not, Satan will be put down under your feet. Keep the commandments of the Lord. Bring forth fruit worthy of Repentance.

Is one step ahead enough for you?

———— ·❀❀· ————

15ᵗʰ Jan '24 Tuesday

O Though bounteous Giver of all good,
Thou art of all Thy gifts Thyself the crown
Give what Thou canst, without Thee we are poor,
And with Thee rich, take what Thou wilt away.—Cowper

Be affectionate.

You have peculiar gifts.

Use them to the best advantage. Have the Lord your God as Your own. Abstain from Fleshly lusts. Cleave not to the dust. Subject yourself to Christ.

Wash, make clean and learn to do well. The Lord has washed away your sins and you are saved. Hearken unto the voice of the Lord and keep His commandments.

Have faith in the Lord. Judge not one another. The Lord God is mighty to save. *Isaiah 63:1.*

Nothing is impossible with Him. Fear not; only believe. *Mark 5:36.*

Name some peculiar gifts that you have.

16th Jan '24 Wednesday

O Love of God! How strong and true,
Eternal, and yet ever now;
Uncomprehended and unbought,
Beyond all knowledge and all thought.—H. Borar

In the fear of the Lord is strong confidence; and his children shall have a place of refuge.

You have received all from Christ.

Love the Lord. Do little things for the sake of Christ. God is Truth. Do not mind humbling yourself to exalt Christ.

The Lord He alone is God. His service is pleasant. Great is the love of God. Love is patient and kind. Be not jealous. *I Corinthians 13:4.*

Have faith in God. Hope and Love all.

Count some of your blessings you have received from Christ.

———·❧❦·———

17ᵗʰ Jan '24 Thursday

*T*he gate of heaven is love. There is no other. When generous acts bloom from unselfish thoughts the Lord is with us, though we know it not.—L. Larcom

Let everything be done for love, nothing for fear.

The Lord is very merciful. He hears the prayers of them that call on Him. By loving others you will do the will of God.

The Lord God is mighty. He forgives the truly repentant. Repent and return to the Shepherd and Bishop of your soul.
The Word of the Lord is a Lamp to your feet. *Psalm 119:105.*

Put on the armour of Light. Love as many people as you can. Belong to the Lord.

Mighty is God and worthy of praise. Such as trust Him will surely be rewarded.

Why do you prefer to do things for love rather than fear?

⬦⬦⬦

18th Jan '24 Friday

*I*f we love others as Christ loves them we will always seek to please them. We will always be gentle and kind, speaking in love when we must say anything unpleasant, anything that will give pain.—J. R. Miller

Do all things for love. Christ is your Exemplar. He died for you. Seek to please Him at all times.

God hates the proud. Humble yourself and cease from man who is but as a passing breath.

The Word of the Lord is mighty & able to save.

You know not when the Lord will come. Let your lamp be trimmed and bright against His coming.

Love is the Supreme virtue.

Love God, love all. Every man will reap the consequence of his deeds. Have faith in God. Christ is Lord of all.

Read I Corinthians 13, the love chapter.

19th Jan '24 Saturday

*N*one of us can measure the power of endurance in the love of God. It watches over us during the hours of our insensibility to its presence summoning us to arise to a nobler better life, more worthy of ourselves, more glorifying to Him.—F. B. Merv.

Think no evil, much less repeat it. Believe that God hears you. Serve the Lord with humility of mind.

Rejoice in simplicity. Honour all men and you will be honoured. Righteousness will never be unrewarded.

Rise to a nobler, better life; for Jesus calls you to such a life.

Yield not to your wayward desires. The Lord for your sake has suffered and bled and died. Be not proud and lofty. Be not carried away by the world. Seek the Lord and you shall find Him

Appa was named after Rev. Turlington Noble, an English missionary to his State in India. Look him up in the Internet. Noble lived upto his name Noble.

20th Jan '24 Sunday

*G*row three ways, like a tree—downward, in love to Jesus; upward, nearer to God; outward, refreshing others round you.—M. E. Briscoe.

Cast all thy care on God. See that all thy cares be such as though canst cast on God, and then hold none back.—E. B. Pusey.

Let love shine through all your conduct. Love God, and love your brother man. The Lord, Emmanuel, is with you. He is your Saviour. Fear not; for He shall counsel and direct you.

Forget others' weak points. Be loving all the same. Do loving acts and make life a pleasure to all. You are His. He loves you. Glorify Him. Make use of your opportunities and waste them not. The Lord is merciful. Grieve not His loving heart with wayward behaviour.

Pray that you grow three ways like the tree.

————⟨❖⟩————

21st Jan. '24 Monday

*T*hat you may be loved, be worthy to be loved. Deep love can do much, even when in deep poverty.—Selected.

If you do not love, you know not God, for God is love. *1 John 4:8.*

The Lord will help you to walk in His ways. You shall be strengthened. The Lord will refine you for He loves you. Help others to stand.

The Lord God is worthy of praise and exaltation. His works are great and wonderful. Hear the Word, keep it and you shall have eternal life.

Humble yourself under the mighty hand of God. The Lord hates pride. Be contrite and broken in spirit. Be not hasty to get angry. Be loving.

The Lord's upholding hand will be with you. Make good use of all your talents, your sight, hearing, i.e. Let others see it in you.

Do you know God? Do you know how to love?

22ⁿᵈ Jan '24 Tuesday

*T*his God is our God for ever and ever; He will be our guide even unto death.

Whom have I in heaven but Thee? And there is none upon earth that I desire beside Thee. *Psalm 73:25.*

Lean hard on the Lord. Trust also in Him for His mercy endures forever. He alone is God.

Loving is its own best return and reward.

Love is the best thing in the world and is peace. Hear the Word of the Lord and do it. Have faith in Him and He will uphold you.

Holy fellowship with others is always elevating. Cultivate good Christian friendship. Serve the Lord conjointly.

Be anxious to do good acts and to hide yourself. Be it not known that you have done it. Give all the glory to Christ to whom it is due.

Ask God to help you love, not expecting anything.

———⟨❸⟩⟨❿⟩———

23rd Jan '24 Wednesday

O Love that will not let me go,
I rest my weary soul on Thee;
I give Thee back the life I owe
That in Thine ocean depths its flow
May richer, fuller be.—G. Matheson

Friendship can be firm only on a stock of known and reciprocal merit. Judge not others rashly. Love all.

Trust in the Lord and your mind will be at peace. Christ is your forerunner and surety. Rejoice in hope. Evil will reap punishment.

The Lord is able to do mighty things, only trust in his great power.

If you want to follow Christ, you must be prepared for insult and dishonour.

Glory in the Cross.

If you suffer now, you shall reign hereafter. Consider the greatness of God and His loving care over such tiny creatures as men.

Can you really "Glory in the cross"?

————◈◈◈————

24th Jan '24 Thursday

*W*ish rather to be well spoken of than to be rich.

Presence of mind is courage.

Be strong and of a good courage.—*1 Chronicles 28:20.*

Be true and honest and your character will be sublime. Owe no man anything but love all. Trust in God and go ahead.

The Lord is at hand. Be diligent therefore. Be patient. The Lord God most holy is worthy of all praise.

Go and show your people the great things God has done for you.

Bring forth fruit worthy of repentance and of your Master Christ. Abstain from all fleshy lusts.

Be what you are, say what you think. In all things be sincere. Be not overbearing or arrogant. Do not let down Christ by your behaviour. Serve the Lord.

How about sharing some answered prayers with someone today?

————⋅◈⋅————

25th Jan '24 Friday.

Mother Mary Doraichi's Birthday

$\mathcal{T}$he Lord thy God: He it is that doth go before thee; He will not leave thee not forsake thee.

Rejoice, and again I say unto you, Rejoice. *Philippians 4:4.*

Be single hearted. Take good care of your character. Let your character be solid and full of the Love of God. Christ died for you and saved you from death eternal. Count all earthly things as nothing.

Believe and you shall be established.

Faith can work great wonders. The Master is mighty.

Be a child of God, for He is your Father and you are His son. Serve the Lord with love and joy. Put what you believe into practice. The Lord will preserve you. Be prepared to do great as well as small things. The Lord God is mighty. Trust in His great power. He will provide for you all things.

Write three things you believe about God.

26th Jan '24 Saturday

*B*e wakeful, all you, and keep on praying, that you may not come into temptation. *Mark 14:38.*

Here you have no continuing city. Live as a citizen of Heaven. Serve the Lord at all times honestly. Be not lazy.

Guard yourself against pride. Be watchful. The blessing of the Lord, it maketh rich. Abstain from evil.

Be a worthy disciple of Christ. Pray unceasingly.

The Lord can work wonders. There shall be no weeping in heaven, all will be joy.

Never yield to sloth. Take the Lord your God as your Guide.

Review your acts always at night fall.

Give no place to vengeance. The Lord He is God.

Review your actions of the day—What pleased God and what did not please God?

27th Jan '24 Sunday

*T*he Gift of God is eternal life through Jesus Christ our Lord. *Romans 6:23.*

Mine be the reverent, listening love
That waits all day on Thee,
With the service of a watchful heart
Which no one else can see.—A. L. Waring

Watch. Ponder the end. Keep your eye heavenward but do not fall into sin. Your well-being depends on yourself. Be ready. Never procrastinate. Pass your time here with fear.

Christ was made sin for your sake. If you love Christ, serve Him.

Choose life and not death. *II Kings 18:32.*

You are saved through Christ.

Evil days come as punishment. Take heed to the warnings of the Lord and beware. The way of Glory is through suffering. Be not surprised if you encounter disappointments or reverses.

Any life-changing decisions awaiting you today?

————⟨⟩————

28th Jan '24 Monday

*W*atch! 'tis your Lord's command,
And while we speak He's near;
Mark the first signal of His Hand
And ready all appear.—Dr. Dodding

As thy days so shall thy strength be.

I can do all things through Christ which strengtheneth me.
Philippians 4:13.

Keep out of the way of sin.

You cannot be too careful. Watch your thoughts. Be not anxious about anything. His grace is sufficient for you. Glory in His might.

The Lord God most High and Holy hates hypocrisy. Deny yourself, take up the Cross and follow Christ.

The Lord is a kind father. Affliction is but a forerunner of great blessings. The Lord is your Shepherd. Do nothing inconsistent with the honour of your high calling. Watch and pray.

Get into new forms of service. You are to be a sign and a wonder to all people. The Lord is with you. Pray.

Some sins we can definitely keep out. What are they?

———— ·❸·❀· ————

29th Jan '24 Tuesday

*D*ependence on God does not mean sitting still: it means in part letting God use us to put at man's disposal all the potential service which is still folded in our new knowledge of natural law.—Hefordick.

Understand dependence on God as doing your duty and trusting in Him. He waits to do things through man. Do things rather than speak of them. Deeds never die. The Lord weighs actions. The Lord sees you. The Lord knows all and nothing is hid from Him.

Ponder your actions.

The zeal of the Lord will perform wonders. The Lord gives joy.

What you do in God's name lasts forever. Speak not of those who are your foes. Love them.

Obey the Lord. Praise the Lord at all times. Present yourself to God. Repent and return unto the Lord your God.

Be not faithless but believing. *John 20:27.*

The Lord will honour the faith of such as trust in His Love. All is vanity. Only he that keepeth God's commands shall abide for evermore.

Take time to be holy. Ponder and weigh your actions.

————⟨⊛⟩————

30th Jan '24 Wednesday

*L*et us run with patience the race that is set before us, looking unto Jesus the author and finisher of our faith. *Hebrews 12:1.*

Look to Jesus. Take up your Cross and follow the Lord. Be temperate in all things.

Rise and be doing.

Act well at each moment. Be gentle in thought. Doing good is a happy thing. Have good friends. Go and preach the gospel to all men. Fear no ill. Humble yourself for you are only an instrument in God's hands. Be childlike and a ministering angel.

Keep your sympathies awake. Scatter joy all around. Be steadfast in the hour of need, gentle in thought and benevolent in deed. Do good. Humble yourselves under the mighty hand of God. Walk in the laws of the Lord from your youth up. Use your money for the service of God. The Lord is not angry forever.

He is kind and merciful. Be not harsh but humble and loving.

Who and What are involved in "Rise?"

———•❧❦•———

31ˢᵗ Jan '24 Thursday

*K*eep true, never be ashamed of doing right; decide on what you think is right, and stick to it.—G. Elliot

Count your many blessings name them one by one
And it will surprise you what the Lord hath done.—*Johnson Oatman Jr.*

All you do and say you will have to account at the last day. Return good for evil. Do the right and fear not. Fight the good fight of faith. You are a conqueror through Christ's Love. Oust the evil one. Harness your skill and knowledge to the greater usefulness of mankind and glory of God. The knowledge of the Lord will drive out all evil. Hesitate not to follow the Lord. Go forward. He will lead you on.
If God is for you, you need fear nothing. Christ justifies you through His Blood.

You are responsible for your actions.

Be not restless. Trust God for guidance in your thoughts. Do good to all. Be a spiritually minded man of the World! Be alive to the needs of all men. Serve. The Word of the Lord is sure and man in trying to disprove it only proves himself foolish. Pray more and work more.

Have you taken responsibility for your actions?

———◁◈▷———

Eliezer

My God is Help   February

First Day in the Month of February. Friday

I will go in the strength of the Lord God: I will make mention of Thy righteousness, even of Thine only.

We walk by faith, not by sight. *II Corinthians 5:7.*

God is Love. Dwell in God. Blessed are you if your hope and trust is in the Lord. Do everything in the name of Jesus Christ. Yield entirely to Him. Mind your business. Do things in the best way possible. Your desire to help others must be coupled with knowledge as to how you can do it. The Lord JEHOVAH is your strength. He is great. Rejoice in that your salvation is secure.

Jesus Christ is yours.

Follow the Lord in His forward movement. Serve Him with an open and eager mind. You are clothed in the Righteousness of God and henceforth you are not your own. Count all things but loss. Let God dominate your actions. Your deeds are your angels, good or bad. It is better to be envied than pitied! Terribly will wickedness be punished if unrepented. He will not leave things alone. Do not forget the many privileges you have. Make the best use you can of them.

How did Jesus become yours?

———◈◈◈———

2nd Feb '24 Saturday

O let Thy sacred will
All Thy delight in me fulfil!
Let me not think an action mine own way
But as Thy love shall sway,
Resigning up the rudder to Thy skill.—G. Herbert

Ask for grace so to live and die as to be Christ's in heaven. Forget injuries. Do any action which makes you better, fearing none. The Lord will deliver you out of temptation. Be content with what God gives you. You have to advance with time in all things of morality or else you will be thrown out of the march. The Lord turns tables. Keep His Laws of Love and you will have Eternal life. Love God and man as self.

Humble yourself under the mighty hand of God. *I Peter 5:6.*

Serve all mankind as Jesus your Master has done. Forget yourself. Be not a slave to evil but a Victor through Jesus. Praise the Lord for his great acts. Go forward, not lagging behind. Keep company with your unoppressive God. Rejoice not in iniquity. The Lord God omnipotent reigneth.

Be a Good Samaritan to someone. Go.

Thank God for your good Samaritan.
Think about how you can be one.

————— ⦿ —————

3rd Feb '24 Sunday

I can do all things through Christ which strengtheneth me. Philippians 4:13.

Strengthen ye the weak hands, and confirm the feeble knees. Say to them that are of a fearful heart. Be strong, fear not.

Be not weary in well-doing. *Galatians 6:9.*

The Lord will give you victory. Be strong in the Lord. Abide in Him. Search your heart and remove all evil in it. Self-examination is good. Is your life pleasing to God? Use all your new powers in the service of God. Advance, for 'tis your Lord's command. The Lord punishes sin.

Sit at Jesus' feet and learn of Him.

Be not anxious about many things.

Man cannot hide himself from God. The Lord watches over you and no evil shall befall you. Be a true child of God. Your heart is open before God. Put your sins aside.

Make use of science to help mankind. There is fresh power in it. Evil certainly will be punished. Ask Him to teach you to pray.

When was the last time you were at Jesus' feet?

4th Feb '24 Monday

*N*o man, having put his hand to the plough, and looking back, is fit for the kingdom of God. *Luke 9:62.*

He which hath begun a good work in you will perform it until the day of Jesus Christ. *Philippians 1:6.*

Always go forward, holding the Banner of Christ before you. Seek a better country and be not satisfied with the present one. Bear patiently all that others inflict on you.

Be kind. Realize the power of kindness and do good. Be not slack in your work. Make the best use of all that is put within your reach. Look unto the Lord your Maker. He is mighty to save. Except He bless, all is vain. Ask earnestly and you will get the Holy Spirit. Be not slack.

Take heed lest you fall. Judge not one another. Forbear. Strengthen the weak and feeble. Reprove others meekly. Try kindness with all as a remedy for a while. Be slow to anger.

Take advantage of up-to-date means and work out the salvation of all. The Lord is mindful of them who fear Him and He punishes iniquity.

Be on Christ's side taking part in His work.

Have you ever gone to the other side? How do you come back?

———⋅◈⋅———

5th Feb '24 Tuesday

*N*o earthly father loves like Thee,
No mother e'er so mild,
Bears and forbears as Thou hast done
With me Thy sinful child.—Fabey

In Christ Jesus you have life eternal. He is your Saviour and verily you are His. *Our* life and actions should be in harmony with each other. Do your duties, pleasantly and humbly.

He gives you sense and strength enough for your tasks.

Trust and go ahead. The Lord God, just and right is He. His majesty how great! Hear the Word of the Lord and keep it. Learn to be what you ought to be. Advance with the times in your area of service.

If you are out and out for Christ, you shall shine in His glory. The chastening of the Lord works salvation of the soul. Consider your duty as your Father's Business. Harbour no malice against any. Finish the work you have begun. The age of miracles has not passed away. God can work through man's knowledge of laws for the service of humanity. The Lord abhors sin. Repent and return unto the Lord. Let others see your light.

Rejoice in the Lord your God. *Joel 2:23*.

For what job do you need extra strength from the Lord today?

6th Feb '24 Wednesday

*T*he task of Thy wisdom hath assigned,
Oh, let me cheerfully fulfil;
In all Thy Works Thy Presence find,
And prove Thine acceptable Will.—C. Wesley.

The Lord is exceedingly gracious and by His mercy hath He visited us. Consider the condescension of Jesus and His Love to save humanity. Meet your daily duties with pleasure and the day will leave you happy. Work for the kingdom of God. Bring the strong tower of Satan into the notice of Jesus Christ your Captain and He will help you to pull them down. Watch. The Lord hates hypocrisy. Rise, play the man and serve the Lord. Face life and its great possibilities hopefully.

Watch for you know not when the Son of Man comes. *Matthew 25:13.*

Put on the armour of Light. *Ephesians 6:11.*

Pray without ceasing. Work for God's Kingdom. Commit yourself to the Lord. Be not a stumbling block to any. Let your words and deeds agree. Live for great things not only for eating and drinking. The Lord's eye is not blind. He knows all. Be of the maximum use to all mankind. Live to serve others.

Master your wayward self.

What wayward behaviour can you identify and change?

———⊰⊱———

7th Feb '24 Thursday

*M*ake my mortal dreams come true,
With the good I fain would do:
Clothe with life
the weak intent;
Let me be the thing I meant.—J. G. Whittier

Trust the Lord. Be not anxious about things beyond your reach. Work steadfastly. Be in all things a man of honour. Praise the Lord at all times. Be thankful and not *ungrateful.*

The Blessing of the Lord makes you rich. *Proverbs 10:22.*

Bless the Lord. The Lord exalteth and He alone abaseth. Fear the Lord your God. Be not a hypocrite. The Lord is able. Do not sleep over matters. Work whole-heartedly and be not behind the times. The Lord is gracious and full of mercy. Watch and pray. Jesus Christ is ever the same and ready to uphold. Receive all with joy.

Be in all things a man of honour.

Submit your will to God. New occasions teach new duties. Christ raises all the forces you have and makes the best use you can with them. The Lord rules over all. He is indeed mighty. The Lord is very mindful of you. Confess Christ before men.

Be not anxious about anything. *Philippians 4:6.*

What does being "a person of honor" entail?

———◈◈◈———

8th Feb '24 Friday

*B*e not downcast at present disappointments, but consider them as God's appointments. They forebode great success in after life, which if used aright would help the brotherhood.

Work and leave the rest into God's hands. Be what you ought to be.

Care more for the quality rather than the quantity of your work.

Keep the commands of Jesus. You should know the will of God. Keep your hands clean. Trust in God and do the right. He will guide you. Be anxious to do good. Be not self-centered. Fear not to serve the Lord. Pray more.

Care for the weak and maimed in your acquaintances. Do your best to bring them to Jesus Christ. You are built up a glorious edifice in Jesus. Praise and magnify the name of the Lord. You are saved because of Blood and Atonement. Do God's work in your daily tasks with joy and earnestness.

God works along with you if your work be for the advancement of public weal.

Seek the Kingdom of God first. *Matthew 6:33.*

Is your work more quantity rather than quality?

9th Feb '24 Saturday

O Saviour, give us then Thy grace
To make us pure in heart,
That we may see Thee face-to-face
Hereafter as Thou art.

The Lord is He that comforts you. Fear not, only lean on His Love. Work strenuously. In serving God you find great delight. Do your work with honesty. The Lord's counsels are always faithfulness and truth. He is your one God. The Lord is your Refuge in the storm. He will quell your enemies.

The Lord is very mindful of you. *Psalm 115:12.*

Trust and obey. Pray more. Let not your manhood be un-rich. Let not prosperity or riches turn your head. Be simple and childlike.

Be prepared to meet the Lord. Whatsoever you find to do, do it honestly and wholeheartedly. Praise the Lord at all times. Rest will follow labour. Receive all with thanksgiving from His hands. The Lord will reward your labours.

Pray and work for peace and justice. Work against poverty but rooting out the causes of it. The Lord is with you. The Lord is Himself Victory. He will save you. Be glad and rejoice in His Name. Have faith in God for He is very mindful of you and is your Guard. Trust and Rejoice.

Why is God mindful of us?

———⟨❊⟩———

10th Feb '24 Sunday

*T*he night cometh when no man can work. *John 9:4.*

With smiles of peace and looks of love,
Light in our dwellings we may make;
Bid kind good humour brighten there,
And do all, still for Jesus' sake.—C F. Alexander

Be angry and sin not. *Ephesians 4:26.*

Stay the angry blow and fight the evil-one. You suffer for your anger. Make yourself what you wish to be. Keep your eyes open to the beautiful things of God's Word. Keep your mind and body holy.

Do your best to stand by the wronged and oppressed.

Trust in the Lord Jehovah for ever. Your father knows what you need. Be calm.

Forsake not your Lord and Master. He suffered and bled and died for you. Raise your soul so high that offence cannot reach you. Be not a slave to sin or anger. Strive for equality. Serve the Lord and mankind. Desire to be like your Master. The Lord is mighty to save. Seek the kingdom of God and His righteousness. He will bless you abundantly. He is ready to bless.

Can you think of ways in which you can stand by the oppressed?

————·❧❦·————

11th Feb '24 Monday

*B*lessed is the man that trusts in the Lord, and whose hope the Lord is. *Jeremiah 17:7.*

Ah Lord, I have such feeble faith,
Such feeble hope to comfort me;
But love it is, is strong as death,
And I love Thee.—C. Rossetti

The Lord is with them that fear Him.

Exhort one another. *I Thessalonians 5:11.*

Let not the deceitfulness of sin entrap you. Take great care of your words for you will have to give account of them. Forgiveness is giving. Love your brethren even as Jesus Christ loved you. Go and follow the Maker faithfully. The Lord will ordain peace for you. Obey and serve Him alone. Call on Him for succour. Watch and wait for the coming of the Lord. Try and be like Christ and you'll win men.

Let the Christianity you profess drive out all ignorance and evil.

Serve the Lord by doing all the good you can. The blessing of the Lord makes you rich. Trust and put your hope in His goodness. No duty is hard if you trust and obey. Love all. Return good for evil. The Lord will watch over you and keep you. Be ready; for the Son of Man comes at an hour you do not expect Him.

Name an ignorant belief in you that Christianity drove out.

———⬦⬦⬦———

12ᵗʰ Feb '24 Tuesday

I love to think that God appoints
My portion day by day;
Events of life are in His hand,
And I would only say,
Appoint them in Thine own good time
And in Thine own best way.

Fear the Lord and be wise. Persevere and hope. Give reproof gently and in the right spirit. Be careful in your speech. You are Christ's and Christ is God's. Be truly His. Be prepared to meet the Lord. Be very cautious as to how you do things. Wound none unnecessarily. The Lord is just and righteous.

The more you are given the greater will be your responsibility.

Prepare the Way of the Lord. *Matthew 3:3.*

Put the glorious maxims of Christ unto practice. That would be true Christianity. Think twice before you speak once and you will not regret your words. Love the Lord and serve Him. Thirst after the true and living God.

You shall be like Him when Christ appears. The Lord will give you rest. Learn hard and study His Word. Be not surprised if you find diversions on account of the Christ. Be watchful for the Lord comes soon.

How are you giving back?

———⟨③⧈⟩———

13ᵗʰ Feb '24 Wednesday

O Lord! My best desires fulfil,
And help me to resign
Life, health and comfort to Thy Will
And make Thy pleasure mine.—Cowper.

Take instruction and be wise. Admire great things. Learn the price of a blessing before it is removed from you. Be grateful. You live this out. Forget not that your life should be in harmony with His. Let not the love of money drag you into all sorts of sin. The Lord is wonderful in counsel and excellent in working. Except you repent too, you shall also perish.

The Word of the Lord quickens you. *Psalm 119:107.*

You are Christ's and hence a conqueror. Let your speech be better than silence or be silent. Cultivate such silence as is golden. The Lord is your judge. Economic struggle is ingrained with selfishness.

Fear not the opposition part. It is the devil which leads and he must go down before the Triumphant Christ. The Lord is the great Judge and He orders all sentences. Trust in His infinite wisdom. Make use of the time given you. Repent ere it be too late.

He waits for fruits.

Meditate on the "fruit of the Spirit" as found in Galatians 5:22, 23.

————⋅◈⋅————

14th Feb '24 Thursday

I delight to do Thy Will, O my God, yea;
thy law is within my heart. *Psalm 40:8.*

In the way that God shall choose,
He will teach us;
Not a lesson we shall lose,
All shall reach us.

The Lord's doings are always for your very best. Rejoice and be glad. Be wise and helpful. Waste nothing but gather knowledge. Choose and do. Christ is your end. Be like Him.

You cannot serve two masters. *Matthew 6:24.*

Let the spirit of service take possession of you. Jesus will free you from the hands of Satan.

God is the strength of your heart. He is yours forever. Hope in Him. Thirst after the Lord. You are His. Rejoice. The dealings of the Lord are always best. Add daily to your stock of knowledge. Do all things in the best manner possible. Keep true to your youthful ideals. Try and serve mankind by love and sympathy. Be meek. Be filled with the Holy Spirit. The Lord will aid and support you. Trust in His Love.

Throw off all cloaks of hypocrisy.

Serve the Lord faithfully and do good.

Check the Dictionary definition of hypocrisy.
Does that apply to you?

———— ·❸·❽· ————

15ᵗʰ Feb '24 Friday

*W*ait on the Lord, be of good courage and He shall strengthen thine heart. *Psalm 27:14.*

Have the courage to be true,
Steadfastly the right to do,
Loving him that wrongeth you-
Play, play the man.

Do your little hourly duties well and when the enemy comes stomp him under your feet. Be brave & fearless. All mankind is sinful and straying. Make your heart clean before God. Christ will do it. There are certain things which a society has to conform to and certain which an individual has. Your business should be of use and service to mankind. Strive to enter in at the straight and narrow gate. Bring others too.

What time you are afraid, trust in the Lord, for He is with you as long as you seek and serve Him. The Lord is mighty. Play the man. Love the wrongdoers. Be true.

Cause none to stumble.

Countenance nothing which will degrade manhood or womanhood. Be calm, work confidently and the Lord will aid you. Be willing to be received under the protection of God. He can take the best care possibly of you.

Bring others as well to Him.

Has somebody made you stumble spiritually and vice versa?

————◁◈▷————

16th Feb '24 Saturday

*I*f ye love me, keep my commandments. *John 14:15.*

They took knowledge of them that they had been with Jesus. Emmanuel—God with us!

The name of the Lord is a strong tower. *Proverbs 18:10.*

Take refuge in it and be saved. Conquer Satan. Go firmly onward. Be ready for genuine hard work. Be true and exact. The Lord will be very gracious to you. You will be led by God if only you are willing to hear His word. Do good to all be it Sunday or Monday. Try your best to help others.

Call upon the Lord. *Psalm 18:3.*

Your groanings are not hid from God.

He will deliver you from all mishaps. Death and sin will be conquered. Be strong and of a good courage. Be firm and fearless. Honour God, and love humanity. The Lord is with you always. Carry the Lord Jesus in your heart and actions and you will be honoured of all men. Leave Him behind and nobody will care to look at you. Pray more, watch more and serve all.

Meditate on the following Bible verse—Romans 8:26.
"But the Spirit itself maketh intercessions for us with groanings which cannot be uttered."

————◆◆————

17th Feb '24 Sunday

*I*t is God's Hand all the time
Urging upward ever,
Oh be brave thro' faith and trust
Rising by endeavour.
Are the steps dark? Yet go on
Every step is victory won.

Go out bearing the cross and reproach of Jesus. Be not ashamed to own Him who is King of Kings. Be courageous. See danger and conquer it. Never be discouraged. Hope on and you will succeed. Therefore honour your work and be diligent about its performance. Humble yourself in due time. Christ will enable you.

If you overcome, you shall also be like Jesus and with Him. There is a crown for you. Go on and victory will be yours. Be not mean but courageous. Be a great man. Set a good example. Consider no thing secular.

Bring the Spirit of Christ to bear upon all you do and are and you will be a glory to Christ.

Do good to such as cannot return it. Depend not on one man for help. Call upon the Lord for help.

When was the last time you were a glory to God?
Don't be modest. Repeat the behaviour again.

18th Feb '24 Monday

*I*t matters not how deep entrenched the wrongs
How hard the battle goes, the day how long,
Faint not, fight on, tomorrow comes the song.

Be of good courage and He shall strengthen your heart, all you that hope in the Lord. *Psalm 27:14.*

Fear not. Go out into the storms of life, with God as your guide. Fight the battle bravely. Call upon God to aid you. Your sorrow shall be turned into joy. The Lord is your Hope. The Man Christ Jesus is your shelter in the time of storm. Come for the Lord bids you and bring others with you into His Kingdom. Try your best to understand others and to bring in a better spirit among all classes.

Though you were a sinner and lost, Christ wagered His Precious Life for yours and has at the risk of His, saved your Life. Show your gratitude to Him by your life. Spurn all that is vile and base and play the man. Fight on bravely and victory will come when it is due. Bring changes for the betterment of all people. Fear not.

To take interest in public weal *(prosperity or well-being)* is good. Serve all. Righteousness shall work peace and happiness. Be not hasty.

Compromise not with Satan.

Forsake yourself and follow the Lord. Be like salt on the Earth. Hear, read and follow.

What does "compromise with Satan" mean?
How can you avoid compromising?

———◦❈◦———

19th Feb '24 Tuesday

*I*f on our daily course our mind
Be set to hallow all we find,
New treasures still, of countless price
God will provide for sacrifice.—Keble.

Apply yourself to your duty with exactness and in peace. Neglect nothing; be violent about nothing. Waste no time. Mend. Trust in the Lord.

Keep watch over your lips. *Psalm 141:3.*

Seek guidance of the Lord. Call upon the Lord for support. He will be gracious to you. Bring the straggling ones to Jesus. There will be joy in heaven then. The Lord will help you if you ask Him to. Be not disheartened by monotony. Persist and you will be blessed.

You shall partake in the Resurrection of your Master. Prepare yourself to be forever with the Lord. Your Redeemer is Mighty. Be cheered with God at your side. Arise and begin to do all you can to serve the Master. Be prepared to meet all sorts of troubles.

Whether slighted or honoured fearlessly and light spiritedly, go on with your duty.

The Hosts of Heaven rejoice in the Home Coming of a sinner. Strive to bring some at least to Jesus. He is the one that repays people.

What are some of your duties today?

20th Feb '24 Wednesday

*G*od is my strength and power, and He maketh my way perfect. *II Samuel 22:23.*

May the end of a perfect day be yours
When the evening stars appear;
And may every day be a perfect day
To the end of a perfect year.

You are chosen and seated unto the Day of Judgement. The Holy Ghost will lead you into all truth. Jesus suffered to give life to you.

Whatever your hand finds to do, do it with your might and do it at once. *Ecclesiastes 9:12.*

Be thorough in all you do. Be not afraid of obstacles. They will make a man of you. Think of the martyrs. Walk righteously and uprightly and the Lord will uphold you. Return to your Father.

You are tempted when drawn away by your lusts. The Lord is able to succour you.

He makes intercession for you to uphold you.

Call on Him. Pretend not. Be brave and fight manfully. Put on the complete armour of God. Minister to the unlovely and bring them to Christ. Try to make the place you live in better. Hearken unto the Lord your God. Serve Him faithfully. Rejoice in bringing men to Christ. The Lord will bless your efforts.

Think about this fact. "Almighty God who made heaven and earth is making intercessions" on your behalf?

————— ·❈· —————

21ˢᵗ Feb '24 Thursday

$\mathcal{W}$hatsoever thou doest, do it heartily,
If it be worth the doing. Nothing great
Was ever yet coined by indifference
Half done is undone.—S. W. Partridge.

Only your very best will do "very well." Do wholeheartedly whatever you undertake. In thoroughness is virtue. Be holy unto the Lord. His peace will keep your mind. You are His property.

Contribute your quota toward the world-salvation.

Be not discouraged but go forward.

The Lord is long-suffering. *Numbers 14:18.*

He should punish evil considering that He is Holy and Jealous. Be faithful in all your dealings.

The Lord will surely grant good harvest if you go and sow His seed. Your trial of faith is for your good. Cultivate all your talents. Do all things as for the Lord. Strengthen the weak hands. Be strong. Fear for God will come and save you. The ways of the Lord are right. God knows your hearts. You cannot serve God and the world. Choose life and live.

Be not discouraged with the world. Rather work for it. Knowing that your labour shall end profitably.

How have you contributed to spreading the good news?

————⸱⧓⸱————

22ⁿᵈ Feb '24 Friday

*L*et us do our work as well,
Both the unseen as the seen,
Make the house where God may dwell,
Beautiful, entire and clean.—S. Longfellow.

Whatever you begin, finish.

What may appear to be of little use now may be your good angel in the future. Do all things first rate. Trust in the Lord and mercy shall surround you. Be glad and shout for joy. The Lord directs each step. You have been loved by God. Show your love to others by seeking their welfare. Fear not, the Lord your God is mighty. Beware of all you do. You shall have to reap the consequences.

Your sleep shall be sweet if you trust in the Lord.

Be anxious for nothing. *Philippians 4:6.*

The Lord's Spirit will grant you peace. Death is only translation. Take pains and trouble. Work bravely and steadfastly.

The blessing of the Lord it maketh rich. *Proverbs 10:22.*
Do at least what is required of you. Remember that you owe all you can give to the World and your duty is only half done if you are self-centered.

Though the Lord be silent, He is not asleep.

He will reward according to the deed. Give not offence to the weaklings of Christ.

How do you handle the Lord's silence?

23rd Feb '24 Saturday

*W*hatsoever I be or do,
Let me honest be and true;
Never wear a false pretence,
Never speak with double sense,
Claim a grace I have not got,
Or look the thing that I am not.

Be governed by your admirations. Covet your neighbour's kindness of heart and manner. Think always of Christ. Be constant.
Walk in the way of the Lord. Prepare yourself to meet God. The Blood of Jesus cleanses you from sin.

It is trouble that makes a man of you.

The Lord will deliver you in trouble. Do at least your duty. Have faith and all things are possible.

God gave you His only begotten Son that you might live. He bore the brunt of God's anger in your stead. Be true to yourself. Be good and true to your friends and God. Treat others as yourself and please your Father.

The Lord is mighty and is able to save such as trust in His care and Love. *Zephaniah 3:17.*

Be grateful for all you receive at God's Hands. Have faith in God. You owe much that you have to your ancestors and to God. Forget not your indebtedness.

Do hardships of life bring maturity of character?

———◆◆———

24th Feb '24 Sunday

*M*en ought always to pray and not faint. *Luke 18:1.*

The Lord heareth and delivereth them out of all their troubles. Ask of God, who giveth to all.

Call upon your God for help. He will bless you. Control your words and thoughts. Say and do only things true. Do not pretend to have what you really have not. Stand firm for the Right. Remember your indebtedness to those gone before you. The Lord God Almighty is able. Trust in His love. The Lord is within you.

Be prepared to receive evil as well from God's hand. Let the Lord do what He pleases with you. You must pass thro' tribulations to Joy and Peace. You should live your Gratitude to God and man.

The Lord is merciful. He will undertake for you.

Call on Him for Help. The Lord comes soon. Get ready to meet Him.

Let not your thoughts and imaginations run riot. Do what you think is best and fear not. Be true to your instincts and to yourself.

'Think of the times you have received mercy from God.'

25th Feb '24 Monday

*H*ave no fellowship with the unfruitful works of darkness, but rather reprove them. *Ephesians 5:11.*

Be sober, be vigilant; because your adversary the devil, as a roaring lion walketh about, seeking whom he might devour; whom resist steadfast in the faith, knowing that the same afflictions are accomplished in your brethren that are in the world.

Resist the Devil and he will flee from you.

Be strong in the Lord. Put on the whole armour of God and watch. Call upon Him for aid. You are only what you are in God's sight. Be true. Be not a hypocrite. Do your best. Praise the Lord! He pardons the repentant sinner.

Forget not your times of humiliation and affliction.

Be steadfast and grateful in life.

The Holy Ghost is with you.

Seek the Lord. You will surely find Him. *Deuteronomy 4:29.*

Trust in the Lord. He will guide. Do what you can do with all your might. Care not for the idle or lazy. Be sincere. Strengthen then the weak-hearted. All flesh is weak. The Word of the Lord abides forever. Pray and do not faint. Call on the Lord and He will avenge you. You can show your gratitude to God and man by being kind to others.

What do you learn from your time of affliction?

———⟨※⟩———

26th Feb '24 Tuesday

Let us not love in words only nor with lips,
but in deed and in truth.
Be what though seemest; live thy creed
Hold up to earth the torch divine;
Be what thou prayers to be made;
Let the great Master's steps be thine.—H. Bonar.

What you practice makes you a Christian. Live Christ. Be sincere in all you say and do. Love in deed. All your thoughts are known to God. Confess. Draw near to God with a true heart. Be clean. The Lord is gentle and kind. He guides you. Be humble and contrite of heart. Implore mercy on you. Confess your sinfulness. All you have received is from God. Show your gratitude in life. Be more worldly.

Jesus Christ the same yesterday, today and forever. *Hebrews 13:8.*

He is your Rock of Salvation and a stronghold. You have received much freely. It remains burden on you to show your gratitude and to help others. Let your work be substantial. Be true to yourself and play the man. The Lord God is great and mighty and man is feeble in His sight. Humble yourself and lay aside pride.

Bring little children to Christ and bring yourself along with them.

Be childlike.

Going to church as a family is a blessing. Is that your practice?

———⟨❂⟩———

27th Feb. '24 Wednesday

*G*uard me, O Lord, that I may ne'er
Forsake the right or do the wrong;
Against temptation make me strong
And round me spread Thy sheltering care.—W. T. Matson.

God pays as He promises but Satan promises the best and pays with the worst. Struggle in your heart with the evil one. Watch and be wary. Be dead to sin. Christ gave Himself for you. Love Him. Be one with Christ.

Your ways are not hid from the Lord. He is great beyond comprehension. Let nothing prove a stumbling block to you in serving God. Remembering your indebtedness, fail not in service to mankind.

God gives liberally and upbraids not. *James 1:5.*

Oh how good He is! How gracious and kind. The Lord is able to strengthen you against temptation.

Watch your hearts.

Associate with the wicked to mix them up. Jesus is full of grace. He the first, suffered for the unjust. Repent and return unto the Lord. The Lord never faints, nor is He ever weary. Trust in Him to uphold you. He gives power to such as wait upon Him. He renews their strength. All things are possible with God. Your labour shall be rewarded. Rest in the Lord.

"Watching your heart" means guarding your emotions.
Why do we need to do that?

———◈◈◈———

28th Feb '24 Thursday

*G*od is love. *1 John 4:16.*

Beloved, if God so loved us, we ought also to love one another. *1 John 4:11.*

Love Divine, all loves excelling
Bread of Heav'n to Earth come down
Spread in us Thy humble dwelling
With Thy faithful mercies crown.—*Charles Wesley.*

You should plead with others in God's stead for the Love of God has been manifest to you. Endure temptation. Instead of looking down, at your temptations, it is better to look to Jesus who will carry you thro' them all.

Watch and pray. *Matthew 26:41.*

Christ has suffered more than you can repay. Offer Him all you can. Help others. You are Christ's slave. Consider the sufferings of the Son of man for you. If you know a certain thing is wrong and then do it, it increases your punishment.

Be pure and all things will be pure.

The Lord tries your heart. Jesus is able to carry on victorious thro' temptation. Yield not to temptation.
The Lord will lead you at all times. He is Love and you are His. Serve Him faithfully. Fear not, for He is your Help. He will support and guide you. He will see that no materially destroying harm touches you. He is able to make you well. Trust Him.

What are the ways you are trying to be pure?

29th Feb '24 Friday

*B*oast not thyself of tomorrow for thou knowest not what a day may bring forth. *Proverbs 27:1.*

The World passeth away and the lust thereof; but he that doeth the will of God abideth forever. *I John 2:17.*

Waste no time for now is the accepted time. Work hard while you can. Be rich toward God and mankind. Never be discouraged.

Conquer old temptations. They are generally hard to overcome.

Call on Christ for aid. When such as trust in the Lord call on Him in trouble, He will not fail them. Lean hard. The Lord knows your desires. Commit your ways unto Him. Fear not; work on.

Fear not: the Lord is from everlasting to everlasting. His mercies fail not. Put your trust in Him. Never feel discouraged for that is caused by the Devil. Take heart for the Lord will stand by you and make you a victor too. Watch. The Christ is meek and gentle. Be like Him. Be faithful in what the Lord has given you, He will reward everyman according to His deeds. All the good you possess is but reflections from the Almighty. Trust in Him.

Old temptations are like die-hard bad habits. How can we overcome them?

———— ◈◈◈ ————

Mizpah

A beacon ⁓ Watch-tower }

March

First Day in the Month of March 1924. Saturday

I shall be satisfied when I awake with Thy likeness. *Psalm 17:15.*

I will go in the strength of the Lord. *Psalm 71:16.*

What is worth doing begin now, today;
What is not worthy, never. Life is short,
Too short, alas, to trifle with the good
Or entertain the bad.—S. W. Partridge

Your whole time is God's and you are to use it as He bid you. Earn what you wish to possess. Do all with might and main. Have fervent love toward all. Walk in love. Sacrifice yourself for Him. The Lord will not forsake such as trust in Him. He is glorious in power. Praise and magnify the Lord. He stands in need of you. What ought to be done, can be done. Trust more.

The Lord is on your side.

Rejoice for none can harm you. Do right and be brave. Whatever you do, do without a thought of fame. Work steadily at improving yourself. Be humble and meek. Pray without ceasing for God dwells in you. Repent and return to your loving Christ. The Lord is able to preserve that which is committed to Him. Trust.

*Have you realized that God is on your side even
when things go wrong?*

———◈◈———

2nd Mar '24 Sunday

*B*e thoroughly warmhearted, the
Lord's own servants.
Guide us through life and when at last
We enter into rest,
Thy tender arms around us cast,
And fold us to Thy breast.

Set yourself right first.

Work enthusiastically. Go ahead. God is mindful of you and ever in your afflictions. He cares for you. Your sufferings are for good. Rejoice and be patient. Be loving, faithful and Christian. Draw many to Christ by your life and service. Fear not, the Lord has redeemed you. No harm shall befall you, for God is with you. Be for Christ out-and-out.

The people of God have an eternal rest where the wicked cease from troubling. Hope. Do not be indolent. Persevere till you reach the summit of Christian experience. Encourage yourself in the Lord.

The Lord has created you for His glory. Fear not: for He is with you. Receive the son into your heart. You shall have to give account for all you receive of Him. Give yourself in service to mankind.

Pause and ponder. Have you set yourself right with God?

3rd Mar '24 Monday

*I*f Thy Presence go not with me, carry us not up hence. *Exodus 33:15.*

Trust in the Lord at all times; ye people, pour out your heart before Him: God is a refuge for us.

The Lord will direct you in the way you should go. *Proverbs 3:6.*

Trust in the Lord at all times. Depend on strength divine. Yield unto God. Let true Christianity take possession of you. Let your religion be practiced. Give yourself in service to others.

Make happiness wherever you go.

The Lord He is God thro' all ages. Besides Him, there is no other. Render to all their due.

Present sufferings are not to be compared to the eternal glory before you. Follow on. Be truehearted, useful and happy. Lend a helping hand to all. Ask Christ to lead you aright. Learn to help. Realize your great weakness. Ask for sufficient grace. Trust in the Lord and do your best. You are required to show for the God's praise. After death is life eternal and bliss for such who love the Lord and seek to serve Him.

Make a habit of spreading happiness wherever you go.

————◦❖◦————

4th Mar '24 Tuesday

*Y*ield to the Lord with simple heart
All that thou hast, and all thou art;
Renounce all strength, but strength divine;
And peace shall be for ever thine.—Mme. Guyon

Come into contact with Christ's rich personality.

He will help you to lead a victorious life. Leave God to order all your ways. Seek to please your neighbour for His good. Be true and honest.

Set your affections on things above. *Colossians 3:2.*

Walk by faith. *II Corinthians 5:7.*

Search after God. The Lord will blot out your sins if you repent and ask Him. The Lord will uphold you.

Be prepared to suffer if you would become Christ-like. Serve Christ faithfully. Be not servile. Build your hopes on God who is firm. Indulgence is never good. The Lord will fill you with His Spirit. You are His witness. Fear not; be brave. Give richly and you will be rewarded.

Your thoughts have a wide range of influence.

Be watchful and see that they please your God and are not selfish.

Since your thoughts influence your behavior so much, how have you controlled your thinking?

5th Mar '24 Ash Wednesday

*R*epent ye, for the kingdom of Heaven is at hand. *Matthew 3:2.*

Yield not to temptation for yielding is sin.
Each victory'll help you, some other to win
Fight manfully onward. Dark passions subdued
Look ever to Jesus, He'll carry you through.

Rejoice in God's salvation. Keep a cheerful face. Get the song and beauty of life into your heart. Get Christ's peace. Lift up your eyes heavenward.

Ask to lead to that Rock higher than you.

Follow Christ's example. Have no one in place of God. Love Him above all. Rejoice in suffering. The Lord will direct you. Be patient and persevering. Beware of thoughts.

Thro' troubles keep firm and fight the good fight of faith. *I Timothy 6:12.*

Be strong in the Lord. The Lord is ready to deliver you. Trust. Keep a cheerful countenance. Let your Spirit be right. Always laugh. Merriment is good all round. Out of the heart are the issues of life. War is not necessary. Educate the opinions of your neighborhood. The Lord He is good. He blotteth out our sins. Only repent and return unto Him. You are His servant. Be prepared, for the coming of the Lord draweth nigh.

What are the ways in which God is higher than you?

———⟨⟩———

6th Mar '24 Thursday

*K*eep a cheerful countenance,
Banish gloomy care.
Forty days and forty nights
Thou was fasting in the wild,
Forty days and forty nights,
Tempted and yet undefiled.

Take the Lord at His Word and love Him sincerely. Recognize and be grateful for the light that is, honour God, help others and be glad yourself. Hope at all times. The Lord your God is in your midst. He will save you. He will deliver you and help you at all times.

There is no God besides you, Lord. *Isaiah 44:6.*

Strive not with your Maker. His ways are hidden from you. Look up for your Master comes soon. Be prepared. Bring people into the transforming touch with Jesus.

Christ was made sin for you. He was forgotten by God, and He suffered for you. Remember your indebtedness to Him and seek to please Him. Be cheerful and virtuous. Be not gloomy for God is *in* all things. Hope. Have a faith which will refuse to grow dim.

Be inwardly victorious.

Be firm in Christ. Look unto God for beside Him there is no Saviour. He is mighty and ready to save. The Word of the Lord abideth forever.

Does "inwardly victorious" mean a happier person?

7ᵗʰ Mar '24 Friday

*A*bstain from fleshly lusts which war against the soul. *1 Peter 2:11.*

Sunbeams scorching all the day;
Chilly dewdrops nightly shed;
Prowling beasts about Thy way,
Stones Thy pillow, earth Thy bed.

The Lord is your Maker. He loves you. Nothing can separate you from His love. Hate sin for His sake. Sow good seeds with grief and sorrow, and you'll have joy. Appear at your best among those who love you best.

Make the best of everybody.

Hope the best; persevere. The Lord is wondrous mighty. He purposes and nobody can gainsay Him. Watch and pray without ceasing. Be prepared to stand before Christ. Be not beaten, but go ahead bravely.

Trust in the Lord with all thine heart. *Proverbs 3:5.*
Cast all your care on Him. He cares for you. *I Peter 5:7.*

Commit your cause unto Him. Look out for the toughest side of things. Persevere. Sorrow will end in joy. Learn to be unselfish. Be not given to pleasure. Return to the Lord your God who is your Redeemer. The Lord knoweth all things from the beginning to the end. Have great ideals. Seek to uphold and live your ideal in life. Serve mankind and forget yourself.

Can you think of someone who makes the best of everything?

———⊰⊱———

8th Mar '24 Saturday

*N*ow, saith the Lord, turn ye even to Me, with all your heart, and with fasting and with weeping and with mourning. *Joel 2:12.*

Shalt not we Thy sorrow share,
And from earthly joys abstain,
Fasting with unceasing prayer,
Glad with Thee to suffer pain?

The Lord will forgive your sins for the Blood of Christ cleanses you. Call upon Him, repent and return unto Him.

Fear not: the Lord is your helper. *Hebrews 13:6.*

Never worry for it will not pay. Inspire people with courage to bear their troubles. Let your ways be perfect before the Lord. Remember the Lord who suffered and bled and died for you. Live and hope for a better world. Serve the Lord.

The Lord is mighty and able to do mighty things for you. Put implicit trust in Him. For He will not fail you. By dint of hard work and perseverance, you'll succeed. Be cheerful and take joy wherever you go. Through affliction you shall be perfected. If you want to be great, humble yourself and serve others.

Spend and be spent for the Master.

Serve the Lord.

Think, how you can be "spent for the Master" today.

9th Mar '24 Sunday

*R*esist the devil, and he will flee from you. *James 4:7.*

And if, Satan vexing sore,
Flesh or Spirit should assail,
Thou, His vanquisher before,
Grant we may not faint nor fail.

Remember that all you possess is from God. Be grateful. Love Him and serve Him alone. Never fail in your duties. Conquer your calamities and get greater power. Fear not. Believe and you will succeed. Forget mistakes. The Lord has interceded for you. He will keep you from falling into temptation. Anything without Christ is in vain. Deny yourself. Never take mean advantage of others.

You are saved by faith. Give glory to God. Sing and rejoice in the salvation God has given you.

Master your misfortunes.

You can conquer fate if you work and trust. Deny yourself. The more you spend for others, the more beautiful will your life be. The Lord is able to do all things. Trust in Him. Christ loves you. Displease Him not. Seek to understand His thoughts and dealings with you.

How have you overcome a misfortune in the past? Explain.

10th Mar '24 Monday

So shall we have peace Divine;
Holier gladness ours shall be
Round us too shall Angels shine
Such as ministered to Thee.

Rend your hearts and not your garments, and turn unto the Lord your God. *Joel 2:13.*

The Lord will provide. He is able.

They that fear the Lord shall lack no thing. *Psalm 34:10.*

He will supply all your need. Speak the truth boldly, committing yourself to God who judges righteously. The Lord will never forget you. He will help you. Rise and pray lest you enter into temptation. Not your will but God's. Seek to serve the World.

If you want to abide in Christ's love, keep His commandments. Bring forth the fruits of the Spirit. Strictly adhere to truth. Crucify not the Lord who has loved and saved you. Let some great good cause wrap your attentions in itself and fill you with zeal in the Master's service. Everyone shall know that the Lord Jehovah is your Redeemer. Trust in Him and you shall never be ashamed.

Betray not the Lord your God by your actions or thoughts.

How can one avoid betraying the Lord?

11ᵗʰ Mar '24 Tuesday

*S*et your affection on things above—
Keep oh keep us Saviour dear,
Ever constant at thy side;
That with Thee we may appear
At th' eternal Easter tide.

The Lord will richly bless such as seek Him. He will preserve your outgoings and down-sitting. Trust, oh, implicitly trust in His loving care. Be sincere and truthful. Be true to thyself. The Lord is mighty to save. He is not disabled. The Lord appoints all things. Dedicate yourself to God's service.

Jesus was touched with grief. He can sympathize with you. Be prepared for suffering and hurt. Jesus loved you. Be sincere always. Keep truth in your life and actions.

Let people rest on your words alone.

The Lord will be your help. If you trust in the Lord, nothing shall you lack. Be firm in your belief. Repent ere it is too late. Betray not the Lord of your soul and body. Remember your indebtedness to Him and be faithful. Be not ashamed of honest hard work. It is a shame to be idle while you can work.

Will others say that "your word is as good as gold"?

12th Mar '24 Wednesday

*E*nter not into judgement with Thy servant;
for in Thy sight shall no man living be justified.
Lord in this Thy mercy's day
Ere it pass for aye away,
On our knees we fall and pray.

Be of good cheer. The Lord will strengthen you. He will make His face shine on you. He is gracious. Grow in grace.

It is good to let your will be lost in God's.

Trust in the Lord. If you have faith and character, you will conquer difficulty and accomplish good. The Lord is your comforter. He is the Son of God. Be modest.

Seek to please the Lord. Be meek and quiet. Order all your conversation with carefulness. Magnify the Lord. Present your body as a holy sacrifice to God. If you understand all God's dealings, you would see they are always the best. Let the Spirit dwell in you. Grow in grace. Jesus the faultless man died for you. Lift up your heart to God. Wish well, be of use of mankind around you, serve and you will be a ministering angel.

Is doing the will of God same as being submitting your will to God?

———— ·❸·❤· ————

13th Mar '24 Thursday

*H*e is able also to save them to the uttermost that come unto God by Him, seeing He ever liveth to make intercession for them. *Hebrews 7:25.*

Holy Jesus, grant us tears
Fill us with heart-searching fears,
Ere that awful doom appears.

Jesus Christ is your Mediator. Look unto Him and be saved. Displease Him not. Never do anything in opposition to better judgement. Be scrupulous about doing your duty. You must be pleasant. Be smart. The Mighty Lord is with you. Be not afraid of man. Be meek. Fear not man's accusations if you are right with God. Faith is the assurance of things hoped for.

Behold, Jesus is with you always. He will never forsake you. Be not faithless but believing.

What time you are downcast, call on the Lord.

Do your duty faithfully and do it cheerfully. Fall in line with God's purposes. Never shirk your duties. The Lord is your Comforter. Be not afraid of frail human beings. Have moral courage. The thought of being answerable for all you do should make you careful how you do things.

Does prayer lift you up when you are downcast?

————⸱⸱❈⸱⸱————

14th Mar '24 Friday

*A*cquaint now thyself with Him and be at peace.
Lord, on us Thy Spirit pour,
Kneeling lowly at the door,
Ere it close for ever more.

Your business is to do your work well in whatever place you may be. Love God. Make the place you live in, pleasant for others. Let the widest good flow from you. Be not a busy body. Let your light shine before men. Think on beautiful things. The Lord will not always chide. He is merciful to those who repent. Weep for your sins and turn to the Lord. Have faith in God, and all will be well.

Take heed to the Word. In the Word is life. Christ loved the world. The love of the Lord constrains you. Seek to be like Jesus. That would do for you. Let your words and character stimulate others to good. Trust in the Lord's guidance. The task before you is that of telling good tidings to others.

Forgive as you hope to be forgiven.

The Lord God is merciful. Be strong to endure. Never lose heart or faith. Be courageous.

Is there someone you need to forgive? Do it today.

15th Mar '24 Saturday

*H*e went a little farther and fell on His face and prayed saying, O my Father, if it be possible let this cup pass from me: not as I will but as Thou wilt. *Matthew 26:39.*

By Thy night of agony,
By Thy supplicating cry,
By Thy willingness to die;

The Lord suffered all thro' His life on earth for you and He died to save you. Forget not how your ingratitude would wound Him. Be busily occupied at all times in the Lord. Work. Don't waste life in doubts or fears. Do your duties cheerfully.

Let nothing unclean touch you, for you are Holy unto the Lord.

Repent and return to the Lord. He will receive and forgive. Trust. Have faith and patience. Pray for the strengthening of the faith of others.

The Lord hath made heaven and earth and all that exists in the Universe. How great He is and yet He considers mankind. Do what you can. Sow good seeds. Serve the Lord. The Lord to save you suffered for you. Forget not His great love. Repent ere it is too late. Have faith in God. Without faith, you cannot please God.

Think of an unclean behavior that you need to confess to God.

16th Mar '24 Sunday

*M*an that is born of a woman is of few days and full of trouble. *Job 14:1.*

By Thy tears of bitter woe,
For Jerusalem below,
Let us not Thy love forego.

Jesus Christ, the same, yesterday, today and forever. *Hebrews 13:8.*

The world passes away, but he that doeth God's will abides forever. Man's life is vapour; only God is abiding. Do bravely what is close at your hand. First duty, then pleasure. You shall be victorious. Be humble and just. The Lord was counted among offenders and bore your sins. Be not afraid of men. They are but a breath. Work for God. Only your faith can appropriate things invisible.

Be filled with the Spirit. Sing unto the Lord praises. Praise ye the Lord.

The Lord is pleased with truthfulness.

There is nothing sweeter than doing the will of God. Obey God rather than man. Fear not, for the Lord will no more remember your evil past. He is merciful. The risen Lord is ever with you. Remember His Presence. Increase in faith day by day.

Besides truthfulness, what else is an offering pleasing to God?

17ᵗʰ Mar '24 Monday

*P*resent your bodies a living sacrifice holy acceptable unto God. *Romans 12:1.*

Grant us 'neath Thy wings a place,
Lest we lose this day of grace,
Ere we shall behold Thy face. Amen.

The Lord is able to keep you from falling. *Jude 1:24.*

You should abhor evil and strive to do the good.

The path of duty is the way to glory.

Let not the fair hours of day be wasted. Do good while you can. Hope always. Have belief in others and in God. The Lord is merciful. He will receive you into His fold. Ask of the Lord *in* faith to conquer the world and to see things transform to God's Honour.

Endure temptation. The Lord was tempted and was victorious. He is therefore able to help you when in trouble. Fear God and keep his commandments. Be sympathetic. Hope for the best. Watch the early dawn.

Do your duty cheerfully. Whatever happens, the mercy of the Lord will not depart from you as long as you love Him. Thro' suffering you get glory. Let the Lord abide with you. He can open your eyes to the glory in the scriptures. Faith in God helps you to live and do something great.

Do you agree that "Duty is the way to glory"?

———⟨✦⟩———

18th Mar '24 Tuesday

*R*eturn, O Lord, deliver my soul; Oh save me for Thy mercies sake. *Psalm 6:4.*

Good it is to keep the fast
Shadowed forth in ages past,
Which our own Almighty Lord
Hallow'd by His deed and word.

You have need of patience. Hope in the Lord. Look steadfastly at Jesus and He will carry you through. Work for the night is coming when you can work no more. Do work in the right spirit. Do your best. Your righteousness is of the Lord. If you are in trouble, the Lord is your Helper. Be not troubled, the Lord is your peace. Life is an adventure and demands faith.

The Lord is your righteousness. You conquer thro' Him.

He is mighty to save. *Zephaniah 3:17.*

Honest and good work is a great boon to mankind.

Occupy yourself with the highest your mind is capable of.

Incline your ear unto the Word of the Lord. Seek for power from above. The Lord will send it *to* you, if you only ask Him. He is your Helper. In every realm of life, you find that faith is greatly needed.

What are some nobler and higher thoughts
your mind can dwell on?

———◈◈———

19ᵗʰ Mar '24 Wednesday

*O*f His fullness have we all we received and grace for grace.

Moses while he fasted saw
God who gave by him the Law,
To Elijah angels came,
Steeds of fire and car of flame.

Be holy, for Christ your exemplar is holy. You are complete in Him. He that gave Jesus will give you all good gifts. Friendship must help you to walk aright. Exhibit kindness of manner and be not conceited. Be full of divine Christ-like love and spirit. Seek the Lord while it is day. Forsake your evil paths. The Lord knows best. Work for Him. The Lord is from everlasting to everlasting. There is great need for faith in everyday life.

Be strong in the Lord and in the power of His might. *Ephesians 6:10.*

The Lord is able to help you.

Be of good courage. *Psalms 27:14.*

Remember the Golden Rule. Be patient, brave, true, faithful and forgiving. Love all. The Lord will reward you. He is faithful that promised. Believe on the Lord and be made in His likeness.

He will endow you with power.

Have faith in God.

Think of a time God has endowed you with power.

————⟨⊰⊱⟩————

20th Mar '24 Thursday

*I*n due season we shall reap, if we faint not.
So was Daniel meet to gaze
On the sight of latter days:
And the Baptist to proclaim
Blessings thro' the Bridegroom's name.

The blood of Jesus Christ cleanses you from all sin. *I John 1:7.*

Walk as a child of Light. The Word of the Lord gives you light. Turn from forbidden ways.

Forgive if you hope to be such as love Him from trouble. Be among his chosen ones.

You have received all you possess from the Lord. Be grateful.

Have faith.

Always try to avoid all appearance of evil though it may be hateful to you.

You must take the opinion of the world's life too but above all see that what you do is right in God's sight.

The just shall live by faith.

You are justified by the faith you have in Christ Jesus as your Saviour.

*'Being justified by faith' was the beginning of
which event in history?*

———⊰◈⊱———

21st Mar '24 Friday

Grant us Lord like them to be
Off in prayer and fast with Thee;
Fill us with Thy heavenly Might,
Be our joy and true delight

The end of all things is at hand; be ye therefore sober and watch unto prayer. Be sober and vigilant for the devil is very deceitful.

Go forward. Slide not back. Watch. Fear not. God is with you. He will uphold you. Be prepared.

Ask the Lord to forgive your weakness and strengthen your purposes.

Repent ere it be too late. Be honest and faithful in your words and deeds. You have need of great faith. Ask it of God.

The Lord is merciful. He will forgive your sins and comfort you so that you may be of help to others. Call upon Him earnestly. Forgive others. Seek to reconcile the world to God.

Die to yourself and live to God. Be contrite and humble if you would have God's blessings. He will make you truly His and heal your sins.

Forget not the Blood of the Lamb of God. He is your Redeemer.

Consider the faith you have in God.

Think of some of your weaknesses that God can strengthen.

22nd Mar '24 Saturday

*F*ather, hear us through Thy Son,
And the Spirit, with Thee one,
Whom our thankful hearts adore
Ever and forever more. Amen.

Come out from among them, and be ye separate, saith the Lord, and touch not the unclean thing. *2 Corinthians 6:17*.

Walk as a child of light. *Ephesians 5:8*.

Be not carried away by the lust of the eyes. Let not company ruin you. Crave forgiveness of God. Be loving. Praise no heart needlessly. Be not angry. Vain fastings please not God. Be a ministering angel and lend a helping hand. Seek the Lord and abide with Him for in Him is life. Faith in God is necessary.

The Lord is with you. Go in His might. He will aid you in your troubles and grant you victory over sin. Fear not, but be brave. Have nothing left over for which you would have to blush. The Lord is kind and forgiving. If you help the needy and oppressed, the Lord will surely bless you. Bring others to Jesus the Loving Saviour of all.

You are a child of the Living God.

What does the "living God" enable you to do?

23rd Mar '24 Sunday

*A*s He which hath called you is holy, so be ye holy in all manner of conversation. *I Peter 1:15.*

Lo! now is our accepted day,
The time for purging sins away,
The sin of thought, and deed and word
That we have done against the Lord.

Your body is the Temple of the Holy Ghost. *I Corinthians 6:19.*

Be holy. Walk with God who is most holy. He is your God. Bear with others. Scorn to revenge yourself. Revenge is hateful. Fill your mind with beautiful thoughts. Keep the day of the Lord holy, for He is well pleased about it. Bring people to Jesus.

Ask Jesus to abide with you. Jesus stands at your heart's door. Jesus is with you always. Find the Lord, and do not let Him go.

Win the heart rather than the head of people.

Fill your heart with holy impulses. The Lord's Hand is not shortened that it cannot save. See that sin does not come between you and God. Whatsoever Jesus says do. Hesitate not to serve Him faithfully. The sublimest virtue of the human mind is to believe in God.

Will kindness win someone's heart? What else does?

———◈◈———

24th Mar '24 Monday

*W*ith God nothing is impossible
For He the merciful and True.
Hath spared His people hitherto
Not willing that the soul should die
Tho' great its past iniquity.

Believe in the Lord your God. He is able to do mighty things.

The just shall live by faith. *Habakkuk 2:4; Romans 1:17.*

Weep for your sins. Be kind to others as well. Be very gentle with your neighbour's failings. The Spirit of the Lord will be upon you. He will aid you in trouble. Fear the Lord. Be zealous for the Lord. Pray often. Your belief in God, supporting you against all evil is a great consolation.

The Kingdom of the Lord is not earthly.

Seek not glory which will perish. Seek eternal glory thro' Christ.

The Lord is merciful yet rouse not His displeasure. Be sympathetic and gentle. You need forgiveness yourself. Rise and shine for the Lord, who is author of your Joy and Light. Do not commit yourself easily. Be cautious, but trust the Lord at all times. A sinner needs faith in God.

What is wrong with pursuing worldly glory?

———·⋆⊛⋆·———

25th Mar '24 Tuesday

*B*e on the alert: stand firm in the faith; acquit yourselves like men. *I Corinthians 16:13.*

Then let us all with earnest care,
And contrite fast and tear and prayer,
And works of mercy and of love,
Entreat for pardon from above.

The Lord will never leave or forsake you. The Lord is your Helper. Be strong and of a good courage. Tho' all forsake, God will be with you and comfort you. Ask for support.

Refuse the first advance of sin.

Fear the Lord. Watch your thoughts. The Lord is your Redeemer. Rejoice and be glad. Be born again if you want Jesus. Faith is to most a matter of life and death.

All power is given to Jesus. He can aid to the end. Your duty is to preach the Word. Be not weary in well doing. God blesses you. Let not evil overwhelm you. Revere God as your Father. The Lord's blessing makes you rich. He is your Light. Be His. Jesus has died to save you. Bring others to the knowledge of the Son. In a Godless world, you die forever. Have faith and you live.

First advance of sin starts with thoughts.
If so, how do you stop?

26th Mar '24 Wednesday

I can do all things through Christ, which strengtheneth me. *Philippians 4:13.*

Yield yourself to the Holy Spirit's guidance
That He may all our sins efface,
Adorn us with the gifts of grace,
And join us to the angel band
Forever in the heavenly land.

Be faithful and fervent unto the end. Do your best and to your utmost ability. Be true to yourself. Persevere in your high purposes. Yield to others when no principle of right is involved. Never deserve contempt. Keep yourself always in the right. The Lord is come to give you beauty and joy. Rejoice in Him.

If you love and honour the Lord, abhor evil.
Distribute to others necessity. Be charitable. Do good and the Lord will not fail to reward you.

Let not ridicule force you to violate your scruples or conscience.

Excel. Never give way to dishonourable dealings. Praise the Lord for His goodness to you. You cannot but acknowledge your debt of gratitude.

The instant you believe on Christ, life everlasting begins. Rejoice in His salvation. God is Real.

How can you avoid yielding to peer pressure?

27th Mar '24 Thursday

*B*ehold, I come quickly; hold that fast which thou hast, that no man take thy crown.
Blest Three in One and One in Three
Almighty God, we pray to Thee,
That Thou wouldst now vouchsafe to bless
Our fast with fruits of righteousness.

Sow righteousness and you'll reap a sure reward. The Lord will be your judge. Keep the faith. Gloomy clouds too will soon pass away. Be active and wise. Fear not. Set your mind to expect difficulties and to surmount them. You shall no more be forsaken, for the Lord delights in you. He will crown you with joy. Make use of every opportunity to serve Christ. Let none go by unused. You can't avoid making up your life.

God is faithful. He is able to preserve you faultless against that day. *Jude 1:24.*

Trust in His love and protection. Practice makes one an expert in many things. Pray without ceasing. The Lord is with you. Partake of the Lord's sufferings if you would receive His rewards. Come to the Lord and He will give you the water of Life. God is Spirit. Worship Him therefore in Spirit and in Truth.

Your actions prove your creed.

Do you agree "handsome is what handsome does?"

———◄❀►———

28th Mar '24 Friday

*C*hristian does thou see them
On the holy ground,
How the troops of Midian
Prowl and prowl around?
Christian, up and smite them,
Counting gain but loss;
Smite them by the merit:
Of the holy Cross.

Be strong and of a good courage. *Deuteronomy 31:6.*

He succours you. Your God. Wait on the Lord and renew your strength. You are a conqueror thro' Christ. Arise and be active. Ask God to direct all you do this day. Please the Lord always. Do not procrastinate. Make good use of your time. The Lord will carry you thro' all troubles. Follow the Lord. Decide and abide by it.

You shall not forever be dead. Jesus is your Resurrection. He is your Witness. Death is but a sleep. Value your time. Let pleasure be only a recreation.

Apply your time well and you will not be troubled about it. The Lord is ever before you preparing your way. Trust in His love. Your business should be to serve the Master. Work and you will be rewarded. Be strong, for the Lord is with you and on your side.

Serve the Lord manfully and with your reason.

How do you serve the Lord manfully?

29th Mar '24 Saturday

*C*hristian, dost thou feel them,
How they work within;
Striving tempting, luring,
Goading into sin?
Christian, never tremble;
Never be downcast;
Smite them by the virtue
Of the Lenten fast.

Suffer to reign with Christ. The Father loves you. The Lord will continue to work in your heart to perform good in you.

Spend every day as if it were your last.

Do thy nearest duty. Go attain. Be not indolent. Seek the Lord while He may be found. You are God's entirely. Let not sin rule over you. Know Christ all for yourself.

Set not your affection on things before. *Colossians 3:2.*

Look up. Let your heart be Christ's. The Crown in Heaven is incorruptible. Do what you can while it is day. Never postpone.

Be not hasty or insincere. Crave for God's company always with you. Love the Lord. Jesus is able to do mighty things. Only trust and all will be well. Walk with Jesus. All that you have is His alone.

If today was your last day, will you change your schedule?

———————

30th Mar '24 Sunday

Christian, do thou hear them
How they speak thee fair?
"Always fast and vigil?
Always watch and pray?"
Christian answer boldly
"While I breathe I pray:
Peace shall follow battle
Night shall end in day."

Meditate upon the works of the Lord.

Spend some time in search with Jesus alone.

Study the Word of the Lord. Waste nobody's time. Be true to your word. Make use of the Present and let it yield you blessings. The Lord has great things in store for you. You are entirely in His Hands. You are His clay. Trust all to Him. The Lord is able to save to the uttermost. Go steadfastly onward in your religion.

The Lord tests your faith by not answering your prayers quickly. Do not get slack. Be importunate. Think most, feel most and act best. Live. Lose no time for doing good. Be thrifty in your use of time.

The Lord will hear you. Seek the Lord and you will find Him. Go and sin no more lest a worse thing befall you. Jesus has made you whole. Ask Jesus to reveal Himself to you.

Pray without ceasing. *I Thessalonians 5:17.*

Be not hasty.

Have you set aside time to spend with God every day?

31st Mar '24 Monday

*W*ell I know thy trouble,
O my Servant true;
Thou are very weary,
I was weary too,
But that toil shall make thee
Some day all my own,
And the end of sorrow
Shall be near my throne. Amen.

Seek first the Kingdom of God and He will give you all things richly to enjoy. *Matthew 6:33.*

The Lord is your Shepherd. *Psalm 23:1.*

Fear not. Seek the Presence of God. Be wise. Your happiness in life depends on the way you pass your days now. Be good and happy now. Be busy about your Father's business. The Lord is merciful to such as fear Him.

Until you know God, there is no peace.

He is yours. Do everything in its own good time. Submit yourself to God and ennobling influences. Rouse yourself from sleep and be earnest. Love is of God. Walk in the way of the Lord. He is your light. The servants of the Lord shall want nothing. Believe in Jesus and you have everlasting life. You can do nothing without your Father in Heaven. Be not lost in doubts. Deal honestly with yourself. Show thankfulness for all you have received from Christ.

How do you find the peace of God in the midst of storms of your life?

———⟨❈⟩———

Photos of Madras Medical College Days

Women and Children's Hospital in Egmore
Madras Medical College, 1930.

Noble in Vishakapatinam in 1932
while doing ENT House surgeoncy

Noble winning doubles handicap Tennis tournament
at MMC 1929-30

Noble bicycling from ICC Lodge to MMC.

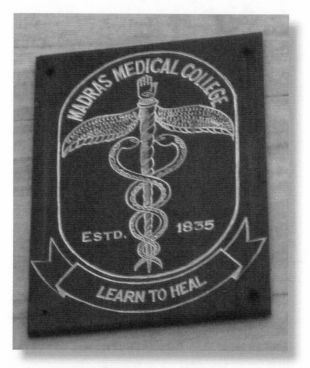

MMC Now. John Prabhakar attended the same Medical
school 1958-64

Photos of Mary and Noble Wedding

Family photo taken at Noble and Mary Kantayya's
wedding in 1932

Bride and groom by the Ford wedding car.

Zion Church, Madras where the wedding took place.

Groom in Indian outfit and the bride in beige silk saree

Israel

A Prince of God   April

First Day in the Month of April 1924. Tuesday

*T*he Fruit of the Spirit is Joy.
Rejoice in the Lord always; and again I say, Rejoice.
Philippians 4:4.

O Thou Who dost to man accord
His highest prize, his best reward,
Thou Hope of all our race;
Jesus to Thee we now draw near,
Our humble supplications hear,
Who humbly seek Thy Face.

Glory in tribulations. *Romans 5:3.*

The joy of the Lord is your strength. *Nehemiah 8:10.*

God shall wipe away all your tears. Waste no time. Life is short.
Improve the present hour. Before you call, God will answer you.
The Lord is with you. Know the Father and Jesus and the Holy Spirit
personally. God holds you to Himself. Have positive religion.

The Lord is your Peace. He will overcome Satan.

Make the best of the present for you may not have it again.

Be punctual.

Incline your ear to the Lord. Until you need God, you will
never find Him. That is, thirst after God and He will be found
of you. Seek the Lord. The fear of the Lord is the beginning of
Wisdom.

*Did you make the best of yesterday? Could you have done
differently?*

2nd Apr '24 Wednesday

*P*eace I leave with you
My peace I give to you. *John 14:27.*

With self-accusing voice within
Our conscience tells of many a sin
In thought, and word, and deed;
O cleanse that conscience from all stain,
The penitent restore again,
From every burden freed.

Love nothing above your God.

You cannot serve God and the World. *Matthew 6:24.*

The Lord knows the secrets of your heart. Serve Him with a perfect and willing mind. Beware of the Devil and of yourself. Stamp and trample down all evil thoughts.

Be frank with your doubts and deal squarely with them.

The Lord loves a contrite and humble spirit. Be not proud or overbearing. Search the Scriptures. Take heed. Watch and pray. Be constant in and out of season. Receive the Son of man into your heart. Look away to Jesus. Be persistent. Think not much of yourself. Humble mindedness is of great value. Be Christ's Disciple. The Lord is your comforter. The Lord will plead with you. Jesus is able to do mighty things for you. Lean hard. God alone is infallible. Trust in His Word and seek to be more like Jesus.

How do you handle doubts about your faith?

3rd Apr '24 Thursday

Not by might, not by power but by my Spirit, saith the Lord. *Zechariah 4:6.*

If Thou reject us, who shall give
Our fainting spirits strength to live?
'Tis Thine alone to spare,
With cleansed hearts to pray aright
And find acceptance in Thy sight,
Be this our lowly prayer.

The Lord will perform His word. He is storing great things for you, but His thoughts are not your thoughts. Be penitent. Cease from anger. The sooner you attempt self-conquest, the easier for you. Fear not; the Lord is with you. He will help you over difficulties. Jesus is able to do mighty things. Trust in Him. Yearn after God.

If you have God on your side, man may fight against you and yet not prevail. He will prosper you. Jesus it is who always comes to the rescue; therefore be not afraid but call on His Holy Name. Be not carried away by impulses. The end is near. Be steadfast in the faith unto the end, for the wages of sin is death.

Jesus is your Deliverer.

Strangle in yourself whatever you abhor, and force yourself to do what you approve of.

Find at least 5 Psalms where God is called "our deliverer"?

4th Apr '24 Friday

*L*et all bitterness and all passionate feeling, all anger and loud insulting language be unknown among you—and also every kind of malice. *Ephesians 4:31.*

'Tis Thou hast bless'd this solemn fast:
So may its days by us be pass'd
In self-control severe.
That when our Easter morn we hail,
Its mystic feast we may not fail
To keep with conscience clear.

The Lord your God is from everlasting to everlasting. He is mighty and He is your Rock of salvation. Fear not. Tho' hard the way, Jesus will carry you over. Shine as lights before the world. Let not your duties accumulate on account of your lazy ways. Watch yourself. Return unto your former state of Innocence. The Lord will receive you. Labour not for meat which perishes. Believe on the Son of God. Ask counsel of the Lord.

Be anxious for nothing. *Philippians 4:6.*

Let your prayer be to God. The Lord knows the way. He leads you. He is your Rock of Ages. Look up to the Lord. Know yourself. Find no fault with others. Be humble but steadfast. Seek the Lord patiently. Come to the Lord. He is the Bread of Life. Do the will of Jesus. He will cast out one. Believe on the Lord and you have life everlasting.

Grow gradually into the likeness of Jesus.

Can you identify one quality that Jesus has, that you have?

———◦❖◦———

5th Apr '24 Saturday

*M*y presence shall go with thee and I will give thee rest. *Exodus 33:14.*

O Blessed Trinity, bestow
Thy pardoning grace on us below,
And shield us evermore;
Until, within Thy courts above,
We see Thy Face, and sing Thy love
And with Thy saints adore. Amen

Leave not the Lord till He bless you. Take hold of His strength. Abide with Jesus.

Ask in faith nothing wavering. *James 1:6.*

Help another. Cheer the troubled. Sympathise with others. Be gentle and Christ-like. Forsake not the Lord. Ask of Him and receive. Go to no other. Jesus is the Bread of Life. He died for the World. Believe in Him.

Know the Lord for yourself.

The Lord works in your heart. Jesus is your sanctifier. He will purge you. He is your end. Sing and pray. See in what you agree with others. Be gentle. Jesus is your Helper always. Bring forth fruit worthy of repentance. Please the Lord. Eat of His Body and drink of His blood and you will have union with Jesus. Call on His precious name. Faith is the Way to Truth.

Do you know the Lord personally?

———◈◈◈———

6th Apr '24 Sunday

*B*ear you one another's burdens, and so fulfill the law of Christ. *Galatians 6:2.*

The Royal Banners forward go,
The Cross shines forth in mystic glow;
Where He in flesh, our flesh Who made,
Our sentence bore, our ransom paid.

Jesus Christ pleads your cause for you in heaven. Be bold and come to Him in prayer. Speak gentle words. Help others in little things. Your progress toward goodness is tested by your sympathy. You must seek to know the Lord through Faith.

You often trespass against the Lord, forgetting to call upon Him.

The Words of Christ are spirit and life.
Make mention of the glorious name of the Lord. Trust in Him. He is mighty and everlasting. You have peace with God.

Loving acts tell greatly on people. Be a good Samaritan. Control yourself. Knowledge comes by faith. Seek the Lord hoping to be satisfied. Confess your evil ways and return unto the Lord your God. Forget not the Lord your God. Forsake not the Lord Who has the Words of Eternal life. Believe in the Lord. Jesus is the Christ.

The less communication with God,
more the chances of trespassing. Do you agree?

———— ·❦· ————

7th Apr '24 Monday

*B*elieving, ye rejoice with joy unspeakable and full of glory. *I Peter 1:8.*

There while He hung, His sacred side,
By soldiers spear was opened wide,
To cleanse us in the precious flood
Of Water mingled with His Blood.

Rejoice in suffering if it is for Christ. Grow in faith. Abound in good works. *II Corinthians 9:8.*

Preach the Gospel. Praise and magnify the Lord. Show your gratitude to Him. You are unworthy of any good thing from God. The Lord is your Guide. Return unto Him. Fulfill the commands of Jesus. Yield not to temptation. Faith becomes experiment, experiment experience, and experience brings forth knowledge.

God's grace is sufficient to sustain you. You can do all things thro' Christ. Live in Jesus. Wait on the Lord and renew your strength. The Lord is your Refuge. Appreciate the good you receive at God's loving hand. Acknowledge your sins. He will put away your iniquities and you shall be whole. Return to the Lord. Fear not mankind. Look up to Jesus for succour and help.

Faith is no makeshift. Rather it is an assurance of things hoped for, conviction of things not seen.

Why do people call "Faith" a crutch or a makeshift?

———◈◈◈———

8th Apr '24 Tuesday

$\mathcal{M}$ost gladly therefore will I rather glory in my infirmities, that the power of Christ may rest upon me. *II Corinthians 12:9.*

Fulfill'd is now what David told
In true prophetic song of old,
How God the heathen's King should be;
For God is reigning from the Tree.

God will freely give you all things. Abide in Christ. In everything Christ has raised you up. Have more of Love. Know how to be serious. Whatever God wills is holy, just and good, therefore fear nothing. You have sinned against the Lord. Come back to Him and He will heal your backslidings. Judge righteously.

Faith is the ear of the soul and the veracity of insight.

Reason is a matter of faith. You take yourself for granted. Achieve something. Abstain from vain thoughts. Put away evil from you and return unto the Lord. Jesus Christ is from above and He is able to save you to the uttermost. The Lord cometh quickly. Be ready to meet Him. You shall see His face. Trust. Deal justly, love mercy and walk humbly with God. Forget yourself. Don't mind pain for the sake of others. Put others first and their good before self-gratification.

How has Faith provided you insight?

⸻◈◈⸻

9th Apr '24 Wednesday

*T*heir Redeemer is strong; the Lord of hosts is His name; He shall thoroughly plead their cause. *Jeremiah 50:34.*

O Tree of glory, Tree most fair,
Ordained those Holy hurts to bear,
How bright in purple robe it stood
The purple of a Saviour's blood.

Fear not. Jesus is on your side.

He is able to keep you from falling. *Jude 1:24.*

Call upon the Lord for aid against the world, the flesh and the Devil. Let your sin make you angry with yourself. Repent of doing evil. It will not pay. Serve the Lord faithfully. Come thirsty soul unto Jesus and He will give you His Spirit. Ask and receive.

Faith plays a great part in every realm.

The Lord has saved you from the depths of hell while you were lost. Forget not His great sacrifice. Let Christ reign in you. Be strictly truthful. Correct yourself. Let no sin hide you from God. Deal justly and return unto the Lord. Stand up for the Truth. Fear not mankind. Call upon God to vindicate your cause. Be not hasty. Faith is supreme everywhere.

How has "Faith" played a part in your physical realm?

⸻⬧⬧⬧⸻

10ᵗʰ Apr '24 Thursday

*W*hen I would do good, evil is present with me. *Romans 7:21.*

Be of good cheer; thy sins be forgiven thee. *Matthew 9:2.*

Upon its arms like balance true,
He weighted the price for sinners due,
The price which none but He could pay
And spoil'd the spoiler of his prey.

You are complete in Jesus. You are sanctified in Jesus. Repent and let Jesus dwell in you. Do every duty aright. Waste no portion of your day.

Be less hasty to scrutinize.
The Lord will surely perish iniquity. Seek His forgiveness thro' Jesus Christ.

Go and sin no more. *John 8:11*

Be more like Jesus. By faith you discover yourself, God and the whole world.
You must suffer persecution for Jesus sake. Be God's friend and care not for man. You should not be of the world. Accept your duties and do them honestly. Do all things well. Be anxious about nothing.

Trust in God and do the right.
The Lord is merciful and slow to anger. Be one with Jesus. Know the Lord. Believe in the Lord, have faith in Him and serve Him with all your heart and soul. Seek Him and you shall find Him.

Read Matthew 7:4 about the beam in your eye.

———— ·❈· ————

11th Apr '24 Friday

*T*o Thee eternal Three in One,
Let homage meet by all be done:
As by the Cross Thou dost restore,
So rule and guide us evermore.

In the multitude of words there wanteth not sin; but he that refraineth his lips is wise. *Proverbs 10:19.*
Be slow to speak and slow to anger.

Ask God to set a watch on your lips. *Psalm 141:3.*

Look at Jesus. Be not turned by failure or success. Be steadfast in the uplift of mankind. Face your actual duties honestly. The Lord is great and mighty. Fear and honour Him. Believe on the Lord Jesus. You need a personal God.

The Lord will instruct and teach you in the way you should go. Be meek and learn of Him. Come to Jesus. Draw near to Jesus. Follow on. Have the highest aims possible. What you have to do is great.

Do your duty and a little more.

Hate evil and do good. Jesus entered glory through suffering. You cannot hope for more. Do always those things which please the Father. Continue in Him. You are not alone. God is your personal friend.

Do you enjoy doing more than your share?

———◈◈◈———

12th Apr '24 Saturday

*F*ierce and dread the tempest gathers
Dark clouds drift across our sky,
All around suspense and tumult,
Waves of trouble rising high;
But our trust is in Jehovah,
Who the wildest storm can still
God has promised to deliver
He is able and He will.

The Lord was like man and suffered in his stead. Consider His infinite stoop. Crave for God Himself. Ask for fresh strength.

Working for God gives you energy.

Rest in the Lord. Do all you can do and leave the rest to God. Things sincerely done have their reward. Strive and achieve. You are to be divine. Do the works of Jesus.

Do nothing of which you will have to repent. Make sacrifices freely. Obedience and duty is your guiding star. Glorify God on earth. Behold the Lord and be transformed. Be firm. Walk worthy of God's gracious hands. Feel your indebtedness to a Personal God. Learn of God ere it be too late. Seek not your own glory. Ask for Christ's righteousness and He will help you.

Have you found satisfaction in working for God?

———— ❖ ————

13th Apr '24 Sunday

*D*ay by day fresh suffering threatens,
Anxious thoughts of peril near,
Grief and pain of separation,

Loss of all one holds most dear;
Yet amid the sharpest anguish,
Perfect peace our hearts can fill,
God has promised to deliver,
He is able and He will!

Whatever you do, do all to God's glory. *I Corinthians 10:31.*

Present your body a living sacrifice to God. *Romans 12:1.*

Let the love of Christ constrain you. Have faith and love.

Continually practice small distasteful duties.

Fail not the demand of the present hour. Have peace of mind from above. Follow Christ. Let not people be disappointed in you. Do good. Confess your sins and be penitent.

Walk as a child of light. Give thanks at all times. The Lord is yours. Order your life well in every single act. Persevere. God wants you to do your duty. Return unto the Lord. Jesus is the Light of the Word. He is able to save you to the uttermost. Be filled with joy. Abound in hope. Wait patiently. Let Jesus come and dwell in you.

How do you make yourself do the "distasteful duties"?

14ᵗʰ Apr '24 Monday

*T*rembling lips are asking sadly
"Why this mystery of pain?"
And our cry goes up to Heaven,
"Lord send peace, send peace again."
Faith and courage must not falter,
Nor cold doubt our spirits chill,
God has promised to deliver,
He is able and He will!—S. B. Kathleen Warren

Jesus is your Beloved Friend. He loves you. Meditate on His love for you. Consider His great goodness. God is working for your best. Do something. Love something and hope for something. Serve God joyously. Scatter happiness wherever you go. Amend your ways and the Lord will bless you. Know your Redeemer. He has saved you. God directs all. Trust.

Though your sins be as scarlet, they shall be as white as snow. *Isaiah 1:18.*

Return. Bless the Lord and forget not His benefits. The Lord is supporting you, you shall be safe.

Do things right and at the right time.

Smile while you can. Serve God joyously. Scatter happiness. Renounce yourself. Keep the Temple of God holy. Do you know your Saviour Jesus? Praise the Lord for all He does for you.

In God's presence is fullness of Joy. *Psalm 16:11.*

Why is right timing as important as the right action?

15th Apr '24 Tuesday

O Lord how happy should we be;
If we could cast our care on Thee,
If we from self could rest;
And feel at heart that One above,
In perfect wisdom, perfect love,
Is working for the best.—J. Austen.

The Lord is mighty to save and to keep you from falling.
Nothing can separate you from Christ. *Romans 8:39.*

Confess and return. Be happy. Happiness is a moral achievement.
Provoke not the Lord to anger. Serve Him faithfully. Believe in
the Son of God. Ask for faith. Have joy and peace in believing.

Seek not great things for yourself. Be meek and lowly. Humble
yourself as Jesus did. Follow in Christ's steps. Be content in
whatever state God places you.

Be broadminded. Feel for others.

Be happy as well as useful. Inspire affection. Obey the voice of
the Lord and be His and it shall be well with you. Be honest.
Jesus is your true Shepherd. Jesus is the Door. Enter in by Him
and be saved. He is come to give you life abundant. Ask and
receive of Him. Ask for vision of God's glory. Rejoice in the
Lord.

Explain "Broadmindedness."

16th Apr '24 Wednesday

*W*ill the Lord cast off forever? And will He be favourable no more? Is His mercy clean gone forever? Doth His promise fail for evermore? Hath God forgotten to be gracious? Hath He in anger shut up His tender mercies? And I said, This is my infirmity; but I will remember the years of right hand of the most High. *Psalm 77:7-10.*

The Lord will uphold you to the end. Be joyful in the Lord. Let your Home be a place of happiness. Love and be happy. Deserve Happiness. Make all happy. Return from evil doing. The Lord hates sin. Jesus is the Good Shepherd. He knows you through and through.

You are God's fellow-worker.

Call upon the Lord, and He will surely answer you. God is ready to give. He will not let man prevail against you if you are on His side.

Rejoice. Love is the true Jacob's Ladder. Seek to be happy.

Think pure and lovely thoughts. Take counsel of a personal God. He is your great ally. Put the yoke of Christ upon yourself. Make the world better for those who come after you.

Yield not to evil thoughts. Ask the Lord to help you against Satan. Jesus has willingly died for you. Forget not His love.

List some of the ways you are God's fellow worker.

————◈◈◈————

17th Apr '24 Thursday

*P*ray with unceasing prayer and entreaty on every fitting occasion in the Spirit and be always on the alert to sense opportunities for doing so, with unwearied persistence and entreaty on behalf of God's people.

Help others. Spend yourself in relieving the wants of others.

Learn the blessedness of giving and serving.

Do all in the name of Christ. Glorify God and be acceptable unto Him.

Boast in the Lord. Be one with the Father. Forsake the old works. Jesus gives eternal life. Forget not God's mercies to you.

Jesus loves you and draws you to Himself. Behold the Lamb of God.

You have Jesus and it is enough. Love Him.

Go onward on your march to Heaven.

Seek not happiness, only do your duties. Be helpful.

Delight in the Lord. Jesus is your Great Physician. Call on Him for aid. All things work to God's glory. Follow after Jesus unhesitatingly, and it will do your soul good.

Think of your last experience of giving and serving.
Was it positive?

18th Apr '24 Friday

*N*ow, my soul, thy voice upraising,
Tell in sweet and mournful strains
How the crucified, enduring
Grief and wound and dying pain,
Freely of His love was offered,
Sinless was for sinners slain.

Christ is your Saviour. Learn of Him for He is meek and lowly. If you would be happy, steep your temper. Keep your word too. Do good to all. Make all around you cheerful. Weep for your sins and the deceitfulness of your heart.

Jesus is the Resurrection and the life. *John 11:25.*

Believe on Him. Worship the Lord Who is worthy of Praise.

Jesus offered Himself once for you. Nothing should separate you from Christ's Love. You are to be forever with Jesus. This is not your rest. Believe not ill. Be just in all you do and say.

Consider happiness as a duty.

Be joyful at all times. The Lord certainly punishes iniquity. Jesus loves you. Believe His Almighty power. He is able to save you to the uttermost. Consider to whom you pray. Try and realize your Personal God.

Is happiness a choice or chore with you?

————◈◈————

19th Apr '24 Saturday

*R*esting from His work today
In the tomb the Saviour lay;
Still He slept from Head to feet
Shrouded in the winding sheet,
Lying in the rock alone
Hidden by the sealed stone.

You have peace with God thro' Christ Jesus. He is your Mediator. You belong to the Lord. Be content with what you have and be happy. Do your duty. To know God and the Lord Jesus Christ is eternal life. Forget not Christ's "infinite stoop" and His loving sacrifice for you.

We put our trust in the Lord who is our Rock of Ages and beside whom we have no other. He will do the best for us. Preach the Gospel wherever you can.

Let the love of Christ constrain you. *II Corinthians 5:14.*

Hide not your talents.

Be troubled about nothing but lean hard on the Lord who is your stay in the Day of Trouble.

Jesus suffered to make you happy. Be prepared to suffer for Him.

What does "leaning on God" mean to you?

20ᵗʰ Apr '24 Easter

*J*esus lives! no longer now
Can Thy terrors, death, appall us;
Jesus lives! by this we know
Thou, O grave, canst not enthrall us, Alleluia!
Jesus lives! for us He died,
Thee alone to Jesus living,
Pure in heart may we abide,
Glory to our Saviour giving. Alleluia!

Abstain from all impurity and fleshly lusts. You shall be like Jesus.

Jesus has risen to grant you franchise from sin.

Choose your friends. Love, trust, and surrender are required for perfect peace with God.

Sympathize with others. Guide others to Jesus.
The Lord is everlasting and almighty. Trust in Him.

Love Jesus and deny yourself to please Him. Experience God.

Nothing can separate you from the love of Jesus but sin. He is with you at all times. Forget not Him. He has saved you from sin.

Avoid battles. Rejoice in the Lord. Seek to help others always.
God is your friend. You be friends with Him.
The Lord orders the footsteps of His children. He is merciful and just. Trust Him. Receive Jesus into your Heart.

Appa used to say, "Easter is more important than Christmas."

———⟨✥⟩———

21ˢᵗ Apr '24 Monday

O Lord of All, with us abide
In this our joyful Easter-tide;
From every weapon death can wield
Thine own redeemer forever shield.

All praise be Thine, O risen Lord,
From death to endless life restored;
All praise to God the Father be
And Holy Ghost eternally. Amen.

Stand fast in the Lord. He will preserve you from evil.

You live by faith. *II Corinthians 5:7.*

Continue in Jesus. Watch. Be brave, overcome. Love Jesus. Little things make people happy. Be not weary of kindness.

Obey the Lord and serve Him. Be anxious to see Jesus as He is. Do all you undertake to please Jehovah. Seek not your own glory. Trust all into the Hands of the Almighty.

Be forbearing.

Never be hasty. Persevere to the end and the Lord will bless you. Sacrifice self for the sake of others. Be accurate and God fearing in all you do.

Let not your friends go astray. Advise and seek to help others.

Look up the word "Forbearing" in the dictionary.

22nd Apr '24 Tuesday

*O*ur fellowship is with the Father, and with His Son Jesus Christ. *I John 1:3.*

Jesus loves you freely.
The Son of God . . . loved me,
and gave Himself for me.
Accepted in the Beloved.

Jesus died that you may live. He is your Friend. Let your thoughts be holy. Let all things be done decently and in order. Waste not words.

Be not inquisitive. Watch your words. Submit yourself to correction. Unless one suffers, others cannot gain. Hate your life and you shall save yourself. Hunger after God.

The Lord is your Saviour and there is none beside you. Trust not in yourself. Lean hard. Jesus has quickened you. Tire none by your incessant talk. Do everything methodically.

Obey the voice of the Lord. Displease Him not. He will not plead forever. Jesus died to save you. God should be your Personal friend. Make Him such.

Realize His Presence and You will find Him holding your hand in the day of trouble.

What comfort does the image of God
"holding your hand" give you?

———— ❖ ————

23rd Apr '24 Wednesday

*G*ive every man thine ear, but few thy voice;
Take each man's censure, but reserve thy judgements.
Sweet as refreshing dews, or summer showers
To the long parching thirst of drooping flowers
Are kind words.

Let all your words be wholesome and for the good of all around you. Be sincere and kind.

The Lord is your Father. The angel of the Lord is with you. Call on the Lord who has made you what you are.

Repent and return to God who is longing for you.

Walk in the Light which Christ gives you. Seek the Lord. He is not man but unimaginably greater.

Return unto the Shepherd and Bishop of your soul. Follow the Master who will give you life-eternal. Learn of the Lord and give to others.
Never play false. Be sincere. Let your words be life giving. The Lord knows your thoughts. He directs your ways if you trust in Him.

Be not enamoured of the prosperity of the wicked. Love not the praise of men. The Word of the Lord will judge you.

God is great beyond your imaginations.

Read the prodigal son story in Luke 15:11-31.

24th Apr '24 Thursday

*T*rust in the Lord at all times, ye people, pour out your heart before Him: God is a refuge for us. *Psalm 62:8.*

Heaven and earth shall pass away, but my words shall not pass away. *Matthew 24:35.*

The Lord is able to deliver you and He is willing. He is faithful. Trust in Him. Speak kindly. Gracious words are precious.

Leave the wrong thing unsaid at the tempting moment.

Watch your words. Leave not hold of your personal God. Obey and live. Humble yourself to the dust. God does all well. Do the works of Jesus and you shall be happy.

The Lord is good to all. Lift up your eyes to Him, for He is your Helper.

Wait on the Lord. Hope and rejoice. Be careful of your conversation. Leave the bitter word unspoken. Speak agreeably with all. Vex not others.

You must be a praise and glory to God. Displease Him not. Betray not your Lord and Master. Seek ever to walk in His ways.

Man is infinitely small. God is wonderful in wisdom and power.

"Words fitly spoken are like apples of gold in a platter of silver." (Proverbs 25:11) Practice it.

25ᵗʰ Apr '24 Friday

*W*ith smiles of peace and looks of love
Light in our dwellings we may make;
Bid kind good humour brighten there,
And do all still for Jesus' sake.

None of us lives to himself, and not one dies to himself.

Every act of yours has some effect on others. Your very words are not weightless. Do all for Jesus' sake. Live unto righteousness. Come to Jesus. Your sins are forgiven you through the life blood of Jesus. You think of God as the best you can know of. The Lord is kind and merciful, yet He cannot leave sin unpunished. Love one another even as Christ loved you.

Your idea about God should be sanctifying mediatory thought. Return unto the Lord. Have nothing to do with sin.

Let not your heart be troubled. *John 14:1.*

Believe in Jesus Who is the Way, the Truth and the life. Know Jesus. You will be able to do Jesus' works because He will support you. Ask and receive.

Beware of unconscious influence. Watch your thoughts.

Sacrifice yourself. All things are yours and you are Christ's. Believe and ask.

How much influence do thoughts have on people's actions?

26th Apr '24 Saturday

*H*elp us to help each other, Lord,
Each other's burdens bear;
Let each his friendly aid afford,
To soothe another's care.

The beloved of the Lord shall dwell in safety by Him; and the Lord shall cover Him all day long, and He shall dwell between His shoulders.—*Deuteronomy 33:12.*

Rest in the Lord, for He supports you. Cast all your care on Him, Who is a mighty God. Mind how you spend your life for it is given to you as a trust. Be pleasant and help others. If you love Jesus, keep His commands. He will not leave you comfortless. You are God's; Call on Him. Man dwells but temporarily in his Body.

Be clothed in the righteousness of God. Christ loved the Church and gave Himself for her. Seek to please Him. Make others happy. Be holy unto the Lord. Be separate from the World. Wait upon the Lord. Ask Him to forgive your sins.

The Peace of Christ should still your murmuring heart in trouble.

Ask for the Holy Spirit. Allow Christ to show Him all of you. Personalities are invisible.

Compare the "Peace of Christ" with worldly peace.

———◆◇◆———

27ᵗʰ Apr '24 Sunday

*T*he world passeth away and the lust thereof; but He that doeth the will of God abideth forever. *I John 2:17.*

The end of all things is at hand; be ye therefore sober, and watch unto prayer. *I Peter 4:7.*

Have patience, never be hasty. Live a Christ-like life. Cast off the works of darkness. Be strong in the Lord. Trust in His strength. Watch your life in small matters. Keep it pure and good for Christ. The Lord certainly will punish iniquity. Abide in Jesus and bring forth fruit to His glory. Love one another. Personality can create. So can God.

The Lord knows all. He will revenge you. **Be proud for you are called by His Name.** Rejoice in the Lord. Love one another even as Christ loved you. Do the Lord's bidding. Ask of the Lord and receive. The ways of the Lord are past judgement. He is great and mighty. Glorify God in your flesh. Be followers of God. Walk as His child. Avoid all evil and grow in His likeness. Do all you can to please the Lord. Let your influence be always for God! Watch the way you speak.

If "Christian" is your last name, how proud
will your heavenly parent be?

———◈◈◈———

28th Apr '24 Monday

*B*ehold the Lamb of God. *John 1:29.*

If you do not shine at home, if your father and mother, your sister and brother, if the very cat and dog in the house are not the better and happier for your being a Christian, it is a question whether you really are one.

All you do affects others. Your deeds travel after and make you what you are. Have a good introspection, for you are full of faults. Delight to do the will of God. Be a slave of the Lamb. The Lord is with you to deliver you from sin. Trust. Mind not the hatred of the World. Let the Spirit help you. God is great beyond human understanding.

Hope in the Lord. Rejoice always. Praise the Lord Who is worthy of all praise. Love Him above all. Be not fond of fault-finding. Shine brightly for Jesus. Make all around you bright and cheery. Repent and return unto the Lord ere it be too late. Seek the Lord while He may be found. Ask for the Holy Spirit's guidance. Be prepared to follow Him. God is supremely good.

How did your actions affect others yesterday?

29th Apr '24 Tuesday

*W*hat should a man desire to leave?
A flawless work; a noble life.

It is good for me that I have been afflicted; that I might learn Thy statues. *Psalm 119:71.*

Before I was afflicted I went astray: but now have I kept Thy Word. *Psalm 119:67.*

The Lord has not punished you according to your deserts. The Lord does all things well. Do submit to His chastening. Let the very atmosphere you are in be holy. Walk worthy of your high calling. Let your influence be in the right direction. The Lord watches your thoughts. He is your Strength and Refuge. All things are yours thro' Christ. You can trust in God.

Jesus will come again. He is your forerunner. Wait for His coming. Long for Christ's coming.

Let your presence carry joy and diffuse peace.

Set a good and holy example to all. Be not sparing of kind acts. Sin brings punishment in its train. Ask of the Lord and He will give. Jesus is with you unto the end of the world. Watch and pray. Jesus is God and the fairest among ten thousand. Love Him above all.

Have you tried peacemaking?

———◈◈◈———

30th Apr '24 Wednesday

*W*hoso keepeth his Word, in him verily is the love of God perfected. *I John 2:5.*

Are you afraid to tell your Lord about your small things as if they were not worth His attending to? Your great things are not any more worth His attending to.

Cast all your care on Him. *I Peter 1:7.*

Abide in Christ. Love Him and keep His word. Do righteousness. The Lord will preserve you. Call on Him in the day of trouble. Be not afraid to tell Him all concerning you. Trust not in man for He will surely fail you, but trust in God who can make all things abound for you. You are not alone. In the world you have tribulation but Jesus gives peace.

Be slow to get angry. The Lord is merciful. He keeps His promise. Follow Him. Love all. Rejoice in suffering when you are in the right. Be angry and sin not. Offer your heart to God. Trust implicitly in Him to order all things for you. He always knows best. Call on Him. Let not your heart deceive you. The Lord searches you thro' and thro'. Know Jesus and you have eternal life.

Opinions about God are a road to understanding Him.

Can anyone really and fully understand God?

———◈◈———

Jehovah - shammah

The Lord is there — *May*

First Day in the Month of May 1924. Thursday

I know whom I have believed, and am persuaded that He is able to keep that which I have committed unto Him against that day. *II Timothy 1:12.*

The pursuit of the Spirit is peace.

Trust in the Lord and be at peace.

Hope and joy at all times. Be not troubled. There is no haphazard in the world. God knows you thoroughly. God is great in Wisdom and Might. With the Lord you are safe. You shall never be ashamed. Glorify the Lord. Receive the Word of the Lord. Trust in your Father's Love.

The Lord is with you. Sing and rejoice. Fear not for He is your Helper. Cast all your care on Him. God knows best how to do things for you. Submit yourself to His Will. Fear not. Nothing can harm you as long as you trust in the Lord and do the right. He is able and make your enemies try to do you good. Trust, only trust.

One of the names of the Messiah is Prince of Peace. Why?

———◈◈◈———

2nd May '24 Friday

*N*ow our wants and burdens leaving,
To His care who cares for all,
Cease we fearing, cease we grieving,
At His touch our burdens fall.—Longfellow.

The young lions do lack and suffer hunger, but they that seek the Lord shall not want any good thing. *Psalm 34:10.*

You are ignorant. The Lord knows the beginning from the end. Leave all therefore in His Hand and be at ease. The Lord loves the humble. You cannot escape Him. He is able to save you. Lean hard on Him. Hearken unto the Word of the Lord and you will be blessed. The Lord will preserve you from evil. Believe on Him. Be one with the Lord. Let your religion be real.

Keep yourself from idols. Love not inordinately. The Lord looketh on your heart. Set your affection on things above. The Lord will supply all your needs. Cast your burden upon the Lord. Endure all patiently. Let your fellowship with God be real and not formal. Lean on Him.

The Lord is able to mould you.

Leave yourself in His Hands.

He is the Potter, you are the clay.

Share the glory of Jesus.

God is the potter and we are the clay.
What does moulding mean to you?

————◆◈◆————

3rd May '24 Saturday

*B*e ye perfect, even as your Father which is in heaven is perfect. *Matthew 5:48.*

Search me, O God, and know my heart; try me, and know my thoughts: and see if there be any wicked way in me, and lead me in the way everlasting. *Psalm 139:23.*

Ye are bought with a price. *I Corinthians 6:20.*

Glorify your Father in Heaven for you have been bought with His Blood and therefore you are His. He careth for you. Seek protection from God. The Lord leads you to your Heavenly Home. The Lord is good and kind. Return unto the Lord Who is the Author and Giver of all good things.

The cup which the Father gives, you must receive.

Neglect not common duties. Humble yourself before God for you are so infinitely small and insignificant. Cast away pride which does not become you. Be wary for your Adversary the Devil goes about like a roaring lion.

Jesus also had to make the decision whether to drink from the cup or not? When was that done? Read Matthew 26.

———— ❖ ————

4th May '24 Sunday

*B*e not Thou far from me, O Lord;
O my strength, haste Thee to help me. *Psalm 22:19.*

Behold, the Lord's hand is not shortened that it cannot save; neither His ear heavy that it cannot hear. *Isaiah 59:1.*

Trust in the Lord your strength. Fear not; only believe.

The Lord will avenge you.

Only call on Him. All will work for your future happiness. Cast all on Jesus. Be anxious about nothing. The Lord is with you. Deny not the Lord who has done such great things for you.

Glorify the Lord on earth. Be about your Father's business. Believe on the Lord. Grow in favour with God and man. Suffer for doing right, rather than for wrong. Cast all your care upon God. Submit to His will. Do your duty, and fight temptations. Look forward hopefully. Abhor evil. Serve the Lord faithfully. Rejoice in His might and seek to do His will. Subdue all pride. Return in humility to your God from Whom flow all the blessings of this life.

What does "avenge" mean personally?
Why is it better to leave it in God's hands?

5th May '24 Monday

Father's 56th Birthday

*N*o good thing will He withhold from them that walk uprightly. O Lord of Hosts, blessed is the man that trusteth in Thee. *Psalm 84:11.*

Have faith in God.

Fear the Lord and you shall want nothing. Be anxious about nothing.

Set all your requests be made known unto God by prayer and supplication.

Be not fainthearted. Play the man. Have presence of mind. Be a hero. Fear to do evil. Deny not the Lord and Master of your Body and Soul. Bear Him out in your life. Seek His pleasure always. Let your Master-motive be for lifting power.

The Lord pities you, for He knows your frame. He is your Keeper. Jesus Christ is ever the same.

Be strong and of a good courage. You have done with the sad and thorny past, fear not. Drink not, be brave. Serve the Lord.

Do not despair. Do your duty and leave the rest to God. If you suffer being innocent, happy are you. Rejoice and be exceedingly glad for great is your reward. Seek for unity with God.

Look up the difference between prayer and supplication.

———————◈◉◈———————

6th May '24 Tuesday

*H*e was wounded for our transgressions, he was bruised for our iniquities: the chastisement of our peace was upon him; and with His stripes we are healed. *Isaiah 53:5.*

The first thing a kindness deserves is acceptance; the next is transmission.

God is just. You, He has forgiven thro' Christ. Go and sin no more. Look for good in everybody. Honour it and try and initiate it. Small kindnesses are the very salt of life. Do something kind to somebody or other. Choose the Way of Life and live it.. Christ suffered greatly to relieve you of pain. Forget not the cause but seek to please Him always. Use your Religion rightly to serve mankind.

Do not meddle with things too high for you. Submit to God who knows all. **Feel your insignificance.** You shall grow into Christ's likeness from day to day. Look always at Jesus. Be transformed into the heavenly. The wages of sin is Death.

When you look at God's magnificent creation,
do you feel insignificant?

7th May '24 Wednesday

*G*od is our Refuge and Strength, a very present help in trouble. Therefore will not we fear, though the earth be removed, and though the mountains be carried into the midst of the sea, tho' the waters thereof roar and be troubled though the mountains shake with the swelling thereof. *Psalm 46:1-3.*

Let nothing trouble you. Your life is hid with Christ in God. Do as much good as you can for others. That will comfort you. Judge not harshly for you are liable to judge amiss. Be not mortally afraid of men.

Trust in God who holds the key of all unknown.

Repent and return unto Jesus. Are you sure you are saved? Do you feel the Presence of God guiding you? Love Him with all your heart. Seek His blessing in all you do, for without Him you are helpless. Trust in the Lord at all times.

Is it difficult to trust God when you don't know the future?

————— ⋅❖⋅ —————

8th May '24 Thursday

*Y*e that are the Lord's Remembrances
Keep not silence.
Looking for and hasting unto thee
Coming of the Day of God.
Come, Lord Jesus.
Make no tarrying, O my God.

Seek to do the Will of God. Delight in His Love. Be kind one to another. Gladden the hearts of all around you for you know not how short your life is. Trust in the Lord at all times. People appreciate little kind acts.

Lose no opportunity of doing good.

Seek the Lord. The Lord knows you and He will aid you in trouble. He is ever at your side. Pray one for another. Prepare to meet your God. Seek to understand men's wants and to help them. Lose no time to show your love for others.

Do good now.

Forsake not the Lord lest you be God-forsaken. Take up your Cross and follow the Lord. Jesus set you an example, and you are not greater than He. Fear God.

Find an opportunity to do good today.

———·⟨⊕⟩·———

9th May '24 Friday

*F*aith is the substance of things hoped for, the evidence of things not seen. *Hebrews 11:1.*

Cast not away therefore your confidence, which hath great recompense of reward. *Hebrews 10:35.*

God has great things in store for you. Do trust in Him. Believe and rejoice. Let your love be sincere. Abhor evil. Do all you can for the Master. Cultivate kindness, for there is nothing so needed as that. Be deliberately kind to all, lest you be cruel to many. Be mindful of the poor. Forget not the Lord who gave His life for you. God is a Person.

Do your duty gladly. Follow the Lord wholeheartedly. Do all things for the love of God. Do good and you will be all the better for it. Fear not. Jesus has taken away your sins. Return unto the Lord. Hear the Word of the Lord. Forget not to serve mankind for Jesus came to save all.

Stand and meditate at the Cross.

Learn of Jesus, for He is your Master. Trust in the Lord.

When I survey the wondrous cross
on which the Prince of Glory died,
my richest gain, I count but loss.
And pour contempt on all my pride.

———— ❈ ————

10th May '24 Saturday

*T*hanks be unto God which giveth us the victory thro' our Lord Jesus Christ. *I Corinthians 15:57.*

If your brother acts wrongly toward you, go and point out his fault to him when only you and he are there. If he listens to you, you have gained him. *Matthew 18:15.*

Behave in such a way to your friends that they may be led to see God's care. Trust all as friends. Have Jesus to do your battles for you, for He has crushed Satan's power beneath His feet. Watch and Rejoice. Fear the Lord and do your duty faithfully. Jesus was pierced in His side for you! You have trust in God, which the Atheist can't match.

Vanity of vanities, all is vanity.

This is not your eternal home. Jesus is the same forever. Trust in the Lord. Be not in haste to spread evil reports. Make friends of all. Rejoice and be glad. The Lord is your Rock. He it is that has saved you. Fear not mankind. Be brave.

One who called everything Vanity in the Bible is a king who possessed everything. What does that tell you?

———— ·❦· ————

11th May '24 Sunday

*H*e shall cover thee with His feathers, and under His wings, thou shalt trust; His truth shall be thy shield and buckler.

He shall call upon Me, and I will answer him; I will be with him, and honour him.
With long life will I satisfy him, and show him my salvation.
Psalm 91:4, 15, 16.
Be proud about nothing. For what you are, you are by the grace of God.

Yield yourself to Him and He will use you to His glory.

Trust Him to do all for you.

Yielding and being used by God comes from daily abiding in the vine.

12th May '24 Monday

*L*ord, Thou hast been our dwelling place in all generations. *Psalm 90:1.*

So teach us to number our days that we may apply our hearts unto wisdom. *Psalm 90:12.*

O earth, earth, earth, hear the Word of the Lord.

Watch your conduct. Be mean to none. Deal gently with those around. Awake to righteousness and sin not. Take the armour of God. Abide in Jesus. Open unto Jesus and let Him in. The Lord is your Lover. Love Him and others. Live in Him.

People abused your Master, yet He was not hasty. Suffer doing the right. That is glory. Be not in a hurry to find faults into others. Ask forgiveness if you are in the wrong. Be generous, speak well of others. Let godly fear rule your heart.

The Lord sees you thro' and thro'.

He is everywhere. Keep the Word of the Lord, for it is Mighty in deed. Seek peace from above. Jesus knows you by name. Serve Him.

Has God seen you through a difficult situation recently?

———•⊰⊱•———

13th May '24 Tuesday

*P*ray everywhere, lifting up holy hands, without wrath and doubling.
I *Timothy 2:8*.

If I regard iniquity in my heart,
The Lord will not hear me. *Psalm 66:18*.

When free from every, scorn and pride,
Our wishes soar above;
We try each other's faults to hide
And show a brother's love.

Ask the Lord in faith. Forgive others. Call on Him in spirit. Put evil away from you. Resolve to do your work well. Be not slothful.

Be always doing.

The Lord will punish them that dishonour Him. Let the peace of Christ abide always in your hearts. He is with you. Get acquainted with God's Personage.

Ask God to lead you to His throne. Jesus is able to support you. The Eternal God is your refuge. Call on Him. Waste not your time. Be not lazy. Be active. Earn your name. Be not a hypocrite. Return unto the Lord with all your heart. Be not faithless but believing. Jesus is your Lord and God. He has suffered and bled for you. Forget not His love to you. Be not puzzled by the world, but put your trust in the Father-heart of God.

Faith followed by works is a good model. Be always doing.

14th May '24 Wednesday

*H*ere have we no continuing city, but we seek one to come. *Hebrews 13:14.*

The habit of viewing things cheerfully, and thinking about life hopefully may be made to grow up in us like any other habit.

You, when you suffer doing the right, have the fellowship of Christ's sufferings. Rejoice and be glad. A cheerful temper is to be coveted above all. Let innocence join cheerfulness. God will certainly punish evil. Believe on the Lord Jesus and you have eternal life. Trouble not about beliefs and creeds, but believe in One.

You can overcome Satan by the blood of the Lamb. Walk after the Spirit. Be prepared for troubles. Jesus will carry you through. Be thankful for all you receive for you are worthy of nothing. Be cheerful for that is what everyone needs. All things work together for good. The Lord will recompense you according to your deeds. All things work together for good. The Lord will recompense you according to your deeds. Jesus is thoughtful and loving. Fear to displease Him.

Belief in a Personality is the search of the Transforming power of Christianity.

Can you think of a person whose life was transformed by Christ?

15th May '24 Thursday

*H*appiness and brightness in God's service is a great gift, and one that wins others to Him. We are told to "make melody" in our hearts to the Lord and how can we do this unless we are bright and cheerful and serve His glory?—Himomell

Persistently look for the good and bright things in your common life and you will be one of the happiest creatures on earth. God Himself is with you to cheer and comfort you.

Rejoice and be exceedingly glad. The Lord will fiercely punish all sin which does not have for forgiveness, the Blood of Jesus, on it.

Love the Lord more than earthly things. Serve Him truly.

You are a part of Christ. Displease Him not by your forward ways. Live for Christ. Let not others know your troubles lest they should be caused needless pain.

Have no eyes for evil. A merry heart is a blessing wherever it be.

Be a faithful minister of God. Admonish and comfort your friends. Submit yourself to the Lord in everything.

Let the Spirit of God work in you, for without it your life will be a cipher.

Can you tell if a person is motivated by the Spirit?

————◈◈————

16th May '24 Friday

*T*ake my yoke upon you, and learn of Me; for I am meek and lowly in heart: and ye shall find rest unto your souls. For my yoke is easy, and my burden is light. *Matthew 11:29.*

Stand fast with Christ Who is your Master and Lord. Follow Him and bring forth the fruit of the Spirit. Pass on kind acts.

Let your laugh ring often, charming others. A cheerful temper is a blessing. Harsh words are often unpalatable.

Fear not man. Go ahead, doing your duty. You shall receive power from on high, for without it you are nothing.

Watch and pray earnestly.

Bless the Lord, your Counselor.

The Word of the Lord is your Lamp. Trust in Him. The Lord will guide you to your hour of Death.

Pray continually. Let joy be one of your hobbies. There is great strength in cheerfulness.

Trust in a Personality is all you need. You don't need hypotheses! The Lord will be for you, if you serve Him truly.

Fear not; to be His servant is a great pleasure.

The Lord will direct you always. Cast yourself under His Protection.

As a servant of God, what will be your goal?

———— ❖ ————

17th May '24 Saturday

*N*ot that we are sufficient of ourselves to think anything as of ourselves; but our sufficiency is of God. *II Corinthians 3:5.*

As He which hath called you is holy, do be ye holy in all manner of conversation. *I Peter 1:15.*

Be mindful how you live, lest you lose your salvation. Walk in the statutes of the Lord. You enter into heaven by free grace.

The Lord's will is better than yours.

Be not conceited. The Lord is great in power and glory. Humble yourself and God will fill you with His Spirit. Be not tossed by every wind of Doctrine.

Jesus humbled Himself and became man to save you.

Be watchful. Perfect your works before God. Despise not instruction.

Think always about others and what you can do for them. Forget yourself in service for mankind.

The Word of the Lord abides forever. Trust in Him.

You have often persecuted the Lord. Repent and turn a new leaf. Call on His name and you shall be saved.

Witness for Him. You know in Whom you have trusted and He is faithful: Rejoice.

Are you willing to surrender your will to God's will?

———◦❸◦❀◦———

18th May '24 Sunday

"We are made partakers of Christ
Partakers of the Holy Ghost
Partakers of the Divine Nature.
Holy, holy, holy, Lord God Almighty,
Which was, and is, and is to come"

Jesus in your life. Hide yourself in Him and let Him alone be seen.

Learn to be humble. Do the best you can each day. Be not greedy of praise.

False words and acts are of little avail. The Word of the Lord abideth for ever. Repent and believe.

Be unified and you will stand.

Let everything be done in lowliness of mind. Be charitable.

Take Jesus' yoke on you and learn of Him. Never despair. Work faithfully and the Lord will reward your efforts.

Think awhile about things of vital importance.

Seek the peace of every place and God will give you peace.

The Lord is able to work wonders on behalf of those who love Him.

Give the chance of Jesus to all.

Lowliness of mind means self takes a back seat. Try that today.

———— ❖❖❖ ————

19th May '24 Monday

*W*ash me thoroughly from my iniquity. *Psalm 51:2.*

Not unto us, O Lord, not unto us, but unto Thy name give glory, for Thy mercy, and for Thy truth's sake. *Psalm 115:9*

Humility is the hallmark of wisdom.

Be born again of the spirit of God.

The Blood of Jesus cleanses you from all sin. *I John 1:7.*

Cast yourself at Jesus' feet. He will forgive and receive you. Humble yourself. Seek the Lord and He will be found of you. The Lord loves you. Jesus is the Prince of Life. With faith in His name mighty deeds are possible.

You cannot explain God, but you can understand His love for you. Serve the Lord. God is faithful. Have fellowship with His Son. Walk in the Light. Jesus supports you by His intercession. Come to Jesus and He will comfort you. The Humble are the great men of the earth. The Lord will certainly punish lying words.

There is victory and power in the Glorious Name of Jesus.

Only trust.

Sing the chorus.
There is power, power, wonder working power in the blood of
the lamb; There is power, power, wonder working power,
in the precious blood of the lamb.

———◆◈◆———

20th May '24 Tuesday

O God, in mercy look on me:
My spirit knows not where to flee;
Yet in its grief I come to Thee—
Oh, cast me not away!

I long to see Thy smiling face,
I long to feel Thy kind embrace,
My Father, in Thy boundless grace,
Oh, cast me not away.—M. F.

Boast in Christ's Cross. Be humble minded. All you do is imperfect. Never be self-conscious. Be loving. Be led by the Spirit of God.

Give time for God's Word. Put on the whole armour of God. Crucify your fleshy lusts. The Lord is merciful. He will not always chide.

Be in Jesus Christ and you will be a new man. Fear not man. Prove all things; hold fast that which is good.

You are the Lord's. Jesus knows you by name. Fear nothing. Trust Him. Never think of yourself. Serve others. Be humble and loving.

Conquer as Christ conquered.

The Lord will correct you, but in measure. He is with you at all times. He is ready to save you.

Put your Trust in Him, for He is your Great Physician.

In what ways is God the heavenly physician?

21ˢᵗ May '24 Wednesday

*P*lant in us a humble mind,
Patient, pitiful and kind;
Meek and lowly let us be,
Full of goodness, full of Thee.—C. Wesley.

For if there is anyone who thinks himself to be somebody, when he is nobody, he is deluding himself.

Humble yourself and in due time God will reward you. People will sooner or later learn to appreciate humility.

The Joy of the Lord is your strength. *Nehemiah 8:10.*

Be strong in the Lord. God will uphold with His grace. The troubles you incur for Jesus' sake will turn to blessings shortly. Be brave and fight manfully. Fear not. The Lord is merciful and kind. Cast yourself on His compassion.

Jesus is your Saviour. Teach others of Christ. Follow in the steps of the Master. Do good to others and never talk of it.

Humility is a road to success. Follow it.

The Lord will have pity if you turn away from your iniquities. Be truthful and honest in all your dealings.

Search after the Lord and He will satisfy you with Himself. He is your only Hope.

Will you consider humility a narrow path or broad path?

22nd May '24 Thursday

*T*he Lord bless thee, and keep thee: the Lord make His face shine upon thee, and be gracious unto thee; the Lord lift up His countenance, and give thee peace. *Numbers 6:24.*

Let the Peace of God abide in you. Be not anxious about anything. Cast all your care on Him. Lay up for yourself riches in heaven. Be quiet and leave all to God. Hold your tongue. Scatter sweet and gentle words wherever you go. The Lord loves thee with a love everlasting. Worship Him. Be truthful whatever be the consequence.

Forget not the great blessings you have received of God's hands. Attain the grace of silence. Give up fault-finding and praise the Lord. Let your words please God. Speak no ill of others. **The Lord is your Hope-Giver.** Trust in Him. He is your shield. The Lord is your Shepherd. He will always do the best for you. Allow the Spirit to work in your heart. The Lord knows your heart. Serve Him with fear and trembling. The Lord permeates all.

Where else do people put their hope, besides God?

———•❖•———

23rd May '24 Friday

*T*he Beloved of the Lord shall dwell in safety by Him; and the Lord shall cover him all the day long, and he shall dwell between His shoulders. *Deuteronomy 33:12.*

Try hard to be humble. Let not pride have dominion over you. Offer unto the Lord all that is worth giving. Prefer others to yourself. Love one another. Jesus is your great Intercessor. Call on Him. The Lord is kind. Grieve Him not. Return unto Him. You are a son of His. The Mighty Lord is on your side and so you have nothing to fear.

Thank God your Father always. All things will work together for your good if your heart is perfect with God. The Lord is on your side. Love the Lord with your whole heart. Praise the Lord. Love all and have no malice against any. Each man is answerable for his own deeds. Be slow at faultfinding.

Obey God rather than men.

Jesus gives you forgiveness. Witness to His Love. Return to and serve the Lord faithfully.

Does obeying God sometimes mean disobeying man?

24th May '24 Saturday

*G*rieve not the Holy Ghost whereby ye are sealed unto the day of redemption. *Ephesians 4:30.*

Walk in the Spirit, and ye shall not fulfill the lust of the flesh. *Galatians 5:16.*

Vex not the Spirit of God. Seek always to please Him. Look unto Jesus. Let not opportunities pass.

Love the Lord and that will keep you from falling.

You cannot analyze God. Trust in His Omnipotence and fear not feeble man. Know the Lord. Keep the Word of the Lord.

Rejoice that you are counted worthy to suffer for Christ.

Let not sin separate you from Jesus.

Forsake not the Lord, for He is compassionate and will receive you back freely. Confess and return.

Love the Lord wholeheartedly with Him on your side all is well.

Obey the Lord, for He is good. Serve the Lord. Give yourself continually to prayer.

The Lord He is alone is God and beside Him there is none. Get to believe in God sincerely.

What else besides sin separates us from the love of God?
Romans 8:38, 39.

———◆◆———

25th May '24 Sunday

*H*ow excellent is thy loving-kindness, O God! therefore the children of men put their trust under the shadow of Thy wings. They shall be abundantly satisfied with the fatness of Thy house: and Thou shalt make them drink of the river of Thy pleasures. *Psalm 36:7, 8.*

Godliness is profitable unto all things. The Lord is very kind to you.
Walk in the path of life and be safe. Do as well as ever you can, whatever God gives you to do. Be lost in Jesus who is yours. God sees your heart.

There is nothing too hard for the Lord, who is great in Counsel and mighty in deed.
Be full of faith and of the Spirit of God. You must have an aching for God.

The Lord searches your heart.

Repent ere it is too late. He is your Good Shepherd.
Choose your companions wisely.
Think humbly of self. Take great care of all you do and your character will take care of itself.
Do good and live.
Nothing is impossible with God. He will always do you good.
Fear the Lord and serve Him faithfully. If you are God's servant, you will grow unto Christ's likeness. You need not prove God, for you can feel Him.

You need the light of God to search your heart. Agree?

———— ⋄⊰⊱⋄ ————

26th May '24 Monday

*T*he Lord is my Shepherd; I shall not want. He maketh me to lie down in green pastures: He leadeth me beside the still waters. He restoreth my soul: He leadeth me in the paths of righteousness for His name's sake. *Psalm 23:1-3.*

Return unto the Shepherd and Bishop of souls, even unto your Saviour Jesus.

Live well each day. Go to the physician for healing.

Grow in Christ's likeness. The Lord is merciful and kind. He will not always chide.

Fear not man. Speak out boldly for the Right, knowing that God is with you. All convictions are amenable to scientific proofs.

The Lamb of God is your Light. Walk as He bids you. You shall enter Glory thro' your Saviour.

Be healed of all your sores for Jesus is ready.

Beware of the company you like.

Lay the foundations of a sound character now.

The Lord will surely keep His Word of Mercy. Depend on Him for the performance of the Word. Glorious is the death of Martyrs. Play the martyr bravely. Resist not the Holy Spirit. Be filled of God. Forgive like Jesus.

Is it ever too late to lay a foundation for a sound character?

———⋅⟨3⟩⋅⟨8⟩⋅———

27th May '24 Tuesday

*W*ho is like unto thee, O people saved by the Lord, the shield of thy help, and who is thy sword of Excellency? *Deuteronomy 23:29.*

I will say of the Lord, He is my Refuge and my Fortress: my God: in Him will I trust. *Psalm 91:2.*

Praise the Lord at all times. There is no Saviour beside Him. Love the Lord and walk in His ways. Abhor all that hinders you in your Christian character. Trust in Him. The Lord will keep His Promises. Man's wrath will work out God's Will. Fear not, but work on. Be firm in your faith.

Be without anxieties, for you have cast all your cares on the Lord who cares for you. The Lord is good. By prayer and thanksgiving make known your requests to God. Grow in holiness. Educate your will to subserve God's purposes. The Word of the Lord abideth forever.

The works of the Lord are mighty unto the saving of the soul. Ask of His Spirit and you will be enabled to do His will.

If you cannot understand God, it does not mean that God does not exist.

Have you ever tried to convince someone that God exists?

28th May '24 Wednesday

*L*ooking for that blessed hope, and the glorious appearing of the great God and our Saviour Jesus Christ: who gave Himself for us, that He might redeem us from all iniquity, and purify unto Himself, a peculiar people, jealous of good works. *Titus 2:13, 14.*

Wait on the Lord. He will save you. Deny ungodliness and all worldly lust. Watch and pray. Try always to hide your anxiety. Be always busy. Overcome thro' Jesus. Do all you can honestly. The Lord hates the oppression of the weak. Repent of your besetting sin. Receive the Spirit.

Persevere. Hope unto the end.

So run that you may obtain.

Be on the alert and work hard for the Master. The Lord knows how to guide you. Just trust in Him. Apart from God, you can do nothing. Rise, for Jesus is your aid. Keep the Word of the Lord. Despise not the day of little things. Believe in Jesus and you have life.

What is the goal of the race of life?

Ascension Day 29ᵗʰ May '24 Thursday

Ye are bought with a price: therefore glorify God in your body, and in your spirit, which are God's.—*1 Corinthians 6:20.*

Strew human life with flowers! Search every hour for sunshine! Exalt your souls! Widen the sympathies of your hearts! Make joy real now to those you love!—R. Jeffries.

The Blood of Jesus cleanses you from all sin. Sin no more. Share Joy and you will be happy.

Keep your face ever toward the sunshine and you will never be sad.

You cannot be satisfied but with God. The effect of righteousness shall be peace. Submit yourself to Jesus entirely. He will show you what to do.

Many are the afflictions of the Righteous, but the Lord will deliver you out of them all if you serve Him. Jesus can aid you.

Glory in the Lord. All pure joys are from heaven.

Fear not man, feeble man.

The Lord hears prayer. Rise and pray.

The Lord has great things in store for you. Work and make life worth living.

Does that mean Christians will never be sad?

————⟨❊⟩————

30th May '24 Friday

*G*ive diligence to make your calling and election sure for so an entrance shall be ministered unto you abundantly into the everlasting kingdom of our Lord and Saviour Jesus Christ. *II Peter 1:10, 11.*

Labour for eternal life. The Lord is your light. Walk in the straight path. God has given you some small sweet way of pleasing others.

Seek to be healthy and joyful.

Hardness of heart is deplorable above all things. The Lord can work wonders. Fear not, but do your duty faithfully knowing that that Lord will reward you. Feel God the glad.

Submit yourself to God. Ask everything according to God's will and He will give it. Have faith in God. Seek the Lord. Jesus is your Intercessor.

Be not sad-hearted. Be cheerful and Christian. Sing as well as pray. Do not brood over things. Displease not the Lord in thought or word.

Be brave, speak for the Master. Walk in the fear of the Lord. Let others be edified by your presence.

The knowledge of Jesus Christ is the hallmark of progress.

Mental health contributes to physical health. True or false?

———·❀·———

31st May '24 Saturday

*H*ave faith in God. *Mark 11:22.*

If thou canst believe, all things are possible to him that believeth. Lord, increase our faith. *Mark 9:23.*

You have power with God through faith. Many things are possible to faith. Take God at His Word. Have joy in your work and it will be done well. Scatter joy wherever you go. Sing and be happy. The Word of the Lord will surely come to pass. Be not stiff-necked but obedient.

Prayer is a mighty weapon. Let it not rust.

Use it daily for Jesus is able. Religion and faith make life glorious to live.

Be not double minded. Abide in Jesus. Go forward. Let nothing draw you back. Sing unto the Lord and rejoice in His might. Remain in God's love and grow into Christ's likeness. The Lord is your help.

Obey the voice of the Lord and your soul shall live. Fear not to do His will, for He always knows what is best for you. The Lord is a prayer-hearing God.

He watches your actions. Man is spiritual and needs Communion with a MORE *(meaning God)*

The phone number of God is Jeremiah 33:3. Try calling often.

————— ❖ —————

Judah

Praise

Jun

The First Day in the Month of June 1924. Sunday

*W*hen the fight is fiercest
In the noontide heat,
Bear us, Holy Spirit,
To our Saviour's feet.
There to find a refuge
Till our work is done,
There to fight the battle
Till the battle's won.

The fruit of the spirit is longsuffering, gentleness.
Galatians 5:22.

'Tis no sin to be tempted, but to overcome. God is faithful and will not tempt you beyond your strength. Be kind one to another. Be patient for Jesus comes soon.

God is essential and life without Him is hell. The Lord will deliver you, because you trust in Him. He will keep you from evil. All things are pure to the pure.

The Lord speaks to you through His Son. Emmanuel is Jesus. The Lord is a mighty Saviour. Be not carried away by the evil one. Be victorious over sin. Run to the Saviour for aid. The Lord can work wonders. Trust in His great power.

Do the work of the Lord fearlessly. Make the best of life's daily occurrences. Be cheerful and happy and Christian.

Which "fruit of the spirit" would you like to grow this month?

———•❂•———

2ⁿᵈ June '24 Monday

*L*et your loins be girded about, and your lights burning; and ye yourselves like unto men that wait for their lord, when he will return from the Wedding. *Luke 12:35, 36.*

Blessed are those servants, whom the Lord, when He cometh, shall find watching.

Be sober and vigilant, waiting for your Lord and master. Press forward to the goal, for this is not your eternal rest. Depart from evil and do good. Be not self-confident, but cast your care on Jesus who will help you to walk aright. Carelessness will never do. Despise nothing.

God is no respecter of persons.

Witness to Jesus' power. Play the game bravely.

All things are yours Jesus. God is the strength of your heart. Fear not: seek the Lord. Turn your face away from evil. Triumph over sin and evil.

Keep the commands of the Lord with zeal and earnestness. Be sincere. Obey the voice of the Lord and it shall be well with you. Be not conservative. Submit yourself to the dispensations of God for He knows best. Be not presumptuous.

How about you? Are you impartial and fair to all?

3rd June '24 Tuesday

*L*et us not sleep as do others; but let us watch and be sober. Watch, for ye know neither the day nor the hour wherein the Son of Man cometh. *I Thessalonians 5:6.*

Abstain from fleshy lusts. Watch and pray that you may be counted worthy to stand before the Son of Man. Spend a great portion of your time in doing kind deeds and making people happy. The Lord is merciful and very kind to you.

Be not afraid of man for the Lord is with you to save and to deliver you. Be filled with the Spirit and work for Jesus. Dare to *attempt great* things for God.

Walk before the Lord and be perfect. Forget the past. Grow in grace. The Lord Jesus will uphold you.

Do worthy actions every day. Love others heartily and seek to help others. Crush all selfishness down and be pure and holy. Speak gentle words. Obey the voice of the Lord, if you desire to live to His honour and your safety.

Pray without ceasing and earnestly.

You shall not find you that have prayed in vain. Make the best of what is left.

Praying without ceasing is difficult to do. Try signing up for one hour in the 24-hour prayer chain groups.

————⸰❈⸰————

4th June '24 Wednesday

*P*ut . . . on the Lord Jesus Christ.
I will go in the strength of the Lord God; I will make mention of Thy righteousness, even of Thine only.
Rise from the dead, and Christ shall give you light.

Glorify the Lord in your life for you are His slave. He will give you peace.

Shed a little heaven around you by your kindly words and sympathizing actions. Be tenderhearted and loving. Never disobey the voice of the Lord. Kill all pride in your heart. The Lord is mighty on behalf of the humble and those who trust in Him.

Never grumble, but make the best of everything.

Walk circumspectly. Have no fellowship with the works of darkness. Put on Christ. The Love of Jesus will enable you to stand.

Take a delight in doing little deeds of kindness.

Encourage and uphold those who are in trouble. Abhor evil and serve the Lord. Be filled with the Love of Jesus and with the Spirit of the Lord. The Lord hates evil and so must you if you are His Child.

Recount some small acts of kindness you did last week.

———·◈·———

5th June '24 Thursday

*T*he Heart of the Eternal,
Is most wonderful kind.
He hath not dealt with us after our sins;
not rewarded us according to our iniquities.
Him who comes to me, I will never on any account drive away.

Be not chary of kind words. They are most healing in their nature. Try it today. Do your utmost to fulfill the Law of Christ.

You are saved by grace through faith. *Ephesians 2:8.*

Boast not but humble yourself. The punishment for sin—Obeying the Lord will surely be great. Reward. Set not yourself against the working of the Holy Ghost lest you be consumed.

The Lord knows your weakness for it is He that hath created you. He pities you. Remember your utter helplessness. Forget not all the good you have received at others' hands.

Use kind words more lavishly.

Seek not great things for yourself. Seek to be a man after God's heart. You are feeble and wayward, but Jesus can train you aright. Have faith in God who does all things well.

Try to be lavish with kind and positive comments all day.

————◦◈◦————

6th June '24 Friday

O Love Divine, how sweet Thou art!
When shall I find my willing heart
All taken up by Thee?
I thirst, I faint, I die to prove
The greatness of redeeming love,
The Love of Christ to me!

The Lord has greatly loved you, though you do not merit it. Forget not your great obligation to Him. If you love God, the duties He sets for you, you will find pleasant.

Do trust in His infinite love. The Lord's purposes will certainly work out. Jesus is the Power of God. Let Him take hold of you and work in you. Trust Him because He knows.

Sin causes suffering, but not necessarily is all suffering a result of sin. Call on the Lord to help the needy.

God's answers may sometimes be in the negative, yet they are always the best answers.

The Lord knows all. Jesus is the Way of Life.

With Him are pleasures forever more. *Psalm 16:11.*

The Promises of the Lord are faithful and cheering. He is with you always.

How did God's answer of "No" to your prayers turn out for the best?

———◦❖◦———

7ᵗʰ June '24 Saturday

$\mathcal{P}$raying always with all prayer and supplication in the Spirit, and watching thereunto with all perseverance and supplication for all saints.

Continue instant in prayer, and watch in the same with thanksgiving. *Ephesians 6:18.*

Be importunate in your prayers. Go away into solitude and spend time in secret with Jesus. All that's good comes from above. Let the love of God shine thro' you. Do little deeds of kindness. Obedience is essential for blessing. Jesus is the Great Sin Bearer.

The Lord blots out your iniquity. Go, sin no more. Confess your sins. Seek after the lowly graces. Keep yourself in the love of God. Let God's love dwell in your heart. The Lord will punish unrepented sin.

Obstruct not the work of the Holy Ghost.

Rejoice and be glad in suffering for great is your reward. Preach the gospel unto all. Be filled with Heavenly Joy.

How is the work of the Holy Spirit obstructed?

————◈◈◈————

8th June '24 Sunday

*B*etter to stem with heart and hand
The roaring tide of life, than lie
Unmindful, on its flowery strand,
Of God's occasions drifting by.

As we have opportunity, let us labour for the good of all, and especially of those who belong to the household of faith. Give yourself time to learn what is good and labour to do good deeds. Let not your youth pass away idly. The Lord your God will prosper you if you walk in His Laws.

Seek first the Kingdom of God. *Matthews 6:33.*

Trust not in your strength. Fear not: be brave. Do the work of the Lord bravely.

Be not carried away by flattery, but be constant in the Service of the Lord.

The end of sin is punishments. Do the work given to you with all your heart. Cultivate knowledge. Be strong in faith for it can work. God will supply all your needs. Give glory unto God at all times. Grow into the full stature of the Divine Man.

Pray for discernment between flattery and honest praise.

———•③•❖•———

9th June '24 Monday

*A*ll life is full of opportunities of choice; and as we choose in them, and abide by your choice, such are we.—Wilberforce.

Someone counsels us to rename own obstacles opportunities, considering each as a gymnasium bar on which to try our strength.—J. R. M.

You are very lucky; only waste not your precious time; let not your glorious opportunities go unprofited by. Let your speech be seasoned with love. Let the word of God abide in you. Subject yourself to God. Go forward in the works of Jesus. Commit all your cares unto God and be at rest. Jesus is your Comforter.

Be sober and vigilant. Resist the Devil manfully. The wicked shall not always prosper for God is on the side of Right. Let no occasions for doing good pass by.

Take time by the forelock. God has a purpose in everything.

Trust in His Almighty and all-seeing power. Commit your cause unto the Lord for He is best able to help you in your troubles. Be full of the Spirit of Christ.

"Take time by the forelock" means, make the best use of precious time.

⊰⊱

10th June '24 Tuesday

*O*mit no opportunity of doing good, and you will find no opportunity of doing ill.

He encouraged them all to remain with fixed resolve, faithful to the Lord. *Acts 11:23*.

Live out God's thought for you. Make the world around you better for your presence. Be good. God is very loving. He hath forgiven your wayward ways and given you Christ while you were yet a sinner.

Be prepared to make the same concessions for others as you make yourself.

Be not selfish but noble hearted. Be of a forgiving nature. Have compassion on others. Charity is the bond of perfectness. Begin, continue and end in the Lord. Scatter sun beams wherever you go. Return unto the Lord who is your Good Shepherd. Abstain from all fleshly lusts. Be true to the Spirit of the Master. You must through much suffering enter into the Kingdom of God.

Read similar thought as found in Mark 12:31

————◆◆◆————

11ᵗʰ June '24 Wednesday

*A*s far as the east is from the west, so far hath He removed our transgressions from us. As a father pitieth his children so the Lord pitieth them that fear Him. *Psalm 103:12-13.*

You are a child of God and He loves you. You are not a stranger, so do what the Lord loves you to do.

Be ashamed of and abhor sin. What you do perhaps do for eternity.

Be careful of your opportunities.

Serve others never seeking to patronize. The fear of the Lord is the beginning of wisdom. As far as lieth in you be at peace with all men. Hold the Cross high in trouble. Rejoice in it.

Be born again. Be rid of the Old Adam and sin. Grow in righteousness and true holiness and fill it nobly. Be humble and loving.

Waste not, want not. The Lord hates the proud. He is the Redeemer of such as trust in Him and seek to do His will walking humbly before Him.

Hearken unto the voice of the Lord and preach the Word. You cannot understand God's dealings. Only trust.

What do you think is meant by being careful of opportunities?
Is it missing, abusing or making the best of them?

————·❦·————

12th June '24 Thursday

*E*very day is of the utmost importance of you, every friend you make, every hour you waste, every word you hear. At present your whole nature is awake, your mind is active, your interests keen, your passions strong, your feelings quick. Everything that tends to give this nature, form, is of the most vital importance to your future self.—Craig Uton

Never let your day go idly past. Do not postpone too long.

The Lord is with you to prove you and to succor you in trial. Lean hard.

Bring forth fruits worthy of repentance. The Lord is Mighty. It is He that doeth all things in heaven and earth. God is beyond that reach of human understanding.

Put on the Lord Jesus Christ. Let not sin reign in you. Yield yourself to God. Let not the day go unloaded with good deeds. Do all you can to aid and succour to others. The Lord is your shield. Trust always in Him and seek to do His will. He is able to deliver you from your besetting sin.

Read Martin Luther's hymn "A mighty fortress is our God . . ."

———— ·❦· ————

13th June '24 Friday

*A*bide in me and I in you. *John 15:4.*

I am crucified with Christ; nevertheless I live; yet not I, but Christ liveth in me: and the life which I now live in the flesh, I live by the faith of the Son of God Who loved me, and gave Himself for me. *Galatians 2:20.*

If you abide in Jesus, walk in His ways. Prepare for His coming. Ask for peace to sustain you in time of trouble. Consider how much you have left done and how much you could yet do and do it. Do all in Jesus' name. Make the best of everything. Be not carried away by public enthusiasm. Weigh everything. Seek to please Jesus alone and fear not what man may do to you. Rejoice in adversity. Believe on the Lord Jesus and He will do all He can for you for He is able.

You will be responsible for all your talents.

Use your opportunities. Return unto the Lord your God for He is rich in Mercy. The Mighty Lord can deliver you even in trouble. Call on His great name and He will succour you. Be not afraid of Death, Pain and Sorrow, you have no cause of fear. Face them bravely.

Read the parable of the talents that Jesus told in Matthew 25:14-30 to get a better understanding of what this means.

———⋅❖⋅———

14th June '24 Saturday

*E*ach present conviction, each secret suggestion of duty constitutes a distinct and separate call of God, which can never be slighted without the certainty of its total departure or its fainter return.

Never postpone kindnesses lest they should become overdue debts.

The Lord will give you love and courage sufficient unto the day. Rejoice when you suffer, for Christ also suffered. The Lord is your Comforter. Be established in all good works. The Word of the Lord will surely come to pass. Trust Him. The Lord will bless your work.

The Love of the Lord can sustain you in your daily trials. There is no time for sin. Be contented. What is a great blessing! Love not wrong.

Let not the cares of this world beset you. Anchor your hopes on Jesus.

Deal righteously before the Lord if you seek life. If you suffer for right, happy are you.

Seek only to please the Lord. Out of the same door with calamity, walk courage, fortitude, Triumphant Faith and Sacrificial Love.

Have you ever regretted not doing something
before it was too late?
Don't.

15ᵗʰ June '24 Sunday

*I*f ye love me, keep my commandments. *John 14:15.*
Reckon not life by hours, but by good deeds;

Love is grey hairs, and usefulness in age;
He who lived best lives longest.
The Lord knows the secrets of your heart. Nothing can be hid from Him. Cleanse your heart that He may dwell therein. Don't lose the opportunity of seeing beautiful things. Shun idleness. Waste not precious time. Say a kind word. No word of the Lord will fail. Lean on His Loving Arm. Search the Scriptures. Abide by the Truth and by Good for their own sake. God is first and great.

Ask sincerely in God's name and in Christ's and you will obtain. The Lord wills your satisfaction. Rejoice evermore. Pray without ceasing. The Lord hears prayer. Make others happy by your presence and word.

Do not postpone things. Waste not time, youth, and opportunities.

Be prepared for anything. Stand travel to witness to Christ's saving power. Seek to please the Lord always.

If procrastination is one of your weaknesses,
unshackle yourself.

————◆◈◆————

16th June '24 Monday

*M*ake my mortal dreams come true,
With the good I fain would do;
Clothe with life the weak intent,
Let me be the thing I meant.

Gather up opportunities and do all the good you can. Fill your place in life and do not leave it empty. Walk circumspectly.

Abstain from all appearance of evil. *I Thessalonians 5:22.*

Serve the Lord with all your heart. The Lord is merciful and forgiving. The Lord requires worship of the Spirit. **Live in Him.**

All men are one blood. Love all well. Hold fast that which you have. The Lord can make you clean. Have faith in His greatness. Grow gradually in the Lord. So run that you may obtain. Fight the good fight of faith. Be not overconfident. Humble yourself under the hand of the Almighty. Serve the Lord in all sincerity of heart.

What does it mean to "live in God"?

17th June '24 Tuesday

*I*f two of you shall agree on earth as touching anything that they shall ask, it shall be done for them of my Father which is in heaven. *Matthew 18:19.*

Be strong and good.
That life's fair morning may not end in tears,
But in the joy of right and peace of God.

Love the Lord. Use not vain repetitions when you pray. Be sincere. Regulate every act with thought and love. Sufficient strength will be given to do your day's work. Ask. The Lord is your guide. You are often involved in things over which you have no control. Return unto the Lord.
You are but dust and must return unto the Lord.

Be prepared for you know not the hour of your home-call.

Bless the Lord and praise Him at all times. Magnify the Lord for He is worthy. Whatever happens to you, rejoice.

This is another way of saying, "Live each day to the fullest."

———⋅◈⋅———

18th June '24 Wednesday

*L*et us therefore come boldly unto the throne of grace, that we may obtain mercy, and find grace to help in time of need.
Lead us, O Father! in the paths of peace;
Without Thy guiding hand ere go astray.—W. H. B.

Through Jesus' Blood, you are healed, for the Lord is merciful. Draw near with a sincere heart. Do nothing at random. Have the good of mankind in view. Seek the Lord and you shall live. The Lord is your God. Fear not, for He will direct and lead you at all times.

The Lord is mighty above your imagination.

Humble yourself under His greatness. Let His will be done in you. Be not conceited. Stoop to learn of others. Play the man, thro' and thro'. Fear God above all.

Give some examples of the Lord's might and power.

19ᵗʰ June '24 Thursday

*I*f Thou wilt save Israel by my hand, as thou hath said, "Let me prove, I pray Thee" and God did so.

In the world you shall have tribulation; but be of good cheer; I have overcome the world. *John 16:33.*

Carry prayer into all your daily occupations. Pray unceasingly. Seek to set yourself in the right way. Ask for advice from above. The Lord requires holiness of heart and purpose. Yield not to temptation.

God works in ways unknown to you. Bow yourself in submission and trust to His Love. Be not afraid. Speak out for the Lord. Sympathize with others and feel for them. **The Lord will bless the cheerful.** So cheer others up.

Cheerful givers have fewer ulcers?

———◦❊◦———

20th June '24 Friday

*T*he literal soul shall be made fat: and he that watereth shall be watered also himself. Every man shall receive his own reward according to his own labour.

We must pray as if everything depended upon God, and work as if everything depended upon us.—Loyola

Be prayerful. Jesus is by your side ready to carry you and your burden. Seek His fellowship. Do your duty and the Lord will certainly repay you more than you deserve.

Ask and it shall be given you. *Matthew 7:7.*

When you are in trouble, the Lord will bear you. He will temper the storm for His children or be closer to them. God's ways are the Best. Trust Him.

Call upon Jesus who is ready to help you and is always at your side. Let your heart be perfect before God. He will guard you and bless you abundantly. Pray for the faint and weak hearted. The Lord will hear your cry. Let all be done in accordance with God's will.

"We must pray as if everything depended upon God, and work as if everything depended upon us."
Isn't this a great motto to live by?

———— ·◊·◊· ————

21st June '24 Saturday

*B*ear ye one another's burdens and so fulfill the law of Christ. *Galatians 6.2.*

He that saith he abideth in Him, ought himself so to walk, even as he walked. *I John 2:6.*

The prayers I make will then be sweet indeed, if thou the spirit give by which I pray.—M. Angelo.

God hears and answers your desires. Just let Him know all. Ask in Jesus' name. Begin all things with prayer. Follow in Christ's footsteps, looking unto Him. Your faith in God is shown by the banishment of certain evils in the world. Be not passive. Evil will be punished. Hope in Him though all looks dark. Jesus is Lord of all.

Scientists are humble. Be prepared to lay aside all bias and to hearken unto the Lord your God. Cart away evil from your midst. The Lord will then hear you and grant you your prayer. Have faith and your prayers will be answered. The Lord is very merciful and good to such as wait upon Him. **Bear your yoke bravely.** The Lord is your portion.

Do you agree that bearing the yoke bravely is a better option than complaining about it?

22ⁿᵈ June '24 Sunday

*I*f any man be in Christ, he is a new creature; old things are passed away; behold, all things are become new. *II Corinthians 5:17.*

The fear of the Lord is the beginning of wisdom. *Proverbs 9:10.*

Be not self-conceited. Seek to know thyself. Know the right and do it. God knows all your needs. Live unto Christ. Let not sin have dominion over you. Call upon the Lord to aid you. He will make you brave. The Lord is mighty to save. Fear none but your Lord.

Faith and prayer are of great moment in one's life. God blesses those who trust implicitly in Him. **Follow in the saintly footsteps of those gone before.** Never be rude to any. God is love. Keep His commandments. If you are His, you must love too. Do the right at all times.

Remember to thank God for the loved ones
who have passed onto eternity.

23rd June '24 Monday

*R*eflect upon your present blessings, of which everyman has many; not upon your past misfortunes, of which all men have some.—Charles Dickens.

Serve God, love Him, live to Him, and you will be bright, and full of hope, and noble.—F. W. Robertson.

Rejoice always. Abhor evil and do good. A contented heart is a great virtue. Let the Holy Spirit be your strengthener.

Hope in the Lord. Thank God for all you enjoy.

Be largehearted and ready to make allowances for others' weaknesses.

The Lord's work will ever prosper. Hope continually.

The Lord is very mindful of you. Humble yourself before Him for He can bring you to nothingness in no time. Do that which is pleasing to Him.

Come to Jesus who will hide you in safety. You will lack nothing for Jesus is yours. Murmur at nothing for it is ungrateful to do so.

Be happy for the Lord does all things for your best.

*Does making allowances for weaknesses
spoil the other person?*

———⟨❀⟩———

24ᵗʰ June '24 Tuesday

*F*ather, I know that all my life
Is portioned out for me,
And the changes that are sure to come
I do not fear to see;
But I ask Thee for a present mind
Intent on pleasing Thee.—A. L. Waring.

Learn the art of contentment and you can sing in the midst of a deluge.

Be not carried away by the world. Commit all your cares unto the Lord. Let Him lead you. He will do the best. Nothing can harm you so long as you love the Lord.

The Lord leads you in every step of your life. How wonderful is His guidance. Lean on His Wisdom. Be honest in all your dealings. Be thoughtful and kind. Be not selfish and self-centered.

Seek contentment which is a gift from God. Receive it and live it.

25th June '24 Wednesday

*L*et nothing make thee sad or fretful,
Or too regretful;
What God hath ordered must be right
Then find in it thine own delight, My Will.—P. T.

Jesus is preparing a home for you above. Trust in His unchanging love. He is your God. Use to the utmost your present opportunities and God will bless you more. Have a contented mind. Return unto your Saviour and be happy. Jesus is able to do mighty things for you. Trust also in Him and be not afraid.

Deep friendship consists in the intermingling of minds in the noblest things of life, not in the general partaking of common physical tastes or indulgences.

Be a man and one free from evil habits.

How many deep friendships can you count on?

———⋄⊛⋄———

26th June '24 Tuesday

The blessing of the Lord it maketh rich, and He addeth no sorrow with it. *Proverbs 10:22.*

The Lord redeemeth the soul of His servants; and none of that trust in Him shall be desolate.

Ask in faith, nothing wavering. *James 1:6.*

The Lord is with you to protect and shield you. Be contented in the work given to you and do it well, for the Lord is the one Who sets your work for you. Let the Lord your God go before you and lead you. Be not hasty.

Stand fast. The Lord your God has delivered you from many troubles. He is a great and loving God. Forget not all you have received at His Hands. Remember your indebtedness to Him and be content with the lot He assigns you.

Put on the armor of God daily as found in Ephesians 6:11-17.

27th June '24 Friday

*S*tand first therefore in the liberty wherewith
Christ hath made you free.
Let us be content, in work,
To do the thing we can, and not presume,
To fret because 't's little.

Be no slave to sin, rather put on Christ and trample sin under your feet. Give up thinking of what is easy and pleasant.

Give up wishing for things you cannot get and be happy without them. Jesus pleads for you above. Displease Him not. Serve the Lord with all humility of mind. You are victorious through Christ. Forget not His great Love. Just do what was given you to do. Be not lost in grumblings, but remember the fresh mercies you receive at God's hands. Be not lazy, work hard, Jesus will bless your labours.

How do you handle when you cannot get the things you want?

28th June '24 Saturday.

(This page is torn and is being replaced with 2 January 1925 Friday.)

*I*n all your ways acknowledge God. *Proverbs 3:6.*

Never go against the dictates of your conscience. Incur people's displeasure rather than the pricks of your inward monitor.

Be just and true. Yield your soul to God and your whole being to His service. Move at the impulse of His Love.

Walk honestly as in the day. Put on the Lord Jesus Christ.

Be strong and of a Good Courage. Rejoice, God does great things gradually.

Be patient and work with Him. The Lord rules over all things. Lean hard on Him.

Pray without ceasing. *I Thessalonians 5:17.*

Let your prayers ever rise heavenwards. **Never be silent about the good you find in others.** Do that which is right in the sight of God. Yield yourself for God's service. God is very thoughtful, wise and good. Oh seek to do His will and to trust in His care.

When you find good in others, why do we need to tell them?

———— ◆◆◆ ————

29th June '24 Sunday

*L*ove worketh no ill to its *neighbor;*

Therefore love is the *fulfilling* of the law. *Romans 13:10.*

For I delight in the law of the Lord *after the* inward man. Romans 7:22.

. . . in the ways of the Lord,

for His yoke is *easy and the burden is light.*
You are the source of our happiness. Serve the Lord.
Tell others of this news of Jesus.

Be prepared to die for him—and the Lord pardons the sins of those repentant. He is gracious.

Displease Him not. Have a watch o'er your mouth.

Make the best of what you have. Do your duty honouring of Him.

The Lord knows you, loves you. He is responsible for your good.

Return unto him. Forget yourself.

Remember your responsibilities to the Lord. Decide aright to the how

. . . all. Be not conceited or vain. You are answerable for your actions.

. . . in the ways of the Lord. We could not decipher the first part of this line. How will you fill in the blank?

———◆◈◆———

30th June '24 Monday

(This page is torn and replaced with 3rd January 1925 Saturday.)

*T*he fellowship of those who are ready to appreciate and allow for infirmities is very pleasant. Be not carried away by an idea of an "all-serene"-ness!

Our God will never forsake us. He restored our hungry souls. He is our guide continually.

Come to Jesus, just as you are and He will make you whole. The Lord is marvelous in His doings. The wisdom and love beneath His acts are great.

The fear of the Lord is the beginning of wisdom.

Trust in God to guide you through life.

Crave for a clearer sight in matters spiritual. The Holy Spirit can enlighten your understanding. That the Holy Spirit may dwell in you, cleanse your heart and be prepared to receive Him.

Strive to do God's will. Perpetually and sincerely pray to the Lord.

The Lord is loving and kind.

He does that which is best.

Do you believe God's best is your best also?

————◈◈————

The Bible

"The Bible contains: The mind of God, The state of Man, The Way of Salvation, The Doom of sinners, The Happiness of Believers. Its doctrines are holy, its precepts are building, its histories are true and its decisions are immutable. Read it to be wise, believe it to be safe, and practice it to be holy. It contains light to direct you, food to support you, and comfort to cheer you. It is the Traveller's map, the Pilgrim's staff, the Pilot's compass, the Soldier's sword, and the Christian's charter. Here Paradise is restored, heaven opened, and the gates of hell disclosed. Christ is its grand spirit, our good its design and the glory of God its end. It should fill the memory, rule the heart and guide the feet. Read it slowly, frequently and prayerfully. It is a mine of wealth, a paradise of glory, and a river of pleasure. It is given you in life, will be open at the judgment, and be remembered forever. It involves the highest responsibility, rewards the greatest labour, and condemns all who trifle with it holy contents."

Photos of Life in Palayamkottai

Family home, Palayamkottai, built in 1909
by Father-in-law Samuel

Captain's chair decorated for each birthday child with
fresh flowers and fruits

Bullock cart—The second car of the Kantayyas

The happy Kantayya family 1953 with dog Tippu

Photos of Kantayya Children

The six children May 25, 1957
Samuel Nirmalkumar, Mary Suvarnakumari, David
Jayasurya, Esther Kamalakumari, Monica Prithakumari,
Elizabeth Lavanyakumari.

The six children, January 1986, the last time
the 6 of them were together

Photos of Birthdays and Anniversaries

Parents' 25th Wedding Anniversary. 1957

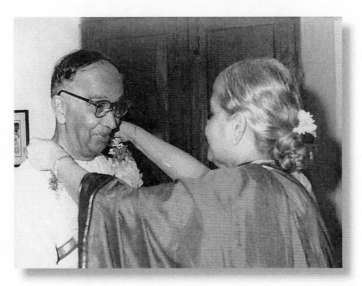

Parents' 60th birthday. 1965

Immanuel

First day of the Month of July 1924. Tuesday

*B*e ye followers of God as dear children.
The fruit of the Spirit *(light)* is in all goodness and righteousness and truth. *Ephesians 5:9.*

How shall He not with Him also freely give us all things. *Romans 8:32.*

Love your enemies. Do good to all. Be like Jesus always in all you do. Be the best you may be. Increase the happiness of all. You are responsible for yourself only. Watch your actions. Realize the beauty of the Lord and Prayer. Say it from your heart. Witness bravely for the Master. Fear not. He is with you.

The Lord knows you through and through. Trust in Him to guide you. He it is that has had mercy on you and has done great things for you. Forget not His benefits.

Remember your responsibilities.

Make the best of all you have and serve the Lord.

*What are your responsibilities toward God, others
and yourself?*

2nd July '24 Wednesday

*L*ife is not made of money, and friendship and talents and patronage, and family influences, and good chances and good positions, and good health and good nature; it is made out of faith, virtue, knowledge, temperance, patience, godliness, brotherly kindness and love.—Inninger.

You are a member of Christ. Serve Him honestly and well. Find content wherever you are. Help those who are in trouble.

Be at peace with all. *Romans 12:18.*

Return unto the Lord who has saved you all along. Live in accordance with God's will. Be not hasty.

Continue always in prayer and the peace of God will keep your mind. Delight in the word of the Lord. Commit your all to Him and He will watch over you. Do your duty.

Mistake not life's best things.

Live at peace with all men. Be contented with your lot. Make the best of what you have.

What are some of "life's best things"?

———·❸·❸·———

3rd July '24 Thursday

*S*eek the Lord while He may be found, call ye upon Him while He is near. *Isaiah 55:6.*

To him that overcometh will I grant to sit with me in my throne, even as I also overcame, and am sit down with my Father in his throne.
Revelations 3:21.

You are a child of God. Walk worthy of that designation. Overcome evil. Give your heart to Jesus. See God in everything. Do right, whatever be your lot. The Word of the Lord will surely come to pass. Trust in Him and fail not.

The Lord chooses the weak and poor to perform great things. Trust in the Lord and He will raise you up to do great things. Abide in Jesus and you will bring forth much fruit. Let your life be exemplary. Tell others of Jesus.

What are you doing today that is worthy of a child of God?

———◈◈◈———

4th July '24 Friday

*C*an a woman forget her suckling child, that she should not have compassion on the child of her womb? yea, they may forget, yet will I not forget thee. *Isaiah 49:15.*

The Lord comforts and upholds such as do not trust in themselves or in the arm of flesh. He is your Redeemer. Choose the best mode of life and practice it. Acquire right habits. Jesus gives you living water. Come and receive of Him freely. Know that the Lord God is Kind and His will is supreme. Lean hard on the Lord and you will never be disappointed.

All have sinned and come short of the glory of God's Son. Return unto the Lord and be purified, for He is merciful and will forgive your manifold sins. Talk sensibly. Your little acts decide your dealing. Attend to the needs of your moral nature. Live in Jesus and lead others to Him. Be not narrow-minded. Realize how small your angle of vision is.

You cannot prosper in sin.

Jesus knows all your troubles. Consult Him.

Sin may bring physical prosperity but not peace of conscience.

5th July '24 Saturday

*G*od so loved the World, that He gave His only begotten Son, that whosoever believeth on Him should not perish but have everlasting life. *John 3:16.*

The Lord is good to all and His mercy endures forever. Believe and find God's promises true in your life. Do each duty as it comes bravely & well. Love all. Treat all nobly. Have a conscience void of offence toward God and man. Fearlessly serve the Master. The Lord can do all things. Trust.
Let all you do, be done honestly and beautifully.

The best things are nearest you; therefore throw not away your opportunities.

Treat people nobly. Have a glorious ideal before you. Seek not your own interests. Be large-minded and help others as well. Be not self-conceited. Be content and happy with all you receive.

*Dwell on some blessings that are close to you
that you may fail to see?*

6th July '24 Sunday

*L*et your speech be always with grace. *Colossians 4:6.*
Let no corrupt communication proceed out of your mouth, but that which is good to the use of edifying, that it may minister grace unto the hearers. *Ephesians 4:29.*

Speak like Christ. Be holy in all you do. The Lord knows your inmost heart. Stand firm for the Master. Cast your confidence on the Lord. Be filled with the Spirit of the Lord.

Never postpone the doing of things right.

Prepare yourself to meet Jesus at the Table.
Be ye merciful as Christ is merciful. Follow after God. Love your enemies and do good to them. Choose and cherish all good things. Stand firm for the Master. Seek the Lord who knows your inmost soul. Abhor evil which the Lord also hates. Worship the Lord with heart and soul and honesty.

Think of a task you postponed, which you can do today?

7th July '24 Monday

O Lord my God, in Thee do I put my trust; save me from all them that persecute me, and deliver me. *Psalm 7:1.*

My Grace is sufficient for thee, for my strength is made perfect in weakness. *II Corinthians 12:9.*

Yield yourself entirely unto the Lord and be happy.

Let God come to you and dwell in your heart. He will aid you in your trials. He will support and advise you, for Jesus knows your infirmities. The Lord hates evil. Abhor it and do the right. Be not hasty. Let the Lord direct you at all times. Trust in the Lord.

Jesus Christ gave Himself for you. His life for yours. Show your gratitude by right living. Come to Jesus. Return, put away iniquity. Yield to God, and you will be safe in His care. Do as the Lord bids you to, not caring for man. He is your Master and you are His slave.

Does "yielding entirely" mean same as perfect submission?

————·◈◈·————

8th July '24 Tuesday

*T*hen will I sprinkle clean water upon you, and ye shall be clean. *Ezekiel 36:20.*

They shall walk with me in white; for they are worthy. *Revelations 3:4.*

Acknowledge your iniquities and receive forgiveness for your sins for Jesus' sake. Go and sin no more. Whatever be your work, do it honestly and in the best means possible. Be zealous and courageous, strong to bear. Fear not when you are dragged before the Counsel to witness for God & Christ.

Call upon the Lord, and He will give you strength to do your work. Bear what the Lord sets for you. Be diligent and serve the Lord. You are born of God; therefore sin not. Have no fellowship with darkness. Hope in the Lord.

He is your comforter. Lean hard on God. Tell Him all your troubles.

Whatever may happen to you, know that God is your father and He doth lead you.

Can you think of a comforting Bible verse or hymn?

9th July '24 Wednesday

Cousin Bhasker's Birthday

I will greatly rejoice in the Lord, my soul shall be joyful in my God; for He hath clothed me with the garments of salvation, he hath covered me with the robe of righteousness. *Isaiah 61:10.*

Your sins are forgiven you. Henceforth you should not sin. Put on Christ therefore and shine for Him. Your most secret thoughts are known to God. Never flatter or provoke others. Have principles and stick up to them. Be earnest and zealous about the word of God. Seek to bring others to Jesus. Fear none, but be brave and truthful.

Judge not one and other. The Lord will recompense you, for He knows all the secrets of your heart. Confess. Walk worthy of your high calling. Be governed by the Spirit of God. Conquer your passions. The Lord will give you His Spirit. Call upon Him. Keep His statutes. **Everything has its place. Keep everything where it ought to be and all will be right.**

One of Appa's favorite saying is "A place for everything and everything in its place."

10th July '24 Thursday

Sis. Sundaramma's Birthday

'*T*is far better to educate the tongue to kindness, wisdom, and wise reticence, than to idly waste its capabilities in senseless volubility.

For as much as Christ hath suffered for us in the flesh, arm yourselves likewise with the same mind. *I Peter 4:1.*

No cross, no crown. Be prepared to suffer for Jesus' name. Do not say all which comes into your head, not believe all which you hear. Keep your tongue from evil. You are God's and Him must you serve. Abide in Him or else you are lost. Tremble before the Wonders of God.

Be quiet, low and gentle in your speech. Be not vulgar. Be true and Christian.

Ask the Lord to watch over your lips.

Give your heart into Jesus' keeping. Be not at enmity with the Lord. Yield yourself up. Do all as unto God. The Word of the Lord never faileth. Lean hard on Him. The Lord is with them who fear Him.

At present, we can add our fast Internet communications as well as spoken words to our watch list, right?

11th July '24 Friday

I will contend with him that contendeth with thee.
And all flesh shall know that I the Lord am thy Saviour and thy
Redeemer, the mighty One of Jacob. *Isaiah 49:25, 26.*

Jesus feels for you. Tell Him all your troubles. The Lord will
direct and uphold you. He is with you to save you. Fear not. Be
perfectly truthful in all you say or do. Commune with the Lord
and you will be kept from speaking untruth. Know that the Lord
God reigneth. The Lord ordereth all things. Lean hard on Him.

The Lord satisfieth the soul of such as seek after Him. Long
after Him. The Lord is good. Thirst for righteousness. Do not
give the lie to your actions. Free yourself from falsehood and
work for the truth. Put on the breastplate of uprightness. The
Lord does what He will. **Speak and witness for the Master.
Fear not what man can do to you.**

*Have you ever held back talking about God
because of what people will say?*

———— ❖ ————

12th July '24 Saturday

O Lord, I know that the way of man is not in himself; it is not in man that walketh to direct his steps. *Jeremiah 10:23.*

My times are in thy hand. *Psalm 31:15.*

The Lord's presence abideth with you. He will not leave you nor forsake you. Run not into temptation. Be sure to speak the truth. The Lord will uphold the truth-speaker. You have received a commission from God. Be faithful unto the end. The Lord hates vanity. Be not proud.

Provoke one another unto Love. Bear one another's burdens. Put not a stumbling block in other's way. Use the right words at the right time. Grow up in union with the Lord Jesus and in truth. **Put away all idols from your heart.**

Pray one for another and so fulfill the Law of Christ. *Galatians 6:2.*

Be anxious for the safety of others.

What may be the "idols" in your heart?

13th July '24 Sunday

*W*hether we live, we live unto the Lord and whether we die, we die unto the Lord; whether we live therefore or die, we are the Lord's. *Romans 14:8.*

I am my Beloved's and His desire is toward me. *Song of Solomon 7:10.*

Delight in the Lord. His Love toward you has been great and unwavering. Trust in Him forever. Think innocently and justly. Be truthful. Be true to yourself to others and to God. The Lord is your own God. Serve Him faithfully. Be not ashamed of the Cross for Jesus was on it and Jesus is yours.

Put on Christ forsaking the old man and his works**.**

Be true to yourself. Speak sincerely.

Hesitate not to tell the truth. Hope in the Lord. Dwell on the words of the Book of Life. Walk in the law of the Lord. The soul that sinneth, it shall die. Seek to renew the perishing. Honour the Lord. Never be hasty to jump to conclusions.

Do you feel good when you put on airs or act hypocritically?

14th July '24 Monday

*L*et no corrupt communication proceed out of your mouth, but that which is good to the use of edifying, that it may minister grace unto the heavens. *Ephesians 4:29.*

Watch over your tongue. Keep your heart with all diligence. Confess Christ and be not afraid of men. Be entirely truthful. Be frank in your dealings. **Beware, for life hath quicksands.**

Watch and pray. The Lord hates iniquity and hypocrisy. Repent ere it be too late and return unto the Lord your God. Science and religion have their own provinces. Religion solves many problems which Science out of ignorance does not comprehend.

You shall see Jesus face-to-face. Thirst for His Presence. Love Him ardently. Let all you do be pleasing to Him. Sacrifice not truth even in small things. Hate a liar and love the truth-teller. You have received all at the hands of God. Forget not His many blessings. Be not ungrateful, for He has loved you. Return His love. Judge not others. Be tenderhearted. Forgive.

Add to the list of life's quicksands . . . bad friendships,
inappropriate reading . . .

15th July '24 Tuesday

*A*s the heart panteth after the waterbrooks, so panteth my soul after Thee, O God. My soul thirsteth for God, for the living God; when shall I come and appear before God? *Psalm 42:1.*

Do good for you know what the good thing is. Be transformed by the renewing of your mind. Delight to do the will of God. Be most scrupulously truthful. Be straightforward. Return unto the Lord. Serve not other Gods. Love Him alone. The Lord will reward you according to your deeds. Be careful what you think, say, or do.

Judge righteous judgement. Let the word of Christ dwell in you. Prove all things. Hold fast that which is good. Be merciful and truthful. Be honest and above-board in all your dealings. Shirk from telling a lie. The Lord is merciful, and though you stray from His paths, He seeks to bring you back.

Whatever you preach to others, see you do.

Practice what you preach.

———◈◈———

16th July '24 Wednesday

*N*o sinful word, nor deed or wrong,
Nor thoughts that idly rove;
But simple truth be on our tongue,
And in our hearts be love.

The best policy is simplicity and truth.

Lay the foundation of truth deep and strong in your character.

A look may be a lie. Beware. You are a priest of God and are his workmanship. You are the temple of God. Glorify Him by your lips and conduct. Bring forth fruit worthy of Christ's blood. Walk not in the way of Hell. Repent and return, and the Father is ever ready to forgive.

Make your prayer to God and set a watch against the evil one. Choose to speak the truth. In everything, trust your Father and be not anxious, for He careth for you. Be honest in all your dealings. The Lord exalts and abases. Humble yourself under His mighty hand. Be not proud, for all you have received is of free grace.

Who is the cornerstone of your life?

17ᵗʰ July '24 Thursday

*H*elp us, O God of our salvations, for the glory of Thy Name; and deliver us, and purge away our sins, for Thy name's sake. *Psalm 79:9.*

The Lord is a God of Mercy. He will forgive your iniquity. Repent and serve Him faithfully. Be diligent and zealous in good works. Waste not your time and the Lord will bless you. Do good and live. If you sin, you die. You are forgiven and received out of free grace. Have faith and cast out fear.

Sorrow after a godly sort and you will be the better for it.

Have love, joy and peace in your heart. Let the Spirit sanctify your heart. Be not beaten back. Strive. Aim at the highest and the noblest. Be alert and alive. You will have to die for your sin unless you get forgiveness thro' Christ. Have faith in God even when all is dark. In all moods, lose not your trust in the Father.

What is the meaning of "sorrow after a godly sort"?
Is it repentance?

18th July '24 Friday

*T*he Lord is good, a stronghold in the day of trouble; and He knoweth them that trust in Him. *Nahum 1:7.*

Be not hasty to take offence. It betrays conceit and pride of spirit.

Depart from iniquity and serve the Lord with humility of mind. Seek others' welfare, not your own. Kind words make others happy and good natured. Use them freely. Seek to give pleasure every hour of your life. Each one has to give account for himself. Walk in the right paths. Even while you were in sin, the Lord died for you.

Do all the good you can and in Christ's name.

Do your very best and with a cheerful and willing mind and confess your weaknesses. Be sympathetic, and do your best to make others happy. The Lord wants you to return from your evil ways and to serve Him faithfully. Jesus has died for you even while you were in sin. Show your gratitude to Him by striving to do good.

Write down some good you will do today.

19th July '24 Saturday

A day well begun is itself a blessing.
Strive hard to redeem the time for you know not what a day may bring forth. Do all to the glory of God.

The mighty God had done great things for you. Glorify His Name. Yield your soul to Him and be at Rest. Resolve not to be useless. Be sympathetic. Restrain your temper and make others happy. Smile. Except the Lord bless it, nothing will come to pass. Fear not. Have faith, and all will be well. Ask of the Lord and receive His spirit. You have received everything from Him; forget not His mercies.

The Word of the Lord abideth forever and is never void of effect.

Be docile and Christian in your acts. Be not proud and self-centered always.

Do you try to abide in the Word of God daily?

20th July '24 Sunday

*Y*e are the light of the World. A city that is set on a hill cannot be hid. Let your light so shine before men, that they may see your good works, and glorify your Father which is in heaven. *Matthew 5:14.*

Be not of the Word, 'tho' in it. Be blameless and spotless as sons of God. Make it a habit to see the heart sorrows and needs of everyone and to reckon it a privilege to relieve them. Scatter blessings wherever you go. You were baptized in Jesus. Rise therefore and live in Him. The Lord hates iniquity. Have faith and rejoice. Be not afraid.

Tho' in sorrows, be always rejoicing. Glory in tribulation, if you suffer for the right. Be glad always in the Lord, for He is your strength. Be filled with the Spirit. Return unto the Lord and He will guide you. Make your life a sweet song.

Comfort others. Lift little burdens away.

Keep the Sabbath of the Lord. Be dead to sin and alive unto righteousness. Live to Christ's Honour and glory.

Whom can you comfort today with a visit, phone call, or a card?

21ˢᵗ July '24 Monday

*P*ut off concerning the former conversation of the old man, which is corrupt according to the deceitful lusts; and be renewed in the spirit of your mind; and put on the new Man. *Ephesians 4:22.*

Live in Christ. Forgive others. Live the Gospel of Love. Be perfectly true in all you say. Live up to your words and ideals. Cheer the suffering and help the needy. You are not alone, but bound up with rest. Discharge your responsibilities faithfully. Sin shall not have dominion over you, for Christ has redeemed you.

Through the Body and Blood of the Lamb of God, you are saved. Be up and doing.

Do something worth living for and worth dying for.

Have a heart for others. Be cheery. The Lord will certainly punish such as break His Laws, but He is merciful on those who fear Him. The wages of sin is death. Forsake evil and return unto the Lord.

Is there anything you will die for?

22nd July '24 Tuesday

*H*e that hath suffered in the flesh hath ceased from sin; that he no longer should live the rest of his time in the flesh to the lusts of men, but to the will of God. *I Peter 4:1.*

You are dead to sin; therefore live unto Christ. You are justified thro' Christ. Seek to please Him. Try and like what you have to do. Be unselfish and observant. Help others for that is a debt you owe them. The Lord will certainly punish iniquity. Ask grace to help in time of need. Jesus is ready. Put first things first and self always last.

Abide in Jesus, and your fruit will be pleasing. Continue in His love. Love one another as Christ loves you. Do what lies in your power and God will bless it.

Command honours, as well as bestow them.

The Lord works wonders in earth and heaven. He is Almighty. Yield yourself to Him. Ask for help to crush the evil in you which makes itself manifest often. Jesus can give you victory.

Think of someone you can bestow honor today?

———— ·❧· ————

23rd July '24 Wednesday

*S*urely I come quickly. *Revelations 22:20.*

Seeing that all these things shall be dissolved, what manner of persons ought ye to be in all manner of holy conversation and godliness? *II Peter 3:11.*

The end of all things is at hand. Prepare to meet Thy God. Wait and watch, for the day of the Lord is at hand.

Do not get angry quickly. Fight against evil in yourself. Strive hard and achieve.

Allow the Spirit to create in you a clean heart. Walk after the Spirit of Christ, and none can condemn you. The Holy Lord hates evil.

Be a messenger of mercy from God to the fallen and falling.

Pray one for another, that you may be healed. Pray with all prayer and supplication. Watch your thoughts. Strive after high things. Curb your wayward desires. Do not dream of things. Live up to the mark.

They who are in the flesh cannot please God. Be not carnally minded. Look up and be filled of the Spirit.

Do you like being a messenger of mercy? Do it more often.

⋅⟨❂⟩⋅

24th July '24 Thursday

*I*n the world ye shall have tribulations; but be of good cheer; I have overcome the world. *John 16:33.*

It is the Lord; let Him do what seemeth to Him good. *I Samuel 3:18.*

They most hypocrites are,
Who others hypocrites call.

Be strong in the Lord; be patient and longsuffering with joyfulness. Submit gladly to God.

Speak gently. Let the Lord guide you. Consider Jesus and his vexations and be not hasty to get offended. Thro' the Spirit mortify the dead of the body. Be led by the Spirit.

Care not for the fleeting world. Wait for the eternal joys.

Fear not. Hope in the Lord and have faith. Rejoice.

Be not angry or worried about anything. Commit all to God who judges righteously. Have faith in God. Without faith it is impossible to please God. Nothing is too hard for God. Lord, increase my faith.

Forget not the Lord God and His laws. The Lord intercedes for you and knows the secrets of your heart. Be not carried away by moods. Have more faith.

Isn't it difficult to wait for things? Why?

25th July '24 Friday

*T*hine, I am, O Lord forever
To Thy Service set apart;
Suffer me to leave Thee never;
Seal Thy image on my heart.

No more can you yield to sin for you have pressed from death unto life. Be quickened with Christ. Govern your self and your behaviour to others. Be calm and good tempered. The Lord tries you to remove the dross in you. Submit. All things will for good work together, if Him you serve.

God is for you, who can prevail against you?

The Lord knows the best way for you, and He will lead you aright and keep you from falling. Lean hard on His guidance. Watch your thoughts and character. Never be hasty to reply. Ask for pardon from above. Jesus is the one mediator. In all temptations you are more than a conqueror thro' Christ. Let nothing separate you from Christ.

Memorize this Bible verse. "Greater is he that is in you . . ."
I John 4:4.

26th July '24 Saturday

I am the Lord thy God which teacheth thee to profit, which leadeth thee by the way thou shouldst go. *Isaiah 48:17.*

Arise ye and depart; for this is not your rest: because it is polluted, it shall destroy you, even with a sore destruction. *Micah 2:10.*

Have faith. Be not lost, but seek the Kingdom of God first. Let the Lord choose all things for you. When you are tempted to be angry, try and be very meek. Have no unholy tempers. Control yourself. The Lord hates alienation from Him. Remember that He overrules all things. Be holy in all manner of conversation, for you are the Temple of God.

Let no corrupt communication proceed out of your mouth.

Grieve not the Holy Ghost. Humble yourself before the Lord. Be not in a hurry to take offence. Jesus is your soul's Preserver. He will save you. Let your thoughts and words and deeds be filled with one Spirit of Love.

What do you see as corrupt communication?

———◈◈———

27ᵗʰ July '24 Sunday

*K*eep a strong curb, however, on your youthful cravings; and strive for integrity, good faith, love, peace, in company with all who pray to the Lord with pure hearts.—*II Timothy 2:22.*

Let the glory of the Lord be seen in you. Jesus was made manifest that you might partake of joy and glory. Live up to the mark. Conform to the Will of God in small things. **Self-control is a virtue.** The Lord is a jealous God and hates His servants worshipping idols. Keep your heart free. The Lord is supreme and can do what He will with man.

Take you the whole armour of God. The Lord can fill you with strength. Go in His Name. Trust in His Might. Put not your trust in vain things. Ask the Lord to show you the way. He is your Guide. Never prove a stumbling block. Self control is pleasant after a while. The Lord knows what is best. Believe on the Lord and you shall have no reason to be ashamed.

Is self-control out of style?

28th July '24 Monday

*A*bove all things have fervent charity among yourselves; for charity shall cover the multitude of sins. *I Peter 4:8.*

If it be possible, as much as lieth in you, live peaceably with all men. *Romans 12:18.*

Love in deed and truth. Be kind and tenderhearted, ready to forgive as you have been forgiven. Retaliate not, but commit all to God. Win honour by worthy deeds. All shall work for your good. The Lord is never hasty. Trust in His judgements. You are sign unto the Rest. Show forth God's dealings.

Pray for the salvation of India earnestly. Be not halfhearted in your prayers. Let your requests be made known unto God, for His Grace is sufficient for you. Pour out your hearts before Him. He will do the very best for you. **Be not carried away by praise.**

Know that all things will work together for your good. The Lord God Almighty reigneth. Believe and live. Confess Christ. Be not led away by appearance.

What are the dangers of being carried away by praise?

29ᵗʰ July '24 Tuesday

*M*ake haste, my beloved,
and be thou like to a roe or
a young hart upon the mountains of spices.
Surely I come quickly
Even so, come, Lord Jesus.
Our conversation is in heaven.

Thirst after the living waters which Jesus gives you. He is your life. Let Him be your guide. Be brave and never a coward. Choose the narrow way which will lead you unto life everlasting. Submit to discipline.

The Lord works mysteriously. He will see that justice is done. There is no caste in Christ. Seek the Lord and find Him.

Fear not: so long as you fear the Lord, all things shall work together for your good. Nothing can harm you. Be prepared for trials and temptations. Be brave and face the devil squarely.

The Lord is not slack in the fulfillment of His promises. *II Peter 3:9.*

Trust in His infinite Love.

What promise has the Lord fulfilled or not fulfilled in your life?

————◈◈————

30th July '24 Wednesday

*S*eek those things which are above, where Christ sitteth on the right hand of God. *Colossians 3:1.*

Above all, make your own life, a pattern of right conduct.

Lay aside all which besets you and follow after the Lord. Grow into the likeness of Christ. Get wisdom from above. Since you know not the way before you, ask God for guidance. He is ready to aid you. The Lord is a jealous God. Serve Him alone and with sincerity. Follow after and you shall obtain.

Put your trust in the Lord and fear not what man has got to say. Confess Jesus before man. Follow in His steps.

Make good use of your free will.

Jesus will carry your troubles. Make all known to the Loving Saviour. Be not conceited, but work out your salvation with fear and trembling. Serve the Lord. Fear not if you have your moods of unbelief. Call on the Lord to aid you against the evil one.

How can one abuse free will?

31st July '24 Thursday

*T*he God of all grace, who hath called us unto His eternal glory by Christ Jesus, after that ye have suffered a while, make you perfect, establish, strengthen, settle you. *I Peter 5:10.*

The Lord is ever with you supporting you. Serve all in the Lord's control. He will choose aright for you.

Accept your round of duty, and you will grow into Christ-like and noble characters.

The Lord looks far into the future and orders all things. Be not high-minded. Be a Christian. Keep the Word of the Lord.

Dwell in unity and peace with others. The Lord loves it.

Love one another with a pure heart. Jesus is your Mediator. Patiently endure all and share the joys of the kingdom.

Life is your school.

Bear yourself up like a man. Do your work well and to your best. All things are of God.

Commit your soul unto God's Hand and He will bring about all things. Do not be Anxious.

Name things you have learned in your school of life.

The fruit of the Spirit is...faith.

The First Day of the month August '24. Friday

*F*ight; Do not think the strife to *last;*
Soon shall victory crown you.

Principle is a higher thing than feeling, and will stand life's *terrible test* far better.—F. W. R.

Without faith it is impossible to please God. *Hebrews 11:6.*

Walk by faith.

Love the Benign Saviour. Show the faith and love in your life and conduct. Keep the Word of the Lord. Be not *terribly upset* about receiving or exacting your dues. Leave that to the rest of the world. Forget your right. Forget yourself and you will be greatly appreciated by all. Be transformed into the likeness *of Christ.* Present your body and mind and soul to God, *in simplicity* and love. Lord, help thou my unbelief.

The Lord is pitiful and of tender *mercies.* He is gracious and compassionate. He *leads* you. Trust and be glad. Be affectionate and self-possessed. Be not forward and *self-righteous.* Rejoice to do the will of God.

The Lord is mighty to save.
Be affectionate and kind.

Let your *love be without* dissimulation.
Be sincere in everything and serve God with a right spirit.

Walking by faith is like learning to play a musical instrument or riding a bicycle. Practice, practice, practice.

———— ⋅❊⋅ ————

2nd Aug '24 Saturday

*T*o one who is well principled, existence is victory. Having nothing, this spirit hath all.—Emerson.

Be strong, be good, be pure!
Right only shall endure.—H. W. F.

Nobleness of character is nothing but steady love of Good and steady scorn of evil.—J. H. F.

Jesus died for you and bore your sins. Henceforth you should sin no more, for you are now your Master's and not your own.

Jesus is the same forever and ever. Strive to be like Him.

Be not misled by the craving for success. Be not slothful in business. Be fervent in serving God. Rejoice and continue in prayer. The Lord, He alone is God. Draw upon God's Resources in times of trouble and stand firmly on the Rock.

You are more than a conqueror thro' Jesus Christ. Sing and rejoice in His marvelous aid. Develop your character.

Make your road pleasant by doing your best and see all things aright.

Overcome evil with good. Live peaceably with all men. Be not wise in your own conceit. Abstain from all appearance of evil. Hope, hope, hope.

How can your road be made pleasant not only for you, but others also?

———— ·❂· ————

3rd Aug '24 Sunday

*T*he Lord is nigh unto all them that call upon Him . . . in truth. He will fulfill the desire of them that fear Him.

Happiness is not the end of life, character is.

Oh how great is Thy goodness, which Thou hast laid up for them that fear Thee!

Serve the Lord with sincerity. Be His child wherever you are and bring glory to His Name. Be up and doing. Deal honestly.

Be patient for the Lord knows what He is about. Be subject unto authority. Consider what is the thing to do, and do it. The Lord will bless you. Religion is your best home.

Endure and come unscathed from this temptation like a soldier of Christ. Be faithful unto death. Affliction works marvelous good in a man.

Spend more time in secret. Seek to do good to all. Be kind and humble. Be not overbearing. Love all. Never postpone. Trust in the Lord.

Why is character so important?

4th Aug '24 Monday

*G*reater love hath no man than this, that a man lay down his life for his friends. *John 15:13.*

Be thou prepared for the fight if thou wilt have the victory. If thou desire to be crowned, fight manfully, endure patiently.

Faint not, persevere and you must succeed. Press onward and God will be thy Aid. Do the work given to you. Forget not the dying love of Christ. Seek to please Him ever. The punishment for sin will surely come. Love all and serve them. Render everyone their due.

The Lord will be with you when you pass through troubles. He hath quickened you from your sins, so go and sin no more. Strive after for success. Yield not like a fool. **Be prepared to knock down all barriers and to work for the greatest glory**. Cast away the works of darkness. Be born again. Put on the Lord Jesus Christ, for it is high time to awake and to show yourself in your true colours.

What barriers have you knocked down or
will like to knock down?

5th Aug '24 Tuesday

*W*alk in newness of life. *Romans 6:4.*

Do not make resolutions which you know you will not carry out, for thus you weaken the mind and will. Strive hard to fulfill the desires of those interested in you and to do your duty as you ought to do it.

Consecrate your whole self to God and deal honestly with yourself. Cast off the works of darkness and put on Christ. Reach after success, but do not set your heart on it. Persevere in whatever you may undertake. Be not hasty to judge others. Be not a stumbling block to any in the path of Right.

Never be anxious, but ease your burden upon the Lord. You know not what is good for you; therefore trust. He will give you peace, and do the best for you. **Strive hard to win the mastery over yourself. Pray and work**. Give people warning against sin. You are altogether the Lord's. Live for Him. Choose to live in the beauties of Nature.

What does "mastery over self" mean? Do you see a particular area of your life that needs it?

6th Aug '24 Wednesday

*W*hom the Lord loveth, He correcteth. *Proverbs 3:12.*

I know, O Lord, that Thy judgments are right, and that Thou in faithfulness has afflicted me.
Humble yourselves therefore under the mighty hand of God, that He may exalt you in due time.

The Lord loves you and will deal gently with you. Afflictions work marvels in you. Seek the Lord steadfastly.

Attempt great things for God. Be not alarmed by apparent difficulties.

Do not give yourself up to moods. Look at the brightest side of things. You have to account for yourself to God. Let not your good be evil spoken of. Do your duty faithfully.

The Earth is the Lord's and the fullness thereof. You have received all of God. Give Him glory. He is your Lord and Master. Serve Him faithfully. Do not be carried aside by passing distractions.

Turn yourself away from beholding the vanities of the world. Be a child of God. Have faith and use it to the best advantage.

Be not in the way of others. Lead them to do good.

Think of a great thing you can attempt for God.

———◆◈◆———

7th Aug '24 Thursday

*P*ractice thyself even in the things
which thou despairest of accomplishing.
Better to strive and climb,
And never reach the goal,
Than to drift along with time,
An aimless worthless soul.

Persevere. Do not be weakened, but have a strong will to do the right. Ask for strength and God will give you His Spirit. Grieve not the Holy Spirit. The punishment for disobedience will be great. Bear with others. Seek to please others to their edification.

Love Jesus with all your heart. He is your Master and your Lord. He is the King of Kings. Count nothing too much to sacrifice to seek the Lord. Be patient and persevere in all you do. You shall certainly succeed. The Lord will bless you. Do your duties to others. You have much given you and so are answerable for it.

Be of the same mind as Christ.

What would Jesus do in your shoes?

8th Aug '24 Friday

*T*hen shall we know, if we follow on to know the Lord. See that you are prejudiced against nothing that is good. Have an open mind and take all corrections in the true spirit of the student.

You are a child of God. Look unto the Lord and be transformed. Persevere. Make earnest attempts to please others for their good.

Work hard to be master at least of a few things. Concentrate your powers. The Lord knows you thro' and thro'. Seek to help others. Pray one for another and God give you grace to bring Him glory.

Call upon the Lord. Ask earnestly for His Spirit. Prepare your heart by your conduct.

Pray without ceasing. *I Thessalonians 5:17.*

Work with your heart and soul, and God will bless you. Do your best to help others and to see that they by your conduct respect religion and spiritual consolation.

Be brotherly and kindly affectionate to all.

Who deserves your affection and kindness today?

9ᵗʰ Aug '24 Saturday

*W*e are all as an unclean things, and all our righteousness are as filthy rags. *Isaiah 64:6.*

Let the beauty of the Lord our God be upon us. *Psalm 90:17.*

Be not proud and selfish. Walk humbly and in the Path of Christ. Aim high. Let your thoughts be pure, your words gentle, your acts just and your whole life an example. Do the best you are capable of. Sacrifice worldly things to gain spiritual. The Lord will take the part of the weak and needy. Rejoice. He will bruise Satan under your feet. Avoid fleshy feeling.

Set your affections on things above and not on earthly objects. *Colossians 3:2.*

All is fleeting and deceitful. Aim at something higher than success. God will make you perfect and strong.

Test yourself and see where you have set your heart.

God is worthy of all Glory. He is your Lord and your Saviour. Trust.

Where have you set your mind—earthly goals or heavenly minded or . . . ?

⎯⎯⎯⎯⎯⎯·❊·⎯⎯⎯⎯⎯⎯

10ᵗʰ Aug '24 Sunday

*C*onsider well the propriety or impropriety of things and act wisely and kindly. Be not hasty in your choice so that you are forced to repent at leisure.

Ye are the salt of the earth . . . the light of the world. Let your light shine.

The Lord is mighty and cares for His children. He can keep you from sinning against Him. Rest on the Word of God. Watch against self which loves to be exalted. Live with men as if God saw you. The Lord is a jealous God. Serve Him faithfully. Be frank in your utterance. Be Christ-like.

Go forward. Climb upward.

Be patient and discreet. Speak with God as if man heard you. Lean hard on Christ. You are saved by grace. Nothing should separate you from the Love of Christ.

Put your trust in God. Glory in Christ. Be filled with His Spirit. Love with all your heart. Your best hours are those when you realize God's Guiding Hand. Spend much time in secret.

What steps can you take to climb upward spiritually?

11th Aug '24 Monday

*E*very kindness done to others is a step nearer to the life of Christ.—Stanley.

Draw out thy soul to the hungry, and thy soul will grow in generous sympathy.

Fear no evil for the Lord is by you to succour and aid you. He will swallow up death in victory. Strive from this day forward to be more like Him. Do all things faithfully. Follow the Master.

Let your love show itself in deeds.

Many look up to you and trust you. Rise up to their trust. Know Jesus alone and Him crucified. Let not your attention be drawn elsewhere.

God is light, and if you dwell in Him, let your conduct be Jesus'. Fear God and keep His commandments. Do all for love and you will find it pleasant. The Lord will give you His spirit and lead you in righteousness.

Put on the Lord Jesus Christ. *Romans 13:14.*

The Lord trusts in you to fulfill the high hopes He has placed in you.

Faith without works is dead. Let us be alive.

12ᵗʰ Aug '24 Tuesday

God will have nobody despise His workmanship. If you wish to kill love, indulge in sin.

A Good generosity is the child of an enlarged sympathy; and there are two great aids in enlarging sympathy: actual sight and thought over it.

The Lord is very merciful. Fear not: return unto Him and He will strengthen you. Be not wise in your own eyes. Plead for a spirit of meekness. Bear the yoke of Christ and follow on. The Lord can work marvels.

Hope thou in the Lord to the end. Labour together with others and allow God to bless you. The Lord desires you to walk kindly, justly, humbly before Him. *Micah 6:8.*

God's ways are marvelous. He can work wonders with weak mortals, but not by your might, but by His Spirit. Learn to be meek and lowly. Praise not yourself. Bear others' burdens.

You are built on Jesus Christ, who is the foundation stone. *I Corinthians 3:11.*

Remain firm.

A familiar chorus: The rain came down and the water level rose The house upon the rock stood firm.

———⟨◈⟩———

13th Aug '24 Wednesday

*W*hat everyone is in God's sight, that he is, and no more. The perfect Christian is silent about his merits and other's faults. The faulty Christian is silent about his own faults and others' merits.

Be patient unto the coming of the Lord. Here are we no continuing city. Rejoice for your home is above. Be very courteous for you cannot say how much evil will otherwise be caused. Be gentle and never rude. The Lord is merciful and He forgives the truly penitent.

You are God's Temple. *1 Corinthians 3:16.*

Be holy and displease and disgrace not God.

Be earnest about Social Righteousness.

You can have joy with the Father only if you surrender yourself entirely to Him and kill self. You must be prepared to communicate it to others if you wish your joy to be lasting.

Walk in the unity of the spirit and in the bond of brotherly love at all times.

Is social righteousness the same as social justice?

————•❊•————

14th Aug'24 Thursday

*H*e that can forbear speaking for some time will remit much of his passion.

"I think" says Cato, "the first virtue is to restrain the tongue: he approaches nearest to the God who knows how to be silent, even though he is in the right."

The Lord will never forget such as trust in Him.

Tho' He may be thought to forsake, yet he will never. Only trust. He is your shepherd. You are saved by Jesus and are no more yours. All are one in Christ. In speech, in conduct, love, faith, and purity, be examples to others.

The Lord is prepared to lift you out of your troubles. Call on Him from out of the depths. How great are His works! How puny and little you are in His sight, and yet He cares for you. Return, be brave, and follow on.

Recall a time when God stood by you.

15th Aug '24 Friday

*B*e not hasty to be familiar with those you meet, for your loquacity may be taken for bragging.

Be moderate in all you do, knowing that **"moderation is the silken string running through the pearl chain of virtues."**

Be not carried away by the multitude of your duties. Rather sanctify yourself and go forward and your whole day will be blest. Ask counsel of God in your perplexities.

Be careful how you act. Be courteous and kind. Treat others just as you love to be treated yourself. Be joyful. Strive after perfection. Be courageous and of one mind with others.

Is any aspect of your life needs to be kept in moderation?

16th Aug '24 Saturday

*L*ose no opportunity of seeing the beauties of Nature all around you. Have a reverent and questioning mind which will find cause for praising in all His works.

Seek fellowship with those around you and make the best of your opportunity.

Be thoughtful for others. Be slow to offend. Be courteous and kind. Be prepared to sacrifice your interests for the sake of others. Trust in the Lord and not unto your own understanding. *Proverbs 3:5.*

Serve the Lord in unity of Spirit. Love the Lord more.

Make a covenant with your eyes that they shall not behold evil.

Be pure in both word and deed. Love the Lord. He will give you His spirit. Prepare yourself to receive Him into your heart. Fight for character.

Internet brings many temptations for the eye. Beware.

17ᵗʰ Aug '24 Sunday

*L*et your actions always be straightforward and above board. Do not get yourself entangled in anything questionable and "let not your good be evil spoken of."

The Lord is your Shepherd, providing for you at all times. Oh, be not of little faith, for you dishonour Him. Rejoice to dwell close to Him, for with Him is joy everlasting. Be fearless in the preaching of the Word. The Lord will give you grace to do it right bravely for it is His Word.

Number your days for you know not the length of your life. Man's life is fleeting. The will of God abides forever. Do not abuse the world.

Provoke others to love and not to anger.

Now is the accepted time. Make the best of it. Be pure. Let your love be true and honest. Be noble and sweet in character. Never think of doing evil. Be brave, and God will be with you.

Apply peer pressure to do good.

———◈◈◈———

18th Aug '24 Monday

Sis. Nesamma's Birthday

*P*raise the Lord, oh my soul
Glory Hallelujah;
Praise the Lord, oh my soul,
Praise ye the Lord.

O taste and see that the Lord is good; *Psalm 34:8.*
that His mercy endureth for ever.

Show Christ-like spirit. God keeps watch over you, only consent to be led. Yield not to temptations. God is great and His works are marvelous. Lean on His arm. The Lord governs the World and orders all things.

Follow the Master's example. Pride not yourself. Consider not yourself greater than others. Be humble. Help to bring joy to others.

O God, Thou art mine. O fill me with Thyself. Glory in the Lord.

Rejoice in His Salvation. Be pure in thought, word and deed. Do not run into evil. Be not passionate and hasty.

The Lord is ready to speak to you, if you are willing to hearken.

Abandon evil and do that which is good. You cannot serve God by thinking alone but by taking active faith in His Name.

Can you think of an instance you heard from God?

19ᵗʰ Aug '24 Tuesday

*T*here is no pleasure great than that of having done one's duty well. Be not lured away from your daily work, but fix your mind and steadfastly set yourself to discharge the duties incumbent on you.

Whatever you do, do all to the glory of God. *Colossians 3:17.*

The Lord and Father is holy, so you be holy. Never neglect your opportunities for service.

Make your habits and motives pure, and reduce slothfulness to a minimum.

The sacrifices of God are of a broken and contrite heart. Put away sin from you. Have "fellowship" with God.

Doubt not: only believe and God will bring your desires to pass. Believe and pray earnestly. He will give you a new heart. Let Him work in you. Never yield to the promptings of the evil one for you truly grieve God's Spirit.

Be pure in heart. The Lord is pleased with such as seek to do His will. Evil can have no place in God's kingdom. Act up to the light you have received and then ask for more and God will surely give it you.

Name some good habits you would like to develop.

20th Aug '24 Wednesday

*A*sk the Lord to help you in your daily tasks.
Be earnest in doing them well.
Blessed are the pure in heart,
For they shall see our God;
The Secret of the Lord is theirs,
Their soul is Christ's abode.

Let not evil conversation go on in your hearing. Fear not objections. Refuse to have anything to do with evil thoughts and all you know to be wrong. Love the Lord, delight in His Word and serve all and your faith will get stronger. All things are not expedient to you.

Your body is Christ's, the Dwelling of the Holy Ghost. You are not your own. Glorify God therefore.

Call upon the Lord and He will hear your cry. He will give you power in the day of weakness.

His grace is sufficient for you. *II Corinthians 12:9.*

Good thoughts leave a pleasant impression on you. Don't indulge in anything evil. Seek the Lord's counsel in all you do, for He is best able to direct you.

Let the Lord dwell in you and lead you in the truth. God is in earnest about the Salvation of His children.

Since Christ dwells in our body, how can we take better care for our body?

———— ❖ ————

21st Aug '24 Thursday

*D*well at all times on the glorious possibilities the Son of Man holds out to you. Let not your feet be turned away from His path by the allurements of this world. Walk circumspectly, looking unto Jesus, and you will reach the goal.

God, through Christ, showed His love to you and expects you to be holy. The Lord is your portion and you have nothing to fear. Keep an innocent heart. Ask for a pure mind and honesty of purpose.

The Lord blesses such as fear Him. Continue in that which the Lord has called you. Be earnest in God fearing in whatever you undertake to do.

The Lord will lead you with His own eye. Trust not in yourself.

The Word of God is a lamp to your feet. *Psalm 119:105.*

Ask for purity and love and gratitude. Be innocent and you need fear nothing.

Prepare for your Eternal Home. Those that know not God are foolish and small-minded. God alone is the foundation of Wisdom. Call on Him.

Live with a purpose, and do not drift.

Do you have a purpose-driven life? If possible, take time to read Rick Warren's book by the same name.

———————•⟨३⟩•———————

22nd Aug '24 Friday

O Father in heaven, I am weak and helpless without Thy gracious aid. Come close to me and give me Thy helping hand. Leave, all, leave me not alone. Still support and comfort me. Show me what is Thy will and give me face to do it for Jesus' sake. Amen.

You are crucified with Christ. Hence forth Christ *lives* in you. *Galatians 2:20.*

Forget not your obligations. Seek to help others. Appreciate beauty. Your business is to be good, say people what they will. Go into the World with a purpose, making all happy.

Ask and receive of the merciful God. Be not a stumbling block to any. Seek the Way of Truth. Walk cautiously with the Spirit.

God is the source of Wisdom and Power and He is manifest in Christ. He is the Prince of Peace. If you walk in the Right, you encourage people to do the same. Have a clean and pure heart.

The Lord knows the secrets of your heart.

Let others know of the Love of Christ. Be not a stumbling block to any. Seek to fulfill the purpose God has in sending you.

Is there a secret you are hiding from God?

———⸭⸬⸭———

23rd Aug '24 Saturday

*S*ilence is a friend that will never betray. The deeper the sorrow, the less the tongue hath it. Truth, like roses, often blossoms on a thorny stem. Patience is the key of paradise.

They must often change who would be constant in happiness, or wisdom. God loves you though you are frail and sinful. He knows you thro' and thro'. Give thanks always for His inestimable love.

Let your hands be useful in the service of Mankind. You are God's own. Walk worthy of your high calling. The Kingdom of God endureth forever.

So run that you may obtain. Be temperate in all things. Keep your body under God's care for you. Love Him.

God will never forget you. He has made you and He will carry you thro'! Trust. Jesus is the same kind and loving Saviour.

Be God's own. Come into God's Presence and dedicate yourself. Walk in God's Love.

God takes a real interest in you.

The Lord exalts the humble and meek. Fear the Lord and serve Him with sincerity.

Do you believe that God is taking real interest in you?

24ᵗʰ Aug '24 Sunday

*H*e that knows not, and knows not that he knows not, is stupid. Shun him.

He that knows not, and knows that he knows not, is good. Teach him.

He that knows, and knows not that he knows, is asleep. Arouse him.

He that knows, and knows that he knows, is wise. Follow him.—Selected.

You are as the apple of God's eye. He careth for you. Jesus knew your sorrows. Tell Him all your troubles. You have to fight a great battle and that along with God. Acquit yourself manfully.

The human heart is weak and forgetful. Forget not God's mercies. Beware lest you fall. God will aid you in your temptations. God is everywhere and He sees you.

Be instant in season and out of season. *II Timothy 4:2.*

Labour and be not slothful. The Grace of God will support you. Trust in the Lord at all times.

Consecrate yourself unto God. Worship none but the Father of Jesus, who is God Almighty. The earth and its fullness is the Lord's.

Remember the scruples of others and respect them.

How do you respect the scruples or values of someone else—by not questioning them or listening and asking questions?

———◦❖◦———

25th Aug '24 Monday

I will greatly rejoice in the Lord, my soul shall be joyful in my God.
Rejoice in the Lord always, and again I say, Rejoice. *Philippians 4:4.*

When you were lost and vile, the Lord saved you alive. Forget not your great indebtedness to Him. Wait on others. You owe every man you meet love and service.

Follow in the footsteps of the Master. Be ready to sacrifice yourself. The Son of God is with you in your trials.

Be fearless of man and he will learn to fear God. Whatever you do, do all to the glory of God.

Bless the Lord at all times. Sing and be a glad and cheerful Christian. Be filled with the Spirit. Be Christ-like in your spirit, seek to be of service to all. Forget yourself and have the Lord before you.

The Lord orders every detail of your life. He is your own God.

Remember that all are one in God. Follow in the light you have received. Realize the presence of God always with you.

What detail of your life are you giving to God today?

26th Aug '24 Tuesday

*B*e perfectly honest with yourself. Make allowances for no weakness but do your best in your search after truth and God. Strive for mastery over self.

God is a spirit, worship Him in spirit and in truth. *John 4:4.*

Wherever you are, do little deeds of kindness to all. Faint not. Live and act as a Child of God. Partake of the Lord's supper worthily and to your improvement. Jesus died for you. Walk humbly, lest the Lord bring you down. Be earnest and faithful.

Fear the Lord. His mercies are new every day. Be content in whatever state you are. God will supply all your need.

Do good for the sake of doing good. Submit yourself to God. Let Light radiate from you. The Lord will raise the humble and abase the proud. Humble yourself. Jesus Christ is God. He is your bountiful Saviour. Forsake not His gentle arms.

Realize the presence of the living God.

Practice the "presence of God" in your silent meditation time as well as all day.

27th Aug '24 Wednesday

*M*easure thy life by loss instead of gain,
Not by the wine drunk, but by the wine poured forth;
For love's strength standeth in love's sacrifice,
And whoso suffers most hath most to give.

The Word of God and His Spirit will direct you in the way you must need to go.

Jesus is your light. Follow on. Love work. Pray and praise. Do your duties honourably. Have high ideals and set them into practice. You know little, so trust God. Covet earnestly that which is good. Come to the Saviour; make no delay. Wait upon the Lord. Consecrate yourself afresh to Him.

Set your heart in finding God. Sleep not: rise and pray.

Watch for you know not when the Master comes. *Mark 13:35.*

This is not your rest. Confess Christ. Find your work and do it well. Be a comforter. Behave yourself honourably. Be not conceited. Your breath is in God's hands. Humble yourself. Glorify God.

Love all earnestly and be prepared to serve others. Be not superstitious because your loving God is in earnest and in loving.

Are you anxious about something today? Ask God for direction and leave it at his feet.

———◆◈◆———

28th Aug '24 Thursday

*D*o such things as are worth the time and labour spent on them. Waste no time for you must give an account of it to God. Be wholehearted and sincere in the performance of your tasks.

Put on the whole armour of God. *Ephesians 6:11.*

Christ is your shield. Be filled with the Spirit of God. Search your heart and return unto God. Be thoughtful in the usage of words. They have such wonderful effect. The Lord will exalt the humble. Be kind and slow to anger. Love covereth faults. God is majestic and loving. Serve to please a loving Father.

Overcome the world. Christ is your wisdom. He will help you in your troubles if only you call on Him. Let your heart be right and will come well. Seek to please God. Be ardent and sincere through and through.

Go forward doing the right. Waver not. Be faithful. God will deliver His servants. Follow after character.

Are you wavering about something? Anchor on God.

29ᵗʰ Aug '24 Friday

*W*hoso trusteth in the Lord, happy is he.

God is our refuge and strength, a very present help in trouble. *Psalm 46:1.*

It is better to trust in the Lord, than to put confidence in princes.

Be of a calm and peaceful mind, for the Lord is your God and He will deliver you.

Do your very best. Never appear to be what you are not. Do not neglect little things. Do every thing well. Serve God continually. He is able to deliver you. Never be hasty and then repent too late. Let your heart be guileless. God will order peace for you. Do all things decently and in order.

Lay down thy self in peace, for God watches over you. He will cover you with His wings. Abide in Him and be happy. Trust and obey. Make the best use of your time and talents. Be diligent and honest. Be sincere and thorough-going. Avoid all sin. The Lord ordereth all things in heaven and earth. Humble yourself. Jesus is very God. Forget not His love to you.

What are the marks of a calm and peaceful mind?

———•◈•———

30th Aug '24 Saturday

[. . .] When he crieth, I will hear.

*D*o not be careless about the gifts with which you are endowed.

Draw near to God and He will draw near to you and bless you. Come with a true heart. Walk in faith.

Do the best at every moment and you will be happy. Be careful. The Son of Man will reign forever. Be His and serve Him.

Forget yourself in service.

By the grace of God, you are what you are. There is nothing stronger than love. Love.

Be sincere in all you do. Do not hide your faults. Confess and turn from sin. Lead a *worthy* life. Do your duty with pleasure. Partner with Jesus and live forever.

Seek first the kingdom of God and His righteousness. Be *above* things. Evil shall not triumph again.

Ask God for a noble end and you shall live forever with the Lord. Christ arose that you might have life. Rejoice.

Name a service when you completely forgot yourself.

31ˢᵗ Aug '24 Sunday

*L*ord, if *thou will, I shall be made clean. Luke 5:12.*

A sincere mind with *love*
absorbing hatred for sin *cannot*
But be led in the way of righteousness.

Keep your tongue from speaking evil of others.

Never be anxious for applause. Go straight onward to do your duty. Your sins are forgiven because of your Savior.

Rejoice and be watchful. Right must triumph.

Die unto sin. Be alive unto righteousness.

Service is the end of life.

God's love should make you die for him. Be earnest in actively doing His will. God partakes in your sufferings and your joys.

Make Him your guide and protector. Sincerity is the basis of way of life. Be sincere in your praise. Do your duty. Jesus is your example.

Follow in his steps. You have to render *a service* in all you do. The Lord governs all.

Our mortal body will be glorified in the Lord.

*Can you think of ways you can keep your tongue
from speaking evil of others?*

The fruit of the Spirit is...meekness

September 1924

The First day of the Month of September 1924.

Monday

*T*he ornament of a meek and quiet spirit is in the sight of God of great price.

Christ . . . An example. Reach forward for the things that are before. Commit yourself unto God. Be not hasty to retaliate. Keep your conscience sensitive and watch and pray. Do that which is right only. There are many things that are inexplicable to you. Ask for wisdom of God. He will bless your labours. He will grant you victory. God partakes in your sufferings.

Through good report and evil, hold on to the truth. Be glad and rejoice. If you suffer, you shall reign also with Christ.
Live so as to be an example.
Keep the commands of the Lord.

Watch and pray. *Matthew 26:41.*

Confess your sins and return unto God, for He will forgive.

Have you ever been put up as an example or a mentor to others? Isn't that a great responsibility?

2nd Sept '24 Tuesday

*T*he trying of your faith worketh patience. And let patience have her perfect work, that ye may be perfect and entire, wanting nothing.

Wait on the Lord and be of a good courage. *Psalm 27:14.*

The Lord will uphold you. He is your shelter and comforter. Do not hesitate about difficult things. Worries should bear you up. **Walk in the way the Lord directs.**
Return unto the loving Saviour. He is merciful and kind. Let all things he done in charity. Be strong and acquit yourself like a man.

Come to Jesus and rest. The Lord is very good. He is love to you. Oh forget not His benefits. Through suffering you must enter into joy and glory. Nothing can harm you if your trust is in God. The Lord goes before you. Call day and night upon the Lord. Fear not what man can do to you. Ask and receive. Love your Saviour.

Is it easy to walk in the way the Lord directs?

3rd Sept '24 Wednesday

*T*he fear of the Lord is to hate evil.
Let everyone that nameth the name of Christ depart from iniquity.
II Timothy 2:19.

Let your mind be pure and holy. Jesus was your example. Follow in His steps. Let the Lord lead you aright. Decide early to be on His side. He will sustain you in your troubles. The guileless Lord died for you. Forsake sin and please Him. The promises of the Lord are faithful and true. You stand by faith.

Let not Satan beguile you. Be watchful. Be clothed in the whole armour of God. Let truth, righteousness, peace, faith and salvation be your armour. Let God guide you.

Be pure in thought, word and deed.

You are vile and sinful, yet Jesus saves you. Love and serve Him faithfully.

How are you trying to keep your mind pure?

4th Sept '24 Thursday

*T*ake head, and be quiet; fear not, neither be fainthearted. Said I not unto thee, that if thou wouldest believe, thou shouldest see the glory of God? *John 11:40.*

Be not troubled or hasty about anything. Rest in the Lord and wait patiently for Him. Be not self-willed. Hope and patiently go on with your work. The Lord will give you light for the next step. The Lord knows the thoughts of your heart. He feels in your sorrows. He loves you and He will strengthen you.

Your sufficiency is of God.

People read you. Bear good witness.

The way the Lord leads you is strange, yet it is the best. The Lord loves you with an everlasting Love. Rejoice in His might. Forget yourself in the service of God and man. Be pure in thought and word. Follow the Lord without a murmur. All will be well.

Name a time God has been sufficient for your life.

5th Sept '24 Friday

*F*or one thing only, Lord, dear Lord, I plead,
Lead me aright,
Though strength should falter, and though heart should bleed,
Through peace to light.—Proctor.

The Word of the Lord will guide you. Wait upon Him.

The Lord is mighty and He will choose your lot for you.

You are transformed by communion with God. The Lord gives wisdom to such as ask to Him. You are one with Christ. The search after God is the import factor, not the results therefore.

The beloved of the Lord shall dwell in safety. *Deuteronomy 33:12.*

Come unto the Lord and drink your fill of the Living Waters. Let God direct you in all you do. Obey and reap the reward. His truth will guide you.

Yield not to the promptings of Satan. Ask the Lord for aid and you will surely receive it. Live Christ and preach Him totally.

Are you waiting for the Lord to choose the lot for you—
Your job, life partner . . . ?

6th Sept '24 Saturday

*C*ause me to hear Thy loving kindness in the morning; for in Thee do I trust; cause me to know the way wherein I should walk: for I lift up my soul unto Thee.

The Lord will forgive if you truly repent. Lift up your heart and hand to Him. He will aid you.

Fight the good fight with all your might. *I Timothy 6:12.*

Be brave and fight your enemies, the world, the flesh and the devil. Know God and work wonders.

You are upheld and borne up by the Love of God.

Be not troubled, only trust.

The Lord God Almighty, wondrous in His care for His children, is your own Guide and Counselor. Fear not therefore, only trust and be at rest in His Love.

Read Psalm 78 to see how David reminds himself of the times God upheld his people.

7th Sept '24 Sunday

*L*abour is not only a necessity and a duty, but a blessing; only the idle feels it to be a curse.—Miles

I wait for the Lord, no soul doth wait, and in His word do I hope.

My soul waiteth for the Lord more than they that watch for the morning. *Psalm 130:6.*

I say, more than they that watch for the morning. Watch. The Lord looketh on the heart. Count your mortal loss for Christ. The Lord proves your actions.

You can gain little without some labour and cost.

You will rise into Christ's glory if you are dead unto sin and are alive to His voice.

The Lord is with you if you look for aid to Him.

Is Baptism a symbol of being dead to sin and alive in Christ?

———◈◆◈———

8th Sept '24 Monday

*H*appy we live, when God doth fill
Our hands with work, our hearts with zeal;
For every toil, if He enjoin,
Becomes a sacrifice divine;
And, like the blessed spirits above,
The more we serve, the more we love.

The Lord bless the work of your hands if you do it with a single eye. Forget about pleasing yourself.

Dare to displease man to please God.

The Lord chastens such as love Him. Come to the Lord and He will give you what your soul requires. Do your best to bring many unto Christ. Look forward.

You possess all things if you have Christ. The Lord is very mindful of you. Rejoice in His wonderful care. Labour is healthy and honourable.

You should walk by faith and not by sight. *II Corinthians 5:7.*

Deal justly and the Lord will be with you.

Think about how many times we displease God to please man?

9th Sept '24 Tuesday

*B*e not deceived; God is not mocked; for whatsoever a man soweth, that shall he also reap. *Galatians 6:7.*

The Lord Jesus is the bread of life. Take the Lord for your counselor and guide, and He will direct you in your choices. He will show you that which is good. Work faithfully and you shall be happy. Use God's gifts aright. The Lord hates sin. Oh return ye unto Him and be saved. Let the love of Christ constrain you.

You will be answerable for your deeds.

You are a new creation in Christ.

Jesus intercedes for you so that you shall not yield to Satan. Call on Him and He will aid you. Do your bit honestly wherever you are and that will be honouring for Christ. The Lord loves the industrious. Be reconciled unto God. Plead with your soul and return unto Him. The Lord loves you.

Who are you answerable to, here on earth?

10th Sept '24 Wednesday

*W*hen I am weak, then am I strong. *II Corinthians 12:10.*

Cast thy burden upon the Lord and He shall sustain Thee. *Psalm 55:22.*

They that wait upon the Lord shall renew their strength. *Isaiah 40:31.*

The Lord will give you a clean heart and grant you unity. Walk worthy of your high calling. Be one with Christ. Be cheerful in your service of God and man. Watch yourself in the unnoticed moments and see that you do the right. The Lord speaks kindly to the erring ones and brings them back. Grow in His likeness. Make the best use of your opportunities.

Fight with the powers of evil armed with God's armour. When Christ is with you, you are mighty. Fear not. The Lord values your services to others. Serve Him faithfully. **The Lord wishes you to be His entirely.** Love Him. Be separate from sin and evil.

What does it mean to be God's entirely? Are you withholding some parts of your life from God?

11ᵗʰ Sept '24 Thursday

*B*e not conformed to this world: but be ye transformed by the renewing of your mind. *Romans 12:2.*

The World passeth away, and the lust thereof; but he that doeth the will of God abideth for ever. *1 John 2:17.*

Walk not according to your natural desires, but curb your passions and obey the Lord. Do your piece of work wholeheartedly. Be perfect with God. Share in working for others. The Lord God most holy hates sin. Fear to displease Him and strive to walk worthy of your high calling.

Study to be quiet and work with your own hands. Work while it is day. Be not weary in well-doing. **Rest comes only after labour.** Share in the good work of the Lord. Serve the Lord with a perfect heart and a willing mind. Work on. In troubles, call on the Lord and He will aid you. Godly sorrow worketh repentance. Rejoice and hope.

In what ways do you seek spiritual rest?

12th Sept '24 Friday

*A*ll things are naked and opened unto the eyes of Him with whom we have to do.
If God be for us, who can be against us? *Romans 8:31.*

The Lord knows your inmost thoughts. Return unto Him for He was wounded for your transgressions. Consider how great things He hath done for you. Be examples of a wise, sincere and upright life. Be thoughtful and kind.

The Lord waits for His wayward children to come back.

Rejoice in His love and bring others to Him.

God will deliver you in temptation. He knows your needs. The Lord is on your side. Call on Him. Remain by Him and you will be safe. Be kind and loving and your labours will not be in vain. Sympathize with others. Fear the Lord. Let your work be consecrated. Give yourself unto God. Serve Him with a willing heart and hand.

*Are you a wayward child of God or one
who found the way back?*

13th Sept '24 Saturday

*Y*ou can learn good things from all sorts of people. There is no one so bad but has some good point in Him which honours his Maker.

Bring sunshine and happiness into the lives of others. Be kind and good whatever comes of it. Serve the Lord. Thirst after the Lord. Seek Him right early and He will be found of you. Jesus shed His life-blood for you. The Lord abhors evil.

"Though rich, yet for your sake He became poor. Lose yourself in the service of others." *II Corinthians 8:9.*

You are the salt of the earth. Have the spirit of Christ in you. Let all you say or do be for the edification of others. Do things which are worthwhile.

Show your love to God by your service.

Young or old, we have our own outreach to serve others, right?

———◈◈◈———

14th Sept '24 Sunday

O Jesus who art waiting
Thy faithful ones to crown,
Vouchsafe to bless our conflict,
Our loving service own.

You work in Christ's work. Use your hands in His service. You gain much in serving the Lord. Choose well and stick to it.

Cast all your care on the Lord. I Peter 5:7.

He pities you and loves you. He will aid you. Forget not the Lord. Remember thy Creator in the days of thy youth. Be earnest in serving Thy Lord.

Be a child of God. Sacrifice all you have at the altar of Jesus. He gave Himself that you may give yourself for others. **Take Him with you wherever you go.** Trust in Him. Humble yourself. Forget yourself and let Christ be magnified.

*Will it change your plans for the day if you took
God with you today?*

15th Sept '24 Monday

*MTM to Ellore**

*S*in shall have dominion no more over you for you are not under the Law but under grace. *Romans 6:14.*

Sin no more, for Christ has given you victory. Stand first in the liberty Christ has given you. Become purer and purer.

Get wisdom and grow in Christ's likeness.

Enjoy doing the right thing. Provide for things honest in the sight of God and man. Return unto Him. The Lord is good. Displease Him not.

Abide in Christ. Be steadfast, and work for the Lord for your labour will not be in vain. Love knowledge. Get a wide education. Be zealous in the Lord's work. Do all you do cheerfully. Keep a watch over your tongue.

*Ellore is Appa's hometown in Andhra Pradesh State in India. He had to take the train from Madras to Masulipatnam (MTM.) He was thrilled to be back home from College that he made special mention of it here. Are you thrilled to go back home?

———⦿———

16th Sept '24 Tuesday

Ellore

Search me, O God, and know my heart; try me, and know my thoughts and see if there be any wicked way in me, and lead me in the way everlasting. *Psalm 139:23.*

The Lord knows the secrets of your heart. Do your duty. Work for His eye. Take heed to yourself. Watch.

Correct your mistakes. Grow in goodness.

The Lord loves you. Remember that always and serve Him truly. He sees that all things work together for your good if you love Him.

When God allows you to meet temptation, it is that you might trample down the works of the evil one. Be not troubled by afflictions. God rules all and Jesus has overcome the world. Have faith in God and rest in peace on His Loving breast.

Do mistakes stifle growth? Have you found 'correcting mistakes' help you grow as a person?

————⋘⋙————

17th Sept '24 Wednesday

Ellore

*T*hus saith the Lord, "I will seek that which was lost, and bring again that which was driven away, and will bind up that which was broken, and will strengthen that which was sick." *Ezekiel 34:16.*

The Lord will save you and guide you even unto the end of the world. He is your Rock. Do your acts and life bear witness to Christ? Examine yourself in the light of the Bible. Yield not to sin. The Holy One is in the midst of you. Displease Him not. Bring everything into subjection to Christ.

Persevere. Have power with God thro' faith. Turn unto God and wait on Him. Be not vain. Glory in the Lord. Lean not on your own understanding. **Jesus can renew His Spirit in you and make you His.**

Be not critical. Rejoice in the Lord. He is good. Taste and see that the Lord is good.

Renewal of spirit is as important as renewal of body.

18th Sept '24 Thursday

Ellore to MTM

*L*ord, fill me with Thyself. Empty me of pride, the old Adam and sin.

Renew a right spirit within me and create a clean heart in me. (Amen.) *Psalm 51:10.*

The Lord He is God. There is no Saviour beside Him.

Destroy self and live in Christ.

Your help is in God. Be ready to suffer for Christ. Boast not. Rather consider how great things He hath done for you and how unworthy your actions are. Throw your all at His feet and He will use you mightily in His service.

Cry unto the Lord in the hour of need and He will aid you. Ask and He will give you victory. You are His son, unworthy as you are, and so He loves you. He will uphold you. Neither cry nor keep silent. Be kind to all. Be willing to learn from all. Be not ready for finding faults.

What do you think about the concept of "destroying self"?

————— ·❊· —————

19th Sept '24 Friday

*H*e is gracious unto me and saith, "Deliver him from going down to the pit; I have found a ransom."

By grace are ye saved through faith; and that not of yourselves; it is the gift of God. *Ephesians 2:8.*

Be not conceited. Humble yourself under the mighty hand of God. He will give you grace if you trust yourself to Him. Therefore trust and be not afraid. Get rid of guilt by casting your burden upon God who died to give you salvation. Beware of love of self. Return unto the Lord. He will heal your backsliding and love you freely. **When you are weak, then are you strong, for the Lord's grace attends you.** Boast not.

Remember that you have to render an account for all you do. Consider all you have received at God's Hands. Lift up your eyes unto the Lord. He will help you. Search and try your ways. Let your hearts be the dwelling place of the Spirit.

Read II Corinthians 12:10

20th Sept '24 Saturday

Prize-giving

*B*e quick to hear, slow to speak and slow to be angry.

I will lift up mine eyes unto the hills, from whence cometh my help. My help cometh from the Lord. *Psalm 121:1.*

Win souls and be wise. Glory in your knowledge of the Lord. In God are hid all your treasure. Be docile and let the Lord teach you. Be not hasty in anything. Take time and the Master will guide you. The Lord is your God. He will bless you and prosper you. Lean on His Wisdom. **Be willing to spend and be spent for others.**

All you have received is of the fullness of God. He will supply all your need. God has chosen the weak to do mighty things for Him. Submit yourself. Deliberate much before saying anything. Be humble and learn of the Great Teacher.

Are you willing to be "spent" for someone special? Who?

21st Sept '24 Sunday

*M*y Grace is sufficient for thee. *II Corinthians 12:9.*

Count it all joy when you encounter diverse temptations; Knowing this, that the trying of your faith worketh patience. And let patience have her perfect work, that ye may be perfect and entire, wanting nothing. *James 1:2-4*

All things work together for your good. All things are yours through Christ. God does all well.

Be silent about others if you can say nothing good about them.

Make friends of God's children and walk in the path which Christ has marked out for you. The Lord God is above all. Trust Him.

Your body is the temple of the Holy Spirit. Grieve not the Holy Spirit. Make it a point not to indulge in unnecessary criticism. Be what Jesus expects you to be.

Silence is Golden especially when being critical of others.

————⟨⊰⊹⊱⟩————

22ⁿᵈ Sept '24 Monday

*M*ake Thy face shine upon Thy servant. Lord, lift Thou up the light of Thy countenance upon us. *Psalm 119:135.*

I will be glad in the Lord. Try to say something good of others. Be careful in your friendships. Jesus is your great Friend. Yield yourself up to His guidance; there is none who can be compared to Christ. Love Him. The Day of the Lord is at hand. Repent and return unto the Lord. Examine yourself and try your hearts for God knows your secret thoughts.

Will not to do your will, but the will of your Lord and Sovereign Master Jesus. Learn obedience. Jesus submitted Himself to the Cross. Share your joy with others.

Be intimate but not familiar.

Strive to attain golden friendship. Those that are sustained by the Lord shall be strong and invincible. Be perfect. Live in peace and God be with you. Let God's peace go with you.

How can you be intimate but not familiar? Does it mean be caring but not nosey?

23rd Sept '24 Tuesday

*T*he Lord will not forsake His people His great name's sake; because it hath pleased the Lord to make you His people.

The Lord proves His children to know whether they care for Him really. Have the Lord for your Helper and you can never be depressed. Give freely and the Lord will bless you. Love Truth and Light.

Cherish noble and wholesome friendships.

Rend your heart and return to the Lord. *Joel 2:13.*

He is gracious and loving. Cleave unto the Lord and His Promises.

The Lord Jesus is your Eternal Saviour and Provider. God has great things in store for you. Love His will. Keep company with your Lord and He will bless you and enrich your life. The Lord will do great things in your life. Seek to please the Lord and not man.

Can you think of a noble friendship you have developed?
Name one.

24th Sept '24 Wednesday

*L*et us lay aside every weight and the sin which doth so easily beset us, and let us run with patience the race which is set before us. *Hebrews 12:1.*

Let your heart be sprinkled from an evil conscience. Wait for the Lord and He will be good for you. Rejoice in His love. Draw near unto the Lord.

Speak always with mildness and in a low tone of voice. Judge not others till you stand in their place. Be steadfast in friendship. Know that the Lord your God is in your midst and that He will save you. Live in Christ who gave Himself for you and who love you. God's grace will uphold you in time of need. The Lord is with you unto the end. Be a good steward.

Betray not the secrets of others.

Let God choose your lot and your friends for you. The Lord will pour out His Spirit upon you. He will deliver such as call on His name. Have faith in God.

Are you good at confidentiality?

———————·❸·❽·———————

25th Sept '24 Thursday

*B*uild today, then, strong and sure,
With a firm and ample base,
And ascending and secure
Shall tomorrow find its place.

Do valiantly. Train yourself from the beginning in godliness and hold you apart for sacrifice and service. You attain glory thro' tribulations. Wait and hope patiently. Live by faith. Be a child of God.

Put on the Lord Jesus.

Abhor sin for your Lover hates it. Be one in Christ. Serve the Lord.

The Lord knows the inmost recesses of your heart. Lay your heart before God. Confess all. Strive to walk in the path of the Lord. Live on the Lord's word and you will clearly see His will for you and for others. You are a son. Partake of the Fellowship.

How do you "put on the Lord Jesus"?

26th Sept '24 Friday

*F*orward be our watchword,
Steps and voices joined,
Seek the things before us,
Not a look behind.

Choose the right at the cost of trouble. Serve others sacrificing your selfish interests. Overcome and be a victor. Jesus died. The Wages of sin is death. The Gracious Saviour died that you might live. Remember that Love is the essential virtue and that all else without it is vain.

Put first things first. Seek the kingdom of God and His righteousness first.

The Presence of the Lord shall go with you. He will prepare your place before you and give you peace. Lean not on thine own understanding. Fall back upon the guidance of your Master and by His commands be led.

Examine yourself to see if you are seeking first things first?

———— ❦ ————

27th Sept '24 Saturday

V's Birthday

(V is probably Appa's first cousin Vimala Appasamy, Principal of Vidyodaya High School in Chennai, India.)

*I*n conversation be sincere;
Keep conscience as the noontide clear;
Think how all seeing God thy ways
And all they secret thoughts survey.—Bp. Ken

Read the Bible daily; study and ponder it and store its divine words in your heart.

Do beautiful things, things of love, of unselfishness, of helpfulness, things that are true, honourable, justly pure.

Nothing makes life so sweet in old age as does the memory of right, good, and kindly things wrought along the years.—J. R. Miller.

Cleave to Him. Humble yourself before Him.

Let Him train and lead you.

Conquer Satan with the Word of God. For He cannot stand long against it.

Bear the yoke when young and be chastised in the days of your youth.

Is it easy to let God train strong-willed humans like us?

———•◈•———

28ᵗʰ Sept '24 Sunday

O Lord our God, other lords beside thee have had dominion over us; but by thee only will we make mention of Thy name. *Isaiah 26:13*

Call upon the name of the Lord. He will help us. Run unto your Saviour and rest in His Love. Live for something. Good deeds will shine as the stars of heaven. Do good. Be kind and loving and merciful. Abhor evil and return unto your God. Be free for the Blood of Christ has set you at liberty. No more shall sin have dominion over you.

The Lord is glorious in majesty and His ways are past finding out. Come, fall before Him and worship Him truly.

Put your trust in His mercy and lean hard on His Love, which never faileth.

Be not anxious about anything. The Lord knoweth the desires of them that fear Him. Watch your words.

Read/sing the hymn "Leaning on the heart of Jesus."

29th Sept '24 Monday

2nd Term of Work

*F*ind out your various peculiarities, the special dispensations of God in your character, the variations of type in you. Cultivate them, ceaselessly add to them, never fear to accumulate them.—Mozoomdar.

Cultivate good habits. Never yield to any unholy impulse. Let Christ be with you in all your doings. His Love for you passeth all understandings. Forgive and forget. Be prepared to lay down your life for the brethren. Be tenderhearted and Christ-like. Forget not the benefits God has conferred on you. Let your faith work by Love. Use your liberty to Christ's glory.

Follow in Christ's steps. Develop your character into Christ's likeness. Make it your aim in life to serve the Lord. Wait on the Lord and be of good courage. Lean hard on God. He is your Saviour. Walk with Christ. Yield to His chastisement. Be not desirous or vainglory.

Put away the works of the flesh and bring forth the fruits of the Spirit.

Appa left Ellore to go to college in Madras when the school holidays were over to begin the second semester. Notice his resolve for the new term.

30th Sept '24 Tuesday

"He knoweth our frame." *Psalm 103:14.*

He doth on afflict willingly not grieve the children of men.

The Lord is good and gentle. He it is that does order all things for you.

Control your temper and you will grow day by day into a holy character. Do your best to put up with the ill-temper of others.

Bear one another's burdens and bear your own burden bravely.

Fight manfully against temptation. Jesus and the Spirit will aid you.

Trust in the Lord with all your heart. He will guide you.

Let His Presence go with you. Be not revengeful. Be cautious in your words and actions.

The Lord hates such as crush the needy and think not of their welfare. Be not weary in well doing.

Do good to all men.

Glory in the gospel of Christ. Be a new creature.

Get ready for the new month. Be a new creature.

Photos of Medical Work

The Kantayya Clinic next to the house

Jaya taking X-Ray at the clinic

Branch Clinic

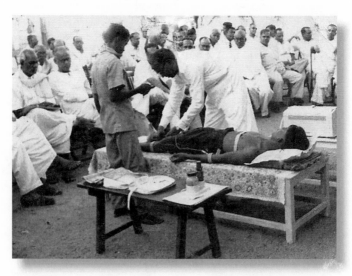

Noble demonstrating EKG to Medical Society
members 1957

Photos of Ordination

Noble with others ordained at the same time.
January 1959

Noble in self-designed Indian style Cassock January 1959

Photos of Pastoral Ministry

Christ Church 2011

Plaque in Christ Church in Appa's honor. Larry & Lorra's family visited the church in 2007

Noble with his two sisters at Clarinda Church after
Wednesday morning communion service

Noble at Varsapathu village church foundation
laying ceremony

Noble flanked by two Bishops, A.J. Appasamy
and David Chellappa

Noble & Mary with Bishop Sunder Clarke, wife Clara
with photo of common ancestors Rev.
& Mrs. W.T. Satthianathan

The fruit of the Spirit is....temperance.

October
1924;

First Day of the Month of October 1924. Wednesday

*I*f any man will come after me, let him deny himself, and take up his cross, and follow me. *Mark 8:34.*

Strive for mastery over self. Be temperate in all things. Be filled with the Spirit. Be sober and vigilant.

Beware of angry words. Be not impatient about anything.

Take all your worries to God in prayer. Return unto the Lord.

Prepare to meet Him. He is gracious and longsuffering. You are accepted in the beloved. The Lord is your Guide. Submit your will to His.

Glory in the Lord. Grow in grace and in the Knowledge of Christ. Never swerve in your conduct from your honest convictions.

Never run the risk of speaking in the excitement of anger.

Yield not to passion. Seek the Lord and you will live. Abhor evil and do good. The Lord is great and good. Trust in the Lord at all times.

How have you tried to control your anger?

2ⁿᵈ Oct '24 Thursday

*A*s far as the East is from the West, so far hath He removed our transgressions from us. *Psalm 103:12.*

Return unto the Shepherd and Bishop of your soul. *II Peter 2:25.*

The Saviour has borne your transgression for you and you are free. Be open and above board in your dealings.

Make others cheerful. Ask for guidance to aid such as are in trouble.

Do good and be of service to others. Jesus reigns. Be His subject. God's trials are with a purpose. He is loving yet He afflicts His children.

All you have is of the bounty of God.

Boast not. Glory in the Lord.

You are washed and sanctified in the name of the Lord. The Spirit will show you what you should do to help the afflicted.

Do good, love the Saviour and live. By grace are you saved, through faith. God is rich in mercy.

Flee youthful lusts.

Write six things God has blessed you with. (Bounty)

———•❧❧•———

B
O
U
N
T
Y

3ʳᵈ Oct '24 Friday

$\mathcal{M}$any waters cannot quench love, neither can the floods drown it.
Song of Solomon 8:7.

Love is strong as death.
Be impelled by love in your actions and thoughts. Jesus lay down His life for you.

By His stripes you are healed. *Isaiah 53:5*

Present therefore your body, a living sacrifice unto God. *Romans 12:1*

Strengthen the fainthearted and inspire new hope. Help others and you help yourself. The Lord loves justice.
Trust in His Arm. Jesus has broken down all barriers between man and man.
Rejoice and Realize the brotherhood of man. Obey God's Laws and grow in Christ.
Let the Spirit work in your heart. Be a good steward of His manifold grace. Love the Lord and serve Him.
Touch others' lives and let them see the Love of God dwelling in you.

Lose self and live in Christ.

The Lord is gentle and waits for you to return unto Him. Grow in grace. You are a fellow citizen with the saints.

Name an evangelist or a missionary who lost his/her self to win souls for Christ.

⸻⟡⸻

4ᵗʰ Oct '24 Saturday

*C*an we be unsafe where God has placed us, and where He watches over us, as a parent a child whom He loves?—Fenelon.

Be clothed with humility. You are the light of the world and yet how black is your darkness! Return to the Saviour. Your help must come from the Lord.

Be not inattentive to the sighs of those around you. Do something to make them happy.

The Lord raiseth up the meek.
You are safe in Jesus' arms. Rest and be at peace. Let one Spirit work in you. Grow into Christ.

Be at peace with all men. *Romans 12:18.*

Serve the Master. Love others more and you will serve them better. Help the needy and succour such as are in trouble. Live in Christ's influence. Seek to understand the Love of Christ. Bring others to Him.

How can you be more attentive to those closest to you?

5th Oct '24 Sunday

*L*ord, Thou hast heard the desire of the humble; Thou wilt prepare their heart, thou wilt cause Thine ear to hear. *Psalm 10:17.*

The Lord will hear your voice and answer you in your distress. Love and serve Him truly. Be not cast down.

Nature is most instructive and wealthy. Learn of it. Be brotherly. Watch for little burdens and carry them away. Do the best you can. The Lord God almighty ruleth the Universe. Humble yourself before Him. Be one with all. Come with a meek spirit to the Bible and be benefited by it.

The Saviour loves and cares for His wayward children. Seek His face and you will find me seeking for you. He is your pilot. Let Him guide and lead you daily. None but Jesus should have room in your heart. Receive him into heart and home.

What are some of the things, nature has taught you?

⸱❸⸱❽⸱

6th Oct '24 Monday

*T*he things which are impossible with men are possible with God. *Mark 10:27.*

The Mighty God. Jesus is the revelation of God. He is God Himself and not a medium. Adore and serve Him. He is omnipresent. Learn true Christian resignation. Bear your cross patiently. Be amiable and gentle. Christ bore a heavier cross. The Lord is gracious beyond your expectations. Oh, seek to please His majesty and Love. Be not lazy.

Deal justly and walk humbly before Thy God.

Live by faith. Let Him speak to you. With patience you can achieve great things and overcome many troubles. Grow into the perfect stature of Christ. Yield not to evil impulses. The Lord bringeth low the conceited. Be thoughtful and kind.

Is there a justice issue that is dear to your heart?

7th October '24 Tuesday

*R*eligion is that nobler half of life, without which nothing stands in a true balance.

Cause me to know that way wherein I should walk; for I lift up my soul unto Thee. *Psalm 143:8.*

Ask of the Lord and obtain. The Lord will teach you what to do. Look up unto Him and wait upon Him.

Be patient in bearing other's failings, for are they not putting up with yours?

Pray and the Lord will give you victory over self. You will reap but what you sow. Be renewed in Christ Jesus. Walk in His love.

Consider the poor. The Lord will deliver you. It is more blessed to give than to receive. Live patiently, lovingly and cheerfully. Be gentlemen. Put away all envy, hatred and anger. Put on Christ. Serve Him with fear and Love. The Day of the Lord is at hand. Forgive all.

Name a failing that you have, which others have put up with?

———◈◈———

8th Oct '24 Wednesday

I will not fear what man shall do unto me. *Psalm 118:6.*

Nay, in all these things we are more than conquerors through Him that loved us. *Romans 8:37.*

Let your religion take entire hold on you. Yield yourself to the working of the Spirit. Witness bravely for Christ. Cling to His Love. Be patient. God only is unchangeable. Be loving and thoughtful. You can hide nothing from God. Love Him and serve Him.

Speak nothing but that which shall edify your hearers.

Be gentle. Grieve not the Holy Spirit, Christ the Saviour.

Be compelled with God's Spirit to work for His glory. Have faith in Christ. Be not worried about little things. Take all to Christ. God only is. Be patient and very loving. Endure trial unto the end. Live as you pray. Call upon your Lord God. He is ready to save you. Be followers of God. Yield not even to the thought of sin.

What kinds of words edify the hearer?

9th Oct '24 Thursday

*W*herever He may guide me,
No want shall turn me back;
My shepherd is beside me,
And nothing can I lack.—A. L. Waring.

Obey and follow on and you will be safe. The Lord is your guide and succour. He is merciful and ready to pardon those who repent. Rend your heart. Be sincere. Wait on the Lord. Be a power for good and be an entity. Walk circumspectly, redeeming the time. Abhor evil. The Lord is ever with you. Do all to please Him. You must see the stars against the night.

Form your opinions aright and stick to them consistently.

Think on lovely things. The Lord's Word will guide you. Submit yourself to the powers that be. Be prepared to follow your Master. Praise the Lord and magnify His name at all times. Rejoice and sing.

Be filled with the Spirit. *Ephesians 5:18.*

What pains do you take to form good opinions?

———◈◈———

10ᵗʰ October '24 Friday

*T*o a Christian man, the end of one duty should be the beginning of another.

On earth and on heaven is but one family. Christ is your elder brother. Do His bidding.

Seek to know God's will, even if it might clash with yours. Be docile. Cry unto the Lord and He will deliver you. Be humble and serve the Lord. Love all. Christ gave Himself for you. Christ delivers you from bondage.

Rejoice. Delight in serving others. Do the will of God. Avoid that which displeases Him. Obey your parents. Ask and you shall receive. The Lord is your Father and all your brothers. Be merciful and never be hasty to judge others or to wish them evil. The Lord is merciful and bears with you.

Live peaceably with all men. *Romans 12:18*.

What guidelines do you use to find God's will?

11ᵗʰ Oct '24 Saturday

*T*he Lord is nigh unto all them that call upon Him in truth. He will fulfill the desire of them that fear Him. *Psalm 145:18, 19.*

Live Christ in your daily life, that others may magnify your Lord. Obey thy Master, that He may show thee His will. Fear not; for the Lord is at your side. Oh sweet privilege! All languish because of sin. Repentance will set all right. God's all-pervading eye is on you. Serve Him and seek to please Him. Jesus has conquered sin. Be thou a victor too, trusting His integrity.

Be a Christian hourly. Be slow to judge and quick to make concessions for their weaknesses. The Lord God is most holy. Laud and magnify His holy name. Thro' Christ is your approach to His Presence. Let your heart be perfect with God. **Be obedient to the divine light shown you.** Cry unto the Lord. The Day of the Lord is at hand.

Be strong in the Lord and in the power of His might. *Ephesians 6:10.*

What is the origin of divine light?

———◈◈◈———

12th Oct '24 Sunday

*L*et us obey; we then shall know,
Shall feel our sins forgiven,
Anticipate our heaven below,
And own that love is heaven.

Be prepared to make sacrifices in little things. Obey and serve the Master. You are reconciled to God through the mediation of Christ. He is your Peace.

Train yourself physically, morally and intellectually. The Day of the Lord, are you prepared to meet it?

Take the sword of the Spirit, the shield of faith, and be girded with truth.

Delight in obeying God's will. Service to mankind should be your prime object in life.

Be ready, for in an hour unknown to you is the hour of the coming of the Lord.

Not by might or power but by God's Spirit. *Zachariah 4:6.*

Seek to live out Christ's Love in your daily life.

How do the following protect you?
Sword of the Spirit:
Shield of faith:
Girdle of truth:

13th Oct '24 Monday

*T*hus saith the high and lofty One that inhabiteth eternity, whose name is Holy: I dwell in the high and holy place, with him also that is of a contrite and humble spirit to revive the Spirit of the humble and to revive the heart of the contrite ones. *Psalm 145:18.*

Seek not after glory. It is fleeting and often brings trouble and heart burning. God works in everything. Do things with a noble intention. Repose on Jesus' love.

Return unto the Lord. Rend your heart, humble yourself and He will bless you.

Jesus gave Himself for you to give you freedom.

Be sincere. The Lord wills your sanctification. Live to the will of God. Lag apart all filthiness. Be holy and you shall live forever.

The Lord will bless such as lay themselves at His feet. Do your bit well and the Lord will give the increase.

Ask the Lord to spare you. Seek not to please man first, rather seek to serve God first.

*What three things are needed to reconcile
and be blessed by God?*

———⬦⬦⬦———

14ᵗʰ Oct '24 Tuesday

*E*very person is responsible for all the good within the scope of his abilities, and for no more; and none can tell whose sphere is the largest—Gael Hamilton

Christ suffered and died. Therefore you are dead to sin and alive unto your Lord and God. Make the most of your little good points. Do not wait for opportunities to do great things.

Do what good comes near your hand.
Know that the Lord God reigns and that He will do great things for you. Lean on Him.

Nothing is impossible with God. *Luke 1:37.*

Ask in faith, nothing wavering. *James 1:6.*

A good beginning is essential.

Work with a will. God will supply all my needs. He will never leave you or forsake you. You live thro' Christ. Trust in Him.

Practice little virtues. Be thoughtful and kind.

The Lord is with them that fear Him. The Lord will pour out His Spirit on such as ask Him. Call on His holy name, the Son of God who gave Himself for you. Be sincere and love Him truly.

Is a good beginning as important as a good end?

15th Oct '24 Wednesday

*W*e are to forgive one another because God, for Christ's sake, has forgiven us, and to the end that we may resemble God.—G. P. Fisher.

The Lord is your rock and fortress. *Psalm 18:2.*

He is your strength and shield. Fear none but trust in Him. You are kept in the shadow of his wings. Be perfect in your sphere. Take care of the little things and strive to attain to perfection in them all. Bring all your troubles and worries to Him. The Lord hates sin. Have faith in God and by it gain eternal life. You are justified by faith.

Sin is mighty in its power for enslaving. Beware.

Be prepared to forgive as you hope to be forgiven. Be kind and tender-hearted. The Lord sympathizes in your troubles. Do your best. Be more Christ-like. The Lord is your Hope. Be strong in the Lord and in the power of His might. You shall live by faith in the Lord. Jesus is your mediator.

What are some enslaving addictions, you need to be aware of?

———◈◈◈———

16th Oct '24 Thursday

*N*ot slothful in business, but fervent in spirit, serving the Lord.
Romans 12:11.

Whatsoever ye do, do it heartily as to the Lord, and not unto men. *Colossians 3:23.*

So run that you may obtain. *I Corinthians 9:24.*

Work the works of your Lord and Master. The Lord will reward you. Rejoice and be exceedingly glad. Guard yourself in little things. Do everything with a loving and earnest spirit. The Lord is merciful. He will bless and not chide forever. You are Abraham's seed of faith thro' Christ. All are one in Him. Trust not in your own strength. Lean hard on God. Be separate from evil. The Lord can aid you in your crushing of Satan. God values your life. Use it to God's glory.

Seek to fulfill God's plan for you.

Repent of sin and return to God. The wages of sin is death. Be a child of God. Abhor sin and seek to please the Lord, Who is your Father and guide. When you yield to sin, you in your turn become a tempter.

Have you found God's plan for your life? Keep seeking.

————⋅❀⋅————

17ᵗʰ Oct '24 Friday

*W*hom having not seen, ye love; in whom, though now ye see him not, yet believing, ye rejoice with joy unspeakable and full of glory. *I Peter 1:8.*

Love God and thus come to know Him. He will be found of, of such as seek Him. Rejoice always in the Lord. Obey the voice of conscience. Be diligent and prudent always.

Smile and do little deeds of kindness.

Sin will ever bring punishment in its train. Be loving and kind in heart. Your sin causes many to suffer and the Son of Man to be crucified afresh.

The Lord is your God. Love, obey and serve Him. All things come of God. To Him all glory is due. Submit yourself to Him. The blessing of the Lord, it maketh rich. Be diligent in service. Be free from guile and the sin that is ready to beset you. Return unto the Shepherd and Bishop of your soul.

Smile often and smile joyfully today.

18th Oct '24 Saturday

*T*he praises of others may be of use in teaching us, not what we are but what we ought to be.

Draw near to God with a true heart and a conscience sprinkled from all evil. *Hebrews 10:22.*

Christ's blood was your life. God can make your little life a power for good. Delight in being ignored, yet do your duty faithfully. The Great and Holy God, worship Him truly. Prepare to meet Him. You are free and a child of God. Jesus came to save you in your struggle for godliness against sin.

God's promises are true and never failing. Lean hard on His Love and Serve Him. Do your duty faithfully. Have great affection for small duties. Be prepared to remain unnoticed and to do good to all. Seek the Lord and you shall live. He knows all about you.

Stand first in the liberty of Christ.

What are some of the liberties you enjoy as a Christian?

————◆◆◆————

19th Oct '24 Sunday

*S*urely the wrath of man shall praise Thee; the remainder of wrath shall thou restrain. *Psalm 76:10.*

Blessed is the man that trusteth in the Lord, and whose hope the Lord is.
Jeremiah 17:7.

Be wise and humble. The Lord is your confidence. He will keep you from falling. He is your Refuge. Rejoice in His protection.

When you stand amongst those ignorant of Christ, remember you should represent Christ.

In difficulties are God's errands. Seek God's will. Do good. Love one another and so fulfil Christ's Law. Have faith in God.

Be humble. Learn of Christ. Carry your cross. Never seek to please yourself, identify yourself with those you wish to help and carry their burdens for them. Then alone can you be a peace maker. You shall be for ease with the Lord. God is your portion. Christ is your Comforter. Overcome difficulties. Go forward. Follow the Christ. Rejoice in the strength of the Lord. Forsake evil and bear the Fruits of the Spirit.

Read how Paul represented Jesus to the people in Athens in Acts 17:16-34.

20ᵗʰ Oct '24 Monday

*D*o the duty which lies nearest to thee, which thou knowest to be a duty; thy second duty will have already become clearer.

Delight to do the will of God. His statutes are right. Love His word. Be filled with praise. Count your many blessings and name them one by one. The Lord hates evil. He will punish. Repent and return unto Him. Bear one another's burden and so fulfill Christ's Law of Love.

God will show you what to do, if you trust Him and do His will first.

Do justly, love mercy and walk humbly with God. *Micah 6:8.*

You are accepted in the beloved. Praise, laud and magnify His Holy Name. Keep touch with Christ. Every day He's blessing. Run not into evil. Be discreet. Walk in the way of the Lord. Be not conceited. Do your duty and so serve the Lord.

Give God your day to do God's will.

———⟨3⟩⟨C⟩———

21ˢᵗ Oct '24 Tuesday

*B*ehold, what manner of love the Father hath bestowed upon us, that we should be called the sons of God! *I John 3:1.*

Be hopeful and live for some great purpose. Be in Christ and you will grow into perfection. Do not lose your birthright of purity, innocence and honour. Cherish and strengthen it. Be cheerful and do the right thing.

The Lord sifts His children but He will never allow the grain to fall to the ground. Sow to the Spirit. Do good to all men as you have opportunity.

Serve others. Be prepared to be neglected and overlooked. Minister unto the needs of others. Let God's love and sunshine dwell in your heart. In the presence of God is eternal joy.

All that men ignore in you, you are worth to God. The Lord will bless such as serve Him. Glory in the cross of the Lord.

Be a new creature in Christ.

What are the signs of a "new creature" in Christ?

22nd Oct '24 Wednesday

*W*hat time I am afraid, I will trust in Thee. *Psalm 56:3.*

The Lord is my Light and my salvation. Whom shall I fear? *Psalm 27:1.*

Trust in the Lord and lean hard on His loving guidance. Let your heart be fixed on God. Receive good and new impressions. Do what you ought, when you ought. Lean not on your own understanding for that would be foolishness. You are saved thro' Christ's Blood. Only turn to God and He'll receive you.

Love the noble idea and cherish the best motive and do the best deed each day. All is left in the hand of the Almighty. The Lord is and there is none beside Him. If God is for you, who can be against you? Choose the straight and narrow way. Learn the best you can, while you can. Man is rewarded for his deeds.

Of Christ's fullness you have received all.

Fall before Him in humility. God hopes great things of you. Rise up to His expectations.

Count some of the blessings and fullness of life in Christ.

———◦❧◦———

23rd Oct '24 Thursday

*G*ive me neither poverty nor riches; feed me with food convenient for me: lest I be full and deny Thee, saying, who is the Lord, or lest I be poor, and steal, and take the name of my God in vain. *Proverbs 30:8.*

Never be idle or lazy. Make the most of your opportunities. Be content with your lot for God will never forsake you. Character and love are of prime import. Follow method in study. Fear the Lord. The Hand of the Lord is in all things. He ruleth over all. Let the Spirit dwell in you. By grace are you saved.

Let Christ live in you and let self be dead.

Oh shun evil, that good may thrive. Be dead to sin. Be filled with the Spirit. Do your best to be informed on all things. You have a great deal yet to learn. You are made nigh unto God thro' your Lord and Master, Jesus Christ. Rejoice in his mediation. Worship and magnify His Holy Name.

When self dies, the new creation lives for God and others.
Is that true in your life?

24th Oct '24 Friday

*F*orgiveness takes the sin away as a barrier to personal friendship with the father.

Your deeds and words affect others. Be watchful and seek to do the right. When Christ comes, all is changed and new creature is created.

Resist evil. Live a good life. Keep the commandment of the Lord. Go from victory to victory. Rejoice in the Lord God, Who is your Hope.

Arise for the Lord will never forsake you. The Lord watches over His children. Live in Christ.

You have to give account for all your deeds. The Lord will uphold all who trust in Him.

Come unto the Lord and He will satisfy your cravings. Long and thirst after God.

Resist the devil and he will flee from you. *James 4:7.*

Let your life be overflowing with power.

Go forward, leaning on God's aid.

Share the Lord's Power and Purity. Christ transforms life and makes it worthwhile.

Check the signs to see if you are moving forward?

25th Oct '24 Saturday

*W*e have not wings, we cannot soar,
But we have feet to scale and climb,
By slow degrees, by more and more,
The cloudy summits of our time.

The Lord is in your midst. Ask and he will hear your prayer. He is able to keep you from falling. Remember God's presence. Make all known to Him. He is wonderful and gracious.

Repent for the day of the Lord is at hand. Bear witness to Christ Who is your Mediator. Choose the highest and the best.

Persevere and you will succeed at last. God is our refuge and strength. Be not anxious in the least. Be hopeful and pray for a better state of affairs. Mighty and wondrous are the ways of the Lord. Desire the highest and the holiest. The Lord loves such as put their trust in Him. Lean hard. Seek to understand the love of God in Christ. Glorify your Lord.

What does spiritual perseverance mean?

———⸱◈⸱———

26th Oct '24 Sunday

*F*ear not therefore, ye are of more value than many sparrows. *Matthew 10:31.*

The Lord reigneth. *Revelations 19:6.*

Be honest with yourself and be true to all. Be not troubled, for God is on your side and He is over all. Rise and be doing. Do what you can and be not idle. Do good. Use the word of God as your sword in the warfare with Satan. You are one in Christ. Be lowly and meek. The Lord is ever ready to help.

Serve the Lord with purity of mind. Be not desirous of vainglory. Love all and be good. Be kindhearted. Pray for God's Spirit over all. Obey the Lord. Look forward unto God. Waste no time.

Turn every minute to good account.

Commit your way unto the Lord. The Lord is your light and Guide. He is your Shepherd and leader.

Are you conscious of time? How do you spend it wisely?

27th Oct '24 Monday

*T*rue worth is in being, not seeming—
In doing, each day that goes by,
Some little good, not in dreaming
Of great things to do by-and-by.

Jesus Himself took your infirmities upon Himself and bore them. **God asks simple faithfulness and the quiet doing of what He allots.** Do your little well. At the Lord's bidding, rise and follow Him. Grow into the perfect man and fullness of stature of Christ. Faith works marvels.

The blessing of the Lord, it maketh rich. *Proverbs 10:22.*

Learn to be meek and to serve the Lord aright. Let your aim be to please God. Trust Him with childlike simplicity. Be prepared to suffer for the Master. Abhor evil and return unto the Lord.

"Is simple faithfulness" same as child-like faith?

28th Oct '24 Tuesday

*T*hey are never alone that are accompanied with noble thoughts.

There is no God beside the Lord our God. Christ became poor that you may be rich. Look up unto Him. Be really humble. Stand steadfast and do the work assigned you. Do your best. Let your light shine before men. Be the salt of the earth. Put off evil conduct and be filled with the Spirit. Be angry and sin not.

Be not dreaming. Do something substantial.

Be sober and vigilant. Take unto you the whole armour of God. Resist the Devil. The Lord is with you. Respect others. Partake in people's sufferings. Be not a stumbling block to any. Serve the Lord in humility of mind. Praise Him ever.

What does it mean to do something substantial—with sharing time, talent, treasure?

———— ·❧· ————

29th Oct '24 Wednesday

*W*e have one thing and only one, to do here on earth—to win the character of heaven before we die.

Be slow to anger. *James 1:19.*

Be at peace with all men. *Romans 12:18.*

Grieve not the Holy Ghost. Let your conversation be helpful to all.

The Lord is adorable. How loving are His thoughts.

Choose the right. Have faith in God. Do your bit thoroughly.

Have faith in God and nothing can be impossible. Trust and obey.

The Lord brings His children into an open space to give them better opportunities of serving and knowing Him.

Bless the Lord at all times. Trust in Him.

Encourage yourself in the Lord.

Submit to the will of God. Do all things with your might. Be scrupulously pure in all you think or say or do.

Put on the Armour of Light.

Have no fellowship with the deeds of darkness. Make the best of your time and talents. Look up to God.

How do you encourage yourself in the Lord—reading good books, listening to Christian music . . . ?

30th Oct '24 Thursday

$\mathcal{W}$ait on the Lord and He shall save thee.

Let us not be weary in well doing for in due season we shall reap if we faint not. *II Thessalonians 3:13.*

Be not conceited and vain. Look unto Jesus for example and precept. The Lord God fights your battles. What need have you to fear?

He is gracious. Come unto Him and let Him work in your soul and life.

Let your words be perfect truth and let no tinge of falsehood creep in. Be filled with the Spirit. Rejoice and be glad. Give glory to God.

Give time for Christ's image to grow in you.

Humble yourself under the mighty hand of God and He will exalt you in due time. Be not proud. By your gentleness overcome force and rudeness. Show a Christ-like Spirit.

Love all even as Christ loved you and gave himself for you. Let your speech be full of grace. Yield not to your evil promptings.

God has a beautiful plan before you.

Submit to His will and He will unfold it to you.

Pray for God to reveal the plan for you.

31ˢᵗ Oct '24 Friday

$\mathcal{N}$ot by might, not by power, but by my spirit, saith the Lord of Hosts. *Zechariah 4:6.*

The Battle is the Lord's.

The Lord God is great and mighty. He orders all things in heaven and on earth. Be not a prey to weaknesses. Be strong in the Lord.

Be merry. Never grumble. Appreciate other people's good qualities. Love and bless them that curse you. Do good to them that hate you. Be perfect even as your Father's perfect.

The Lord makes intercession for you. He will support you in your trials.

Be filled with the Holy Spirit. Be devoted to the fear of the Lord.

The Word of the Lord will surely come to pass. Lean hard on His Loving care. Rise up and go forward, trusting in the Lord.

Be of a pure heart. Be humble and charitable. Be cheerful and kind hearted.

Do good in secret.

Forget self and praise in serving the Lord.

Recall a time you received an anonymous gift/card

Jehovah-jireh.

The First Day of the Month of November 1924.

Saturday

*L*ook out for the bright, for the brightest side of things, and keep thy face constantly turned to it.

Trust in the Lord, and be happy. Your duty is to cheer and make others happy as well.

Pray without ceasing. The Lord is with you. Worship Him in Spirit and in truth.

Let character be your chief aim in life. Forgive others as you hope for forgiveness. Never nurse malice or envy in your heart.

Do your duty and please God. Honour your elders.

Have faith in God and have peace of mind.

The Lord will give you wisdom sufficient for your needs. Ask.

Be not anxious about anything. *Philippians 4:6.*

Be continually happy. Radiate joy around you.

When was God's wisdom sufficient for your need?

———◈◈———

2nd Nov '24 Sunday

*L*ive for something. Do good and leave behind you a monument of virtue that the storm of time can never destroy.—Chalmers

Lay aside every weight and run with patience the race that is set before us. *Hebrews 12:1.*

Let your thoughts be pure and holy. Adorn each day with little sacrifices.

Let the happiness of others be dearer than your own. Seek not praise of man. Lay up for yourself treasures in heaven.

Be strong in the Lord. Put on the whole armour of God. Wait on the Lord.

The Lord is mighty. He speaks to His Children. God is your Salvation. Praise Him ever. He is able to keep you from falling.

Yield yourself, to God and He will use you mightily.

Rise in His love. He is ever with you.

Do you realize that you always rise above with God's love and go down without God's love?

3rd Nov '24 Monday

*I*f any man will do His will, he shall know of the doctrine, whether it be of God.

Hearken unto the voice of the Lord, and do His will. Follow the Master. Never be hasty for you will ever be the loser.

Rejoice because you too can suffer for Christ. Sacrifice yourself that you may love others and serve them better.

You cannot serve two masters. Let God reign in you.

Seek first the kingdom of God. *Matthew 6:33.*

Take the whole armour of God. *Ephesians 6:11.*

The Lord God is everlasting. Learn of Christ.

Do all things after due consideration and be hasty about nothing.

Believe that you can achieve a thing. Work hard for it, and God will so bless you that you will achieve it.

Have patience with all and be slow to anger. Forget self and honour others.

Judge not that you be not judged. Be slow to find faults. Be charitable and generous. Let the peace of God possess your heart.

Haste makes waste. Have you found that to be true?

————⸭⸭————

4th Nov '24 Tuesday

*W*ho is powerful? He who can control his passions. Who is rich? He who is contented with what he has.

Be not vexed with afflictions. God is faithful and He will not over-try your spirit. Jesus is touched with your infirmities. Love is forgetfulness of self. Be affectionate to one another. Be unselfish and true. Seek and you shall find. Remember and put into practice the golden Rule. The Lord is able. He will continue His grace to His children. Jesus strengthens the weak one, giving him power.

Be of good cheer for Christ has overcome the world. *John 16:33*.

Let His peace will fill your heart. Glory to God. Exercise self-control. Be meek and gentle. Be prepared to overlook your convenience for the sake of others. Respect others.

Enter in at the straight and narrow gate and into life eternal.

Be sincere and be filled with the fruits of righteousness. Jesus can fill you with life and vigor.

Why is it hard to choose and enter the "narrow" gate?

———◆◈◆———

5th Nov '24 Wednesday

*G*ive what you have; to someone it may be better than you dare to think.—H. W. L.

Wrestle and fight and pray. Go on from strength to strength. Do small things with a noble mind and so sanctify your labour. The Spirit dwelling in you can change you into Christ's likeness. Never be envious. Bring forth worthy fruit in accordance with your High calling. Let Christ be glorified. Preach Him to all.

With Christ in you, what ought to be done can be done.

Be thoughtful and earnest, kindhearted and true. Life is but a vapour. Make therefore the best use of it. Remember how frail you are. Be wary, the Son of Man cometh. Put what you have to use and increase the common weal. Love. Seek to please God first. Let Christ be glorified in your life. Determine to magnify Him in all you do.

Do you believe that God + you can achieve many things?

———◈◈◈———

6ᵗʰ Nov '24 Thursday

*G*od blesses those who do more than they are required to do. Christ did not seek His own pleasure.

Do all you can to be of use to others. God will abundantly bless you. Be prepared to deny yourself. When Jesus comes, you will be transformed into His glory. Rejoice in hope. Honour the hoary headed. The heart of salvation is victorious power.

Build your life on the Word of God. Delight to serve the Master and to suffer for Him if need be.

You feel comfortable in certain sins, but unless you shake yourself free of them and let Christ take hold of you, you are not going to serve and glorify Him. The Spirit of God will lead you into all truth. Will to do God's will. Jesus wills to make you whole. Yield to Him. Be humble and loving. Forget self in the service of those about you. Be full of Christ. Deny yourself and you will find yourself strong in the Lord.

Try memorizing at least one Bible verse every week?

7th Nov '24 Friday

O taste and see how precious the Lord is: blessed is the man that trusteth in Him. *Psalm 34:8.*

The Lord is good to all and His mercies are great. Praise the Lord for all He has done for you. Be loving and the world will run smoothly. Strive to reach the goal set before you. Be not discouraged but try over again. Success must come. Have confidence in God. His word is mighty indeed. Do all things cheerfully. Shine as a light in your corner.

Let love take possession of you. Forget insults. Humble yourself to the dust.

Let patience have her perfect work in you.

Bravely meet and crush temptation. Let the Lord be your Guide. Go forward leaning on the Master's wisdom. Seek the kingdom of God and His righteousness first. Serve the Lord with heart and soul. Jesus bears your infirmities. Rise on His wings.

Patience is one of the fruits of the Spirit. Ask God for it.

———⋅◈⋅◈⋅———

8th Nov '24 Saturday

*F*aith is the substance of things hoped for, the evidence of things not seen. *Hebrews 11:1.*

How gracious God is! He will wipe off all tears. He will defend His people. Wait upon Him. Take the whole armour of God. Be hopeful and live joyfully. Be not afraid. Jesus is able to quell all earthly storms. Follow Him. Be prepared to sacrifice your life, if need be, in the service of God. Let good become part of yourself.

Let all your actions be set to please God. Forget evil and do good. Be optimistic in your tendencies. You have overcome the world thro' God's aid. Be not dismayed. The world cannot prevail if you but take God's Arm and trust in Him. **Be not proud, for all you have received is of God.** Rejoice always for His blessings rest on you and in His care you are safe.

What are the things you are proud of? Give glory back to God.

9th Nov '24 Sunday

*W*ith smiles of peace and looks of love,
Light in our dwellings we may make,
Bid kind good humour brighten there,
And still do all for Jesus' sake.

People are waiting for sympathy and a few words of comfort. Be not chary of kindness. Jesus humbled Himself to the death of the Cross that He might save you. Realize His sacrifice and life to please Him. Work for the common weal, trusting that God has a purpose for all. What things are gained to you, count them as loss for Christ. Have faith in God. Be a child of God.

Cheer. **The Lord is mindful of you.** He cares for all. Jesus is your Mediator and you are saved by His Blood. Have faith in God.
Follow the Lord.
Be filled with the Spirit. *Ephesians 5:18.*
Have fellowship with Christ. Know Him. Experience Christ and be a power for good.

How do you know God cares for you?

10th Nov '24 Monday

Bro's Birthday. Older Brother G. S. Krishnayya's Birthday

*B*e calm, have courage, be wise, and all will come out right.—Charles Wagner

Be fruitful in every good work, and increasing in the knowledge of God. *Colossians 1:10.*

Christ has chosen you that you should bring forth good fruit.

Yield yourself to His will. Let Him do His good pleasure. Have faith in Him. The Lord will care for you. Use your opportunities.

If God be for you, who can be against you? Be sincere. Rejoice for God is with you. Press forward. Let nothing hinder your progress.

Make the most of your opportunities. Wait on the Lord. Be of good cheer. God will avenge those who trust in Him. Wait and be not impatient.

Let Jesus dwell in your heart. Have faith. Be optimistic, for God will take care of you every day.

Jesus has brought you into the knowledge of God. Your conversation is in Heaven. Have childlike and trusting faith. Be of good comfort.

Did God choose you, or did you choose God?

————⊰⊹⊱————

11ᵗʰ Nov '24 Tuesday

*I*n all their affliction he was afflicted, and the angel of His presence saved them: in His love and in His pity He redeemed them and He bare them. *Isaiah 63:9.*

Let all be the better for your religion.

The Lord is your God. He will ever direct and lead you. Fear not. Trust in Him. God shapes our course and He knows what awaits us.

Serve Him patiently. Have a living faith in God which can work marvels and give you peace. So stand fast in the Lord. Cooperate for the common weal. Know God as your Father.

Make all happy and cheerful. Be a source of joy and happiness.

Draw nigh unto God. He forgives transgressions. You are satisfied through Christ's blood. Let your life be worth living.

Rejoice in the Lord. The Day of the Lord is at hand. Let the peace of God fill your heart and mind. Make all known unto God and lean hard on His care.

Is your religion a stumbling block or stepping stone for others?

———⟨✦⟩———

12th Nov '24 Wednesday

*H*e is happy whose circumstances suit his temper, but he is more happy and excellent who can suit his temper to any circumstances.

Repent of your iniquities and return unto God. He loves a humble soul. Wait on the Lord. Put your trust in the Lord. Let Him think for you. Obey His voice.

Be prepared for action. Be not a child of circumstances. Go out and work for the Master. Pray for workers. Think on things lovely, just and pure.

Let the God you speak of, be experienced by you.

Is it well with your soul? Are you growing or do you remain stunted? Always rejoice for you have great glory in Heaven.

Look at the things which are not seen. Let not untoward circumstances affect your soul. Trust and obey. Go out. Fear none.

Be instant in season and out of season. *II Timothy 4:2.*

Jesus will aid you. Learn in whatever state you are therewith to be content. You can do all things thro' Christ.

Have you tasted and seen that the Lord is good? Tell others.

13th Nov '24 Thursday

*T*he wealth of a man is the number of things which he loves and blesses which he is loved and blessed by.

Be baptized of the Spirit. The Word of the Lord is life giving.

Enrich your minds with noble sentiments. Read good books. Study the Bible. You have freely received of God; therefore freely give to all. Do all you can to help others. Be happy with what you have. Imitate Christ so much until He dwells in you. Be sincere and earnest.

You are accepted in Christ. Grow into godliness.

Ask and receive of God. Be not conservative. Read to weigh and consider. Read with joy and judgment. Be wise and harmless. Rejoice if you suffer for Christ's sake. The Spirit will counsel and lead you. Trust. God will supply all your need. Trust God and be not afraid of man.

Think of ways you can grow in Godliness.

14ᵗʰ Nov '24 Friday

*W*hen alone, we have our thoughts to watch; in the family, our temper; in society, our tongue.

The Lord will order all things for you. Confide in Him.

Be not afraid of frail man. The Lord will never forsake you. Rejoice in Him. Be not satisfied with outward show. Be substantial and sincere. Be prepared to be hated of all men. Be true to Christ. Praise the Lord for the deliverance wrought for you. Have fellowship with the Spirit of Jesus.

Fear no evil though you walk thro' the valley of the shadow of Death for the Lord is with you. *Psalm 23:4, 5.*

Fill yourself with the thoughts of Christ. Think and ponder. Read with care. Man can harm your soul but little. Reverence and serve the Lord faithfully. Seek to please the Lord. The Lord is able to work marvels. His powers are, to us, miraculous.

Does God know everything even before you confide in God?

———◄❀❂►———

15th Nov '24 Saturday

*O*nly be ye gentle hearted;
Beauty rich and wisdom rare,
From a gentle spirit parted,
Earneth hate and causeth care.

Be delicate and perfect in the detail. Never be hasty and impatient. Be steadfast in your love to Christ.

Let the love of Christ dwell in your hearts. *Ephesians 3:17.*

Sympathize with those in sorrow and never despise people. Sacrifice all to follow Christ. Be brave and honest.

Confess Christ before all men. Remember Christ loved you and gave Himself for you. Be crucified to Him and live in Him. Jesus is the Saviour of all. Have faith in God.

Learn to be loving to all and not to fear whom you are inclined to love naturally.

Be broadminded. You are a new creation in Christ. Live to please Him.

Gentleness is very forceful.

Speak sweetly! Do Christ-like deeds and think lovingly. Have faith in God. All are one in the Lord and Master.

Explain how gentleness can be forceful.

16th Nov '24 Sunday

*W*ith my whole heart have I sought Thee. O let me not wander from Thy commandments. *Psalm 119:10.*

Continue steadfast in the Word of God. Walk in His ways.

Be not worried if right fail and wrong prevail—as that's for the time only.

Right must prevail at the end. Be good. Let the vast forever be one grand sweet song to you. Trust and be not wavering in faith. Jesus appreciated your love and motives. Be a child of God. Call upon Him, and He will aid you. Christ is King and Inspiration.

You are fellow citizens with the saints. Walk as becomes those possessing such high honour. Hear the voice of Jesus and go out to do His will as it is revealed to you. Be adventurous. Let the Lord work in your hearts. Be not hindered by anything in your upward way. Be a victor.

Life is not fair. Wicked prosper. The fact that it is only for a short time, does it bring comfort to you?

———◈◈———

17ᵗʰ Nov '24 Monday

*L*et truth, and not opinion, be of supreme concernment. The Lord has great and glorious things in store for you. The Love of Christ passes all knowledge. Desire to do that which is perfectly good. Engage yourself in good. Live in the world, yet be not of it. Have no superstitions. Serve the Lord with Joy. Sow liberally and you will reap plentifully. Sow to the spirit. Be not weary in well-doing. Do good to all as you have opportunity.

Overcome evil by good. *Romans 12:21.*

Shine like the sun and be bright and cheery. Do good but not to be seen. Come unto Jesus who is ready to help you in your troubles. Take His yoke upon you. Forget not all you have received at His hands.

Let His likeness be formed in you.

What quality of God would you like to have first?

———◈◈◈———

18ᵗʰ Nov '24 Tuesday

Parents' Wedding Anniversary Day

*T*he Lord is good. His mercy is everlasting and His truth endureth to all generations. *Psalm 100:5.*

The Lord is mindful of such as put their trust in Him. He keeps them from falling and Jesus intercedes on their behalf.

Try to be very good. People appreciate thoughtfulness and kindness.

Religion and rites are for you and not you for them. Learn of Jesus. Do well. You are free in Christ. Sin has no more dominion over you.

The things God has in store for such as love Him are wondrous and good. You shall see Him as He is which will mean pleasure unbounded.

Have a high aim in life.

Do good while you can. Act manfully. Let the Spirit of God work in you. Jesus is able to work wonders in you. Allow Him to do it. Your faith must show itself in love to all.

What are some high aims and low aims of your life?

19th Nov '24 Wednesday

*H*ave your conversation honest.

You are to be complete in goodness as your Heavenly Father is complete. *Matthew 5:48.*

Do good naturally. Usefulness is cheering. The Lord expects great things of you, for He has spent much on you. Do your best to please Him.

Share your joys with others. You shall have to give account for every idle word you speak. Be careful.

Love your neighbour as yourself. Be steadfast in serving the Lord.

The Lord will dwell with you if you are contrite in heart and humble in spirit. Make clean His abode and repent and return.

Do good hoping for no return. Be substantial in your goodness. Do the will of Jesus your Maker. That is pleasing to Him.

Be not carried away by outward appearances.

Trust in God.

What outward appearance distracts you from truth?

20th Nov '24 Thursday

*P*ass we, then, in love and praise,
Trusting Him thro' all our days,
Free from doubt and faithless sorrow
God provideth for the morrow.

Cleverness is not of such great consequence as goodness. Be thoughtful about the good of others.

The Lord is your strength and light. Fear none. Trust in Him. Let the word of God dwell in you richly.

Walk in the Spirit. Be not vainglorious. Provoke and envy not.

The Lord is merciful and kind to you. *Psalm 103:8.*

Jesus is your mediator. He has washed your sins away.

Be zealous for God. Be good. Work for the welfare of others. Be desirous to help and aid others.

Man is a wonderful creature. Let your eyes be open to see the Love of God in all He does for you.

Be gentle in your rebuking. Bear one another's burdens. Be slow to think evil.

Forgive as you hope to be forgiven.

Does forgiveness involve forgetting also?

21ˢᵗ Nov '24 Friday

I will remember my covenant with thee in the days of thy youth and I will establish unto thee an everlasting covenant. *Ezekiel 16:60.*

The Lord will forgive the past thro' the atonement of His Son, if you are anxious to turn a new leaf. Throw yourself at the feet of God. Choose the good and grow in Christ. Make the most of your opportunities. Be not carried away by the deceitfulness of the world. Look up to God. Mind your business and be not distracted. Be sincere in your devotions.

The Son of God, God is love. Let God do the best for you. **Choose the route to maximum good.** Good thoughts ennoble the mind. Let the Love of God dwell in you. The Day of judgement must come. Watch and wait.

Be not weary in well doing. *II Thessalonians 3:13.*

You shall but reap what you sow.

What route have you chosen? Is it bringing maximum good to you, your family, and family of God?

————◈◈◈————

22nd Nov '24 Saturday

*T*he Spirit . . . helpeth our infirmities.
The Spirit maketh intercession for us.

Worship God with humility of mind and sincerity of spirit. Walk in the Spirit. The Lord will bless all. Make use of your goodness. Spend thought for the benefit of others. Be not selfish. The blessing of the Lord it maketh rich. Glory in the Cross of Christ.

Be crucified unto the World. Let it have no more power over you. Faith in Christ will never be in vain.

Godly sorrow works repentance. *II Corinthians 7:10.*

The Lord has punished you less than you deserve. The Lord will restore your soul. The Lord is great and good. Increase in love and thoughtfulness. Be slow to misjudge people. Serve the Lord. Bear one another's burdens. Let the Love of Christ dwell in you richly.

What words, thoughts, and actions will you crucify?

23rd Nov '24 Sunday

*G*od is our refuge and strength, a very present help in trouble. *Psalm 46:1.*

Be not afraid, but be of good cheer. Anxiety will not help. The Lord is your dwelling place. Pray for new life in the Church. Let a spirit of unity dwell in your heart. Do everything in its time and place. Let your religion help you in your daily duties. Put first things first. Serve the Lord with sincerity. Let the Spirit work in your heart. Yield to God.

Word first—duty second and pleasure next.

Jesus is Lord and God of all. Let Him have the rule of your life and soul. Let the Spirit of God dwell in your heart. Be of use to all. Let your religion be your help and daily comfort. Prepare yourself to meet the Lord. Let the Love of Christ dwell in you richly.

What is your order of being in God's word, duty and pleasure?

24th Nov '24 Monday

*B*lessed are they that hear the word of God, and keep it. *Luke 11:28.*

Let the love of God dwell in your heart and show it by service to mankind. Be sanctified in Spirit. Be free to do what you ought, when you ought. Do not be willful and self-assertive. Have some real Christian experience to share with others. Let not unbelief have room in your heart. Confer not with flesh and blood when the welfare of the soul is concerned. Take it to the Lord in prayer.

Be right toward God and man. Love all and seek the Lord of your soul. Be not weary in well-doing. The Lord pities you in your weakness and is waiting to help you.

Become not the slave of passion. Freedom comes thro' discipline.

Serve the Master. Be not hasty to promise. Stand firm unto the end.

Slave of passion is another name for addiction.
Do you have any?

———◈◉◈———

25th Nov '24 Tuesday

O Lord our God, other lords beside Thee have had dominion over us, but by Thee will we make mention of Thy name. *Isaiah 26:13.*

Follow the Master—abhor evil. Ask for the Holy Spirit. Make the most of the present for you have to render an account thereof to God.

Give with the loving spirit of Christ. Yield yourself to God. Make one person happy every day.

Give liberally, and the Lord will bless your little marvelously.

Be honest and true to your convictions. Let the love of Jesus constrain you. Pray for freedom from sin.

Improve your present and do your very best day by day. Be not slack in discharging your duties.

The Lord is not willing that any should perish. Repent and turn unto God. Try to make others happy. Be loving.

It is more blessed to give than to receive. *Acts 20:35.*

Spend much time with Jesus. Trust in His love. Be more believing. Doubt not the Saviour's love and power.

What have you given to God liberally?

————◈◈◈————

26th Nov '24 Wednesday

*C*ircumstances and internal desires often so disable one, that plans are frustrated and resolutions broken. Strive to be master of your circumstances.

The Lord delights in you. Fear not. He orders all things for you. You are His.

Preserve your self-respect and never do mean things.

Live at peace with all the world. Be content with your lot. Be more particular in matters of the Spirit than of form. All are one in Christ. By faith are you saved.

Take Christ's yoke upon you and learn meekness of Him. *Matthew 11:29.*

Rescue the perishing. Come unto Jesus. Be humble. Love all sincerely. Hate that which is evil.

Be content with your lot. Hope for the best.

Be a peacemaker. Draw friends closer in the bonds of love.

Watch your heart-life. Forget not your sonship in the Kingdom of God.

What is the best way to preserve "self-respect"?

27th Nov '24 Thursday

*P*rejudice should have very little part to play in the formation of your opinions, for it hampers right judgment.

You are partakers of Christ's glory. Let God's light shine in your heart. Praise and laud His Holy Name. Lose not penitence amid the distractions of life. Return unto the Saviour. Ask the Lord to help you in your difficulties and persist in your appeal. Have faith in Him and He cannot turn you aside. Whatever may happen, stand firm unto the end.

Be cheerful and happy, radiating joy whatever you do.

Use not your freedom to cause any one to stumble. *I Corinthians 10:32.*

Your conduct affects others. Consent not to evil impulses. Accept Jesus as Lord of all. Never be selfish. Repent of evil. Jesus is ready to save and to heal. He frees the bound and strengthens the helpless. Call on Him.

Do you know someone who radiates joy? Imitate that person.

28ᵗʰ Nov '24 Friday

*T*he feeling of helplessness should make you cast yourself on the Almighty and trust in Him as the fountainhead of all wisdom

Be a live Christian. Grow in virtue. Have faith in God. Show your faith in your deeds. Long after the righteousness of God.

Avoid doing the easiest thing, but do that which is right.

Cast your burden upon the Lord for He will sustain you. The Lord will uphold you in your infirmities. Hesitate not to call upon Him.

Let not your heart be troubled. *John 14:1.*

Death is no calamity. To be present with the Lord is great and glorious. Jesus has gone before. Carelessness and laziness sometimes cost very high. Watch yourself and be on your guard against them. Yield not to the promptings of the flesh. Be a conqueror.

Name a good deed that is not easy to do.

29th Nov '24 Saturday

A day when you do not engage in any actively good enterprise is, indeed a day to be regretted. Opportunities lie everywhere for one with an eye to seize them.

Be not slack. Rise and be doing.

The Lord is ever nigh. He will not forsake you.

He is the Bread of Life. *John 6:48.*

Look up unto Him and be satisfied with His likeness. Be thankful to God for all blessings He had given you. How many are His mercies.

Deny yourself and follow the Master. Take up your Cross. Crucify the flesh and live in the Spirit. Provoke or envy not.

God is ever with you. You are justified by faith and works.

Know the will of God and seek to do it.

Praise the Lord for all the beautiful things you enjoy at His hands. He is so liberal.

Come apart and rest awhile. Let God speak to you in the silence of the night.

Try meditating on God for five minutes.

———◈◉◈———

30th Nov '24 Sunday

*L*ift up your heart with praise and thanksgiving to God for His wondrous guidance and loving kindness.

Make your life a living sacrifice and a true offering to Him.

Let the peace of God dwell in your heart. *Colossians 3:15.*

Let not your heart be troubled. *John 14:1.*

Rejoice always and specially if you have the chance of suffering for Christ. Rejoice, even if you lose all worldly possessions for you have Christ. Sow good things.

Do all things well. Be honest and prudent. Ask freely and in love.

Be not faithless. Prayer can work marvels.

Spend more time in secret.

Do to others as you would they should do unto you.

*Write some of the ways you prevent your heart
from being troubled.*

Jehovah- Nissi

The LORD our Banner

December

December 1, 1924, Monday

(This page is torn and replaced with The First Day of January 1925)

. . .*f*aithful heart
. . . Likeness to thee,
That each departing day
Henceforth may see
Some work of love begun
Some deed of kindness done.

Look not back but for sound wisdom and experience and not for regret and despair. Press onward to the Goal, looking unto Jesus. Dedicate this year to God. Sanctify your lot by doing it with a noble mind as a service unto the Lord.

The Lord God Almighty reigneth. Rejoice in His loving care of you. Jesus is the fulfillment of the Law and the Prophets.

Resolve to let Jesus take possession of your heart throne for He is worthy of it and is "the Lord of All Good Life."

Let the Lord your God go before you this year, leading you in the right.

He does order all things for you. Let nothing separate you from the Love of Christ. Show your religion by your actions. Give room for the Spirit to work in your hearts.

Read these promises for God's leading.
Psalm 32:8.
Proverbs 3:6.
Isaiah 30:21.

————◈◈◈————

2nd Dec '24 Tuesday

*U*nto whom much is given, of them much is expected. *Luke 12:48.*
Their responsibilities are greater.

Be kind and true. Mortify self and serve others. The Holy Ghost is pleading for you. Displease Him not. Cultivate a quiet submissive spirit. You are entirely in God's hands. Fall in line with His great purposes. Jesus has come to save the lost. Come therefore unto Him. He does not wish any should perish. Be a new creature in Christ. The Blood of Jesus makes you whole. Have your heart sprinkled from an evil conscience.

Submit yourself unto God. He will not cause you needless pain.

Let Him chart out your path for you, for you know not what is best.

The Lord is in the midst of you.

Are you ready to follow the path God charts for you?

3rd Dec '24 Wednesday

*C*ommit thy way unto the Lord, trust also in Him; and He shall bring it to pass. *Psalm 37:5.*

The Lord will hear you before you call on Him. Love Him and make known all your troubles unto Him. Strive after Christ's likeness. Obey the voice of the Lord and serve Him with a single heart. The Lord desires mercy from you, not sacrifice. Forgive from your heart and freely, for have you not been freely forgiven?

Your body is the temple of the Holy Ghost. *I Corinthians 6:19.* Defile it not by impure thoughts. The Lord abhors evil. Take counsel of the Almighty. Live and die to God's glory.

Bend your will to God.

Be holy in thought, word, and deed. Love the Lord and delight in doing His will. Jesus gave His life for you.

Bending your will to God is not an easy task.
Are you ready to do that?

———◆◈◆———

4th Dec '24 Thursday

*D*o your best and never leave any thing to chance. Work ere it be late and ere the work done will be of little avail.

All things whatsoever you ask in prayer believing, you shall receive. Trust in the Lord with all your heart. Depart from evil. Let God's will be done in your life. Be slow to anger. Control yourself and delight in service. Bring young souls unto God.

With God all things are possible. *Matthew 19:26.*

Be not anxious about anything but make known all your requests unto God in prayer. *Philippians 4:6.*

Gain the mastery over yourself. Let the Spirit rule your heart. Be not anxious to do great deeds. Be great in your thoughts and actions. Follow the Master.

What is the difference between Spirit-led and self-led?

5th Dec '24 Friday

*S*et a guard therefore on your actions, words, and looks, for out of these do misunderstandings arise.

Be not slack. Consider the way the Lord has led you. Rejoice that you have been afflicted. Keep the command of the Lord and walk in His Testimonies. **Strive to consecrate your powers to God.** Be resolute in refusing evil. Look up to God for all. With God all things are possible. Sacrifice yourself for the Kingdom's sake. You know God by fellowship.

When you are weak, then are you strong. Man is not saved by His own might. Trust in God. Be unselfish, helpful, and true. Serve the Master. Never waste your talents.

Work for the night is coming. *John 9:4.*

The Lord will amply reward your labour. Work to do that which is right.

Look up the word "consecration."

———◆◈◆———

6th Dec '24 Saturday

*B*e ye strong, therefore, and let not your hands be weak, for your work shall be rewarded. *II Chronicles 15:7.*

Do not err. The Lord is with you. He will give you wisdom. Jesus will light your onward path.

Be strong in the Lord. Pray for wisdom. If you would be great, serve the Master. Minister unto all.

Be not self-assertive and anxious for moments. In joint worship and fellowship is true Christianity.

Work strenuously if you want to secure a good character. Keep your body under.

Spread happiness wherever you be. Seek the Lord both early and late.

The Spirit and the desires of the flesh are contradictory. Call upon the Lord for grace. Jesus will aid you. Confess your weakness and lean on God. Use your opportunities well.

Ask for the opening of your eyes, for they are dim and the scales are on your eyes.

Who had scales that fell off from the eyes when Prophet Ananias prayed for him? Read Acts Chapter 9.

———⚬⚬⚬———

7ᵗʰ Dec '24 Sunday

*M*en need fellowship, not only for the enrichment of their faith, but for its stability.

Have sympathy with all that is good, and even the bad despise not, but strive to rectify. Jesus is your righteousness. He humbled Himself that you may be exalted. Be genuinely human and obedient unto God. Serve much. Join in fellowship that you may be made steadfast in faith. Object not if the Lord requires your services. Forget not His great love for you.

The Lord is gentle and longsuffering, slow to anger and plenteous in mercy. *Numbers 14:8.*

He will care for the brokenhearted and the forsaken.

Live out Christ's life of sacrifice.

He died on the Cross, that you might live. Let the Spirit of God dwell in you richly.

Father Damien, Amy Carmichael, and Rev. Zigenbalg—Look these persons up on the Internet and read about their lives of sacrifice.

———— ·◈◈· ————

8th Dec '24 Monday

Yea, all of you be subject one to another, and be clothed with humility; for God resisteth the proud, and giveth grace to the humble. *I Peter 5:5.*

Owe none anything but to love. Serve one another. Be kind and bear their burdens. Never neglect your duties for you will rue it. Cultivate humility. Seek to be useful. Believe that there is more good in others as well and never be self-righteous. Let not the sacred be desecrated. Praise the Lord at all times. Slide not into evil. Jesus can open your dim eyes.

It is sweet to think of duty accomplished and of the satisfaction there, there is no end. Hope in the Lord, for you will see Him personally.

Have presence of mind and consciousness of purpose.

Man is frail. God resisteth the proud. Make the best use of your abilities. Have faith in God.

Do you have the consciousness of purpose?

9ᵗʰ Dec '24 Tuesday

*(**Anand's Birthday.** Anand is his younger brother G. Anandrao Kantayya.)*

*I*t is God which worketh in you both to will and to do of His good pleasure. *Philippians 2:13.*

The Lord loves such as keep His commands and do His will. Wait therefore on Him and walk humbly. Yield yourself to God that He may work in you. Remember how sinful you are inwardly and never get head-turned at praise. Go labour in the Master's vineyard. He calls you, and you should rejoice in service.

If you would show others what is right, do it yourself. Jesus has gone ahead to prepare a place for you, that where He is, you may also be. With Him, is joy forever. Follow the Lord. Oh humble your evil spirit, crush it, that God may work afresh in you. Hasten slowly. Follow your God and Master. He has come that you might live.

Oh, receive Him into your heart and let Him reign without a rival there.

You are all one in Christ. Be more charitable and broad-minded in your outlook.

Have you received Jesus into your heart?
Make sure he is the only one.

————— ⟨⊕⟩ —————

10th Dec '24 Wednesday

*G*ive us holy love and patience: grant us deep humility,
That of self we may be emptied, and our hearts be full of Thee.

Do everything for the satisfaction of having acted well. Neglect no detail. The Lord will preserve you from all evil. None can harm you, for your life is hid in Christ. Be not forward. God sets Himself against the haughty. Man cannot be happy without religion. To the call of Jesus, give a hearty acceptance and yield yourself to be transformed.

Stand fast in the liberty wherewith Christ has made you free.

By love serve one another. Be a servant of righteousness. Jesus has freed you from the slavery of sin. Rejoice and be exceedingly glad. Hearken unto His voice and do His will.

Liberty and freedom are available to all in Christ. Why don't more people want the liberty in Christ?

11th Dec '24 Thursday

*L*et not your good be evil spoken of. Abstain from all appearance of evil. *Romans 14:16.*

Provide for honest things in the sight of the Lord and of men. Be not a cause of stumbling to any. Put what good you know into practice. Be the dawning, glad or gloomy, go to Jesus and tell Him all. Render to everyone their due. Be of a receptive and appreciative mind. You are a child of God. Rejoice in your great privilege.

The Lord is your Shepherd, and you can nothing want. Lean on His love and fear not to trust Him. Awake. Watch and be sober.

Shine for the glory of the Lord. The Lord is around you.

Let your lights be burning, for behold your Lord comes.

Shining for the glory of the Lord is a responsibility as well as privilege. Do you agree?

———◆◈◆———

12th Dec '24 Friday

*W*ait on the Lord: be of good courage, and He shall strengthen thine heart. *Psalm 27:14.*

The Lord upholds you. Go out and help the weak. God will wipe away all your tears. Rejoice for He is yours. He is in your midst. Your mission is unique. Rise up to Christ's expectations of you. Don't hug your sins. Hold them a small space from you till you can see and loathe them. Love the Lord with all your heart and soul and love your neighbour as yourself.

Form a strong and great character while you are young.

Watch and pray that you enter not into temptation. Be strong and fervent in spirit. Be not slothful. Will to do God's will. You have often dishonoured God. Strive to curb your sins by looking up to Jesus and with the help of the Spirit. Humble yourself that you may be exalted in due time.

What is great about forming good habits while young?

13th Dec '24 Saturday

*F*ight the good fight of faith—in nothing terrified of your adversaries.
Be strong in the grace that is in Christ Jesus. Walk in Him. Be honest and true.

Sow love and peace and reap a happy harvest. Acquire good habits. God abhors hypocrisy. Be sincere in all you do. Have respect for your word. Be kind and thoughtful.

Truth is its own evidence, as the lightning flash is, as the blessed sunshine is.

You are not sufficient of yourself.

Trust in the Lord and lean not on your own understanding. *Proverbs 3:5.*

Keep cheerful. Form good opinions and fine habits. Never be conceited. Humble yourself more.

Do you seek truth, speak truth, and live truth?

———❖❖———

14ᵗʰ Dec '24 Sunday

Who is like unto Thee O Lord, glorious in holiness, fearful in praises doing wonders? *Exodus 15:11.*

Praise and glorify His holy Name, for His mercy toward you is great. Be discreet and never hasty. Beware of bad habits. Let not sin have dominion over you. The Lord hates a show. Love Him and seek to do His will. Be thorough in all you do.

By nature, you are evil. Be born again in Jesus and be born of the Spirit. Keep a guard over your thoughts and words. Cultivate happy habits. Let not sin have dominion over you. Let your life bear witness to your word. Behold the Lord comes. Give Him room in your heart.

Spend more time in secret with Jesus alone.

How much time do you spend with Jesus alone every day?

15th Dec '24 Monday

*I*n all the little things of Life,
Thyself, Lord, may I see;
In little and in great alike
Reveal Thy love to me.

Be faithful in small, obscure, un-praised things. Keep a double watch upon yourself. Bear on another's burdens and so fulfill the Law of Christ. Christ too was a minister.

Love all as brethren. The end of all things is at hand.

Prepare yourself to meet the Judge and Bridegroom and help others as well.

Fight the good fight. Look for the good only in others. There is more than you can easily notice. Yield yourself to God. Be holy.

Abound in the work of the Lord for your labour is not in vain. *I Corinthians 15:58.*

Never despise the day of small things. Lean hard on God. Beware, for you are in the last days. The Day of the Lord is at hand. Be prepared to meet Him in the clouds.

Is God your judge and bridegroom? How have you prepared?

———— ·❀· ————

16th Dec '24 Tuesday

Selfishness will never help one to reach the summit of glory. It is the selfless that are glorious.

Be led by Christ. He is your Saviour and Brother. Do little things with earnestness, for therein is one's ability tested. Never be neglectful. Love one another even as Christ also loved you. Deny yourself in the service of others. Behold the Lord comes. Prepare to give Him a hearty Reception. Yield yourself that the Spirit may work in you.

Be rooted and grounded in love.

Be a friend to all. Shine for Jesus. Care not for demonstrations. The coming of the Son of Man will be unexpected and sudden. Let your soul be prepared to meet Him aright.

Think of many ways you can be rooted in love,
beginning with thought, word and deed.

17th Dec '24 Wednesday

*B*etter is a little with righteousness than great revenues without right. *Proverbs 16:8.*

Be patient at all times. Pray always with all prayer and supplication. Ask according to God's will. Do all things with your whole mind.

Scatter smiles wherever you go.

Watch and be ready. Do faithfully that which is assigned you and be not careless. Be ready for Christ will come soon.

Do every little thing with a regal spirit and you will find enjoyment therein. Be of use to all around you. Set an example to all around you, more by your deed than by your word. Have no fellowship with the works of darkness.

Have faith in God and keep your torch burning, for the Son of Man will come soon. Watch and pray and prepare yourself against that great day.

At the end of the day, count the many smiles you scattered.

———⋅◈⋅———

18th Dec '24 Thursday

*W*e may boldly say, "The Lord is my Helper, and I will not fear what man shall do unto me. *Psalm 118:6.*

A persevering, sustained effort will keep you going onward in your Daily life. Be anxious about nothing. Let the Peace of God keep your heart. Draw nigh to Him with a sincere heart. Begin each day rightly. All sins are bad. Be a victor over private temptations. Be not a wicked, unprofitable and slothful servant. Work for the night is coming. Use your talents well.

Exert yourself so that you may keep up your onward growth. You can never be justified by works for your very thoughts are sinful. Look to Jesus. Take care of little things. Make a great deal of each day.

Omit not to do the little acts of kindness, for in them is life eternal.

Recall a little act of kindness someone did
and send them a thank-you card.

———————⟨⊰⊱⟩———————

19th Dec '24 Friday

*W*ho is among you that feareth the Lord, that obeyeth the voice of His servant, that walketh in darkness, and hath no light? Let him trust in the name of the Lord, and stay upon His God. *Isaiah 50:10.*

Keep a strict watch over yourself in all matters and specially in those which seem insignificant. Keep your lights burning. Fear not, for no man can prevail against you if you trust the Lord. Strive and be earnest in your daily duties and you shall obtain victory. The Lord suffered that you might be saved. Seek His pleasure ever.

Stand firmly on the Rock of Life. Ever follow that which is good. Return unto the Shepherd and Bishop of souls. Fear not, for Jesus has compassion on the erring ones. Watch and pray that you enter not into temptation. **Understand the value of things.**

Fear the Lord. You often betray the Master by your low and evil conduct. Seek His honour and glory ever.

Do you value relationships more than possessions?

20th Dec '24 Saturday

*A*lways there is a black spot in our sunshine, it is the shadow of ourselves.—Carlyle

God had called you to holiness. Abandon therefore the works of darkness. Seek to do His Holy will. Let not self mar your plans. Take care of small sins. Take up your Cross and follow the Master. Remember the sacrificial love of Christ. Be not overconfident in yourself. Be humble. Develop personality. Trust not yourself but God which can raise the dead. He will open heavens and bless you abundantly.

God's thoughts are above yours. *Isaiah 55:9.*

Have faith in God. **Be scrupulously honest with yourself.** When you feel your weakness, let Christ come into you and work. Watch and pray that you enter not into temptation. Submit to the will of God. Rise and go forward.

Don't you agree that it is easier to live with yourself
if you are honest with yourself?

———◦❈◦———

21ˢᵗ Dec '24 Sunday

A forward look is always necessary but a retrospective inward look is not without its advantages.

Do things in the best light that has been shown to you and God will give you greater light and wisdom.

The days of joy God will give you. You must thro' tribulation enter into joy. Work with God and nothing is lost. Toil patiently and God will bless your labours. The Lord has a purpose in all things. Trust in His great loving thoughts. Work united against evil.

Make mighty endeavours toward a joyful Christmas. Give surprises and try to increase happiness everywhere. Enter in at the straight and narrow gate. Sing and rejoice for the Lord is coming to deliver the oppressed.

Finish the Bible verse "Thy word is a lamp . . ."
Psalm 119:105

22nd Dec '24 Monday

*W*e know not what the path maybe
As yet by us untrod
But we can trust our all to Thee,
Our Father and our God.—W. Treers.

The Lord is your rock and fortress. *Psalm 18:2.*

Jesus will lead you on. Oh let Him guide you. Look up. Believe on the Lord. Let your faith show itself in loving works for Jesus came that you might live His life.

Unite in Worship. Be prepared to put up with insults for you deserve them. Jesus the Holy One was so patient, though He did not deserve any.

Behold the Lord cometh! Rejoice and prepare yourself to meet Him.

Be enthusiastic in the cause of Truth. Lean hard on Christ.

Let the Cross shield you from harm.

Look heavenward. Recollect and repent ere the Day of Redemption be past.

Name some other weapons in the armor of God.
Ephesians 6:10-18.

23ʳᵈ Dec '24 Tuesday

*N*o longer forward, nor behind
I look in hope or fear;
But, grateful, Make the good and find,
The best of now and here.

Trust in the Lord forever. Jesus is your peace. The Lord is merciful and He is your everlasting strength. God means you to be happy. Do your duty wholeheartedly.

The wages of sin is death. *Romans 6:23.*

Be not led away by pomp and glory for they are fleeting and deceptive.

Be grateful for all God has given you and seek to do your best.

Jesus is the Resurrection and the Life. Trust in Him for He alone is the Way. Your life is hid in Him. Let nothing hinder your doing your duties well. Let God lead you in the right path. Be submissive and never hasty to take offence.

Name things God has given you alphabetically. A—abundant life. B—beautiful family, etc.

———⸱❈⸱———

24th Dec '24 Wednesday

*W*e should live soberly, righteously, and godly, in this present world, looking for that blessed Hope and the glorious appearing of the Great God and our Saviour Jesus Christ. *Titus 2:12, 13.*

Be chary in the usage of your time. Waste none for there is plenty to be done. Abhor evil and love God.

Let the Spirit work in you that the fruit of the Spirit maybe seen in you. Go forward, each day doing your daily duty and do it cheerfully. Do all with a will.

The Lord bled and suffered for you. Oh, wound not His loving heart.

How does our disobedience wound Christ's heart?

25 Dec Christmas '24 Thursday

*G*od's gift to us a surprise was and we today give presents to others wrapped in an unnecessary bundle of paper just to give them a surprise. Let us fall down and worship Jesus, the Lord of all good life, as our own Saviour and Advocate.

Realize your opportunities, be prepared to take risks to obtain great things.

Be friendly and never conceited and over-reserved.

Write down the opportunities that lay ahead of you in the New Year and pray to God to accomplish great things.

1
2
3
4
5
6
7
8
9
10

26th Dec '24 Friday

*P*ut duty always before pleasure. Be honest. Have the courage of your convictions. Serve the Lord with humility. Do your duties faithfully. Be of a forgiving spirit. By faith you stand. Sow not to the flesh. Your labour will be rewarded.

Come to know Jesus as the Lord of all Good Life. Jesus had a broad heart which embraced the whole world in its love. Know yourself. Seek the Lord while He yet may be found.

Keep a watch over your silly lips.

Though lips get blamed for thoughtless words, it is the thoughts in our minds that form the words. So watch your thoughts too.

27ᵗʰ Dec '24 Saturday

*S*o teach us to number our days that we may apply our hearts unto wisdom. *Psalm 90:12.*

The Lord is your Refuge and strength at all times. Lean hard on Him. He will look after you and bless your work. Nothing is too hard for Him.

Present sufferings are not to be counted. The joys in store are great. Steadily apply yourself to your duty and you will rejoice in the end.

Cleave to God with a set purpose.

Peace I leave with you, my peace I give unto you; not as the world giveth, give I unto you. Let not your heart be troubled, neither let it be afraid. *John 14:27.*

Cleaving to God involves leaving something else.
What are they?

28th Dec '24 Sunday

*S*in shall not have dominion over you, for ye are not under the law, but under grace. *Romans 6:14.*

Being then made face from sin, ye became the servants of righteousness.
Jesus is your Salvation. Let not sin have any room in you.

Keep each day as it passes pure and holy. Leave each day well.

There is life in duty alone. The Lord suffered that you may live.

An utter forgetfulness of self and preparedness for martyrdom and death are absolutely necessary for one who wishes to follow Christ.

Would you be willing to be martyred for Christ? Think about it.

———— ❈ ————

29ᵗʰ Dec '24 Monday

*Y*ou daily duties are part of your religious life, just as much as your devotions are.—H. W. Beecher.

Fall in with the forces at work and do every moment's duty. Work with a loving heart. The Lord wills your salvation.

To know God is life eternal.

The Lord is very mindful of those who are trusting in Him. Lean hard on His Love.

Draw nigh unto God and He will draw nigh to you. *James 4:8.*

Come with a true heart. Keep your body a fit temple for the Holy Ghost.

Accept the redemption of sins through the cross.

What is eternity like? Verse 3 of the Hymn, Amazing Grace says, "When we have been there ten thousand years, we have only just begun!"

———— ⬦❖⬦ ————

30th Dec '24 Tuesday

(This page is torn and replaced with 4th January '25 Sunday)

Set your affections on things above, not on things on the earth. *Colossians 3:2.*

Lay up for yourselves treasures in heaven. *Matthew 6:20*

This is not your rest. With Christ it is far better. Live and die unto the Lord. Let Christ abide in you. Look for that which is good and strong in others. Try to acquire it. Do not that which is forbidden. God knows that which is for your good. Obey His Word.

Fight the good fight of faith. Fear not death for it is the gateway to the visible presence of God. Dwell in love and unselfishness. Be victorious in the midst of temptations. Come before the Lord with a pure and sincere heart. Repent and return for the Day of the Lord is at Hand.

Noble Kantayya certainly did fight a good fight of faith. Praise God for his life and the true devotional model he left behind.

———⟨⊗⟩———

31st Dec '24 Wednesday

(This page is torn and replaced with a letter Appa wrote in 1963.)

G. N. Kantayya B.A., M.B;B.S (Madras) 24-3-1963.
PHYSICIAN & PRIEST. C.S.I.
REGISTERED MEDICAL PRACTITIONER

Return Journey from Madras
Foreword

Dear Children,

God creates our bodies. He puts souls into them & sends them into the world. What for? That we may do His will.

How are we to know what God's will for us is? The DUTY nearest to me & to you—is His will. When we do our duty to the best of our ability—we are doing His will.

As I write this, I am sitting in a Railway compartment and traveling in a train (Trivandrum Fast Passenger.) Now what is the *duty* of the Engine Driver, the Engine and the train? *To run on the Rails* provided and reach our destination or home town or terminal, is it not? The best Engine Driver, the most powerful Engine, the grandest train, cannot move forward without the RAILS! Our duties are like the RAILS. We fulfill God's purposes, we do God's will, we reach our heavenly home—as the train runs on the rails, only as we do our DUTY.

My parting advice to you all is—DO YOUR DUTY to the very best of your ability. Then surely God will bless you richly and you will have the joy and satisfaction that you have fulfilled God's will!

God will surely help you to do your DUTY as you plan your work & work your plan.

Your affectionate friend,
G. N. Kantayya

Amen

Kantayya Preventive Medicine & X-Ray Clinic

G.N. KANTAYYA B.A., M.B., B.S. (MADRAS)

PHYSICIAN & PRIEST C.S.I.
REGISTERED MEDICAL PRACTITIONER

Branch X-Ray Office:-
Tirunelveli Town
TELEPHONE No. 287
PALAYAMKOTTAI
24-3-1963.

Return Journey from Madras

Foreword

Dear Children,

God creates our bodies. He puts souls into them & sends them into the world. What for? That we may do His will.—

How are we to know what God's will is for us? The DUTY nearest to me & to you – is His will. When we do our DUTY to the best of our ability – we are doing His will. As I write this, I am sitting in a Railway compartment and travelling in a Train (Trivandrum Fast Passenger.) Now what is the duty of the Engine Driver, the Engine and the train? To run on the Rails, provided and reach our destination or home town or terminus, will it not? The best Engine driver, the most powerful Engine, the grandest train – cannot move forward without the RAILS! Our DUTIES are like the RAILS. We fulfil Gods purpose, we do Gods will, we reach our heavenly home as the train runs on the rails, only as we do our DUTY.—

My parting advice to you all is —

DO YOUR DUTY to the very best of your ability – Then surely God will bless you richly and you will have the joy and satisfaction that you have fulfilled Gods will!

Photos of Community Work

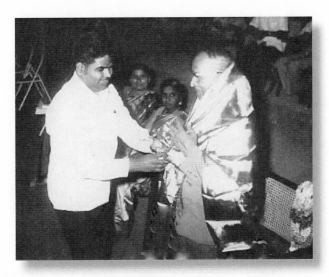

Red Cross of Palayamkottai honoring Noble with a
'Golden Shawl'

Noble as Santa Claus distributing clothes to the poor.
Kamali in half-saree upfront. 1953

Photos of People Helped by Noble.

Servant Sundaram who went to Courtallam to cook for the couple on their Honeymoon, later became a Christian

Young Nirmal with 12 year old attendant Muthiah, who was housed and educated by Noble

Thomas & Dharmaraj, orphaned nephews of Mary,
grew up in the Kantayya home

Noble helped Raja, on extreme left, obtain a job as a
Physics demonstrator in St. John's Collge, Palayamkottai

Noble with indomitable spirit, carrying on ministry using
cycle rickshaw despite leg fracture

Amazing Appa & Amma 1980

Reflections on Noble : Memories Shared by Family and Friends

Mary Suvarnakumari Victor,
Second child of Noble, Palayamkottai, India

I am really happy and privileged to write a few words about my dear father Rev. Dr. G. N. Kantayya.

When we all lived in our ancestral home *Shanti Alaya,* we used to have family meals together. *Appa* used to teach us to talk in English as well as Telugu, which was fun. During holidays, he would organize games like memory testing—keeping a number of articles on the round table and he would cover it up with a cloth after allowing us to see for a few seconds, which we all enjoyed. On Sundays, he would make us memorize the "Collect of the day" (prayer of the day) and repeat it before lunchtime! We would attend morning and evening services at the church where *Appa* was pastor and walk back home after Evensong.

When I was doing my Bachelor of Teaching at St. Christopher's Training College in Madras, Dr. Billy Graham conducted meetings there. My Dad also was there with me. At that time, I was convicted of my sins, and it was my father who encouraged me to stand when the altar call was given. I am really grateful to my father for that. My life changed completely. I shared my experience with my siblings who were at home. He led many people to Christ including Devairakkam, a boy whom he baptized. Devairakkam stayed strong in his faith until he passed away in 2011. *Appa* also helped a blind beggar's family of six by educating the boys and helping the girls with marriage expenses. *Appa* was a very loving, affectionate, and thoughtful father. I praise God for his exemplary life.

Pansy Kantayya,
Wife of eldest son Sam Nirmal, Rockford, Illinois, USA
A Daughter-in-law Remembers

A month or so after my oldest son Vivek was born in my hometown of Cuddalore, I heard a rooster crow very early one morning. It was *Mama* who was standing there in our front porch saying, *Kok Ra Ko Ko*. He had come by train from Palayamkottai to baptize his grandson Vivek that day! He was the one who had fooled us all with his famous impersonation of the rooster's crowing! After Vivek's name was entered in the Baptismal Register at St. John's Church, *Mama* was pleased to turn back several pages and find two of his older siblings' names in the same register—sister Nesamma's in 1897 and his brother Stephen's in 1899—both baptized at the same Church when his father was working for the Revenue Department in Cuddalore before he got God's call!

A few years later, when we were living in Palayamkottai, *Mama*'s example of a compassionate physician would make a lasting impression on young lad Vivek's mind and make him the person he is today. I am grateful to God and *Mama* for that.

David Jayasurya Kantayya,
Third child of Noble, 1939-1988

Jayasurya, as his name signifies, was truly a victorious shining beam of light in the Kantayya household. God endowed Jaya with many talents. He had great memory power, especially for numbers. He was very observant, (can mimic the actions and walks of many relatives) outgoing personality with deep sense of duty and exuberant hospitality which outshone his hearing impairment. *Appa* loved Jaya so much that he provided as many animal friends as he could like sheep, goat, cows, love birds, pigeons, rabbits, chicken, dogs, and cats at one time or other. Jaya had no problem taking care of them or communicating with them.

Jaya remained a bachelor. He loved his family and always wanted the best for all his loved ones. He rejoiced in their good fortune. He loved *Appa*, admired him, and enjoyed being his X-ray technician at the clinic till *Appa* died in 1981. Jaya mourned his loss deeply. Once while visiting *Appa*'s gravesite, he said wistfully, "If I shout *Appa* loudly enough, will he hear me?" Jaya passed away in his forty-ninth year. Even now people who knew him will say that his smile communicated far more than words can say. If Jaya was alive, he will be the first one to write all about his beloved *Appa*.

Dr. John M. Prabhakar (Prabhu)
Husband of daughter, Esther Kamali, Rochelle, Illinois, USA

Dr. Noble Kantayya, my father-in-law, was a pillar of the community of Palayamkottai, my hometown. He was a visionary and a man before his time. He had unique ideas and was a pioneer in many ways in the medical field as well as a pastor of the Church of South India. He boldly encouraged the use of *Carnatic* (South Indian) music in worship while most of the hymns that were sung in churches at that time were translations of English, German, and other Western languages. It is for this reason, the Hoy Trinity Cathedral choir sang the Tamil Christmas lyric, "Samadhanam Ohdhum Yeasue Christu" (Jesus Christ, Prince of Peace) when they came to his house on Carol rounds. People respected him for his efforts. Being an "outsider" in a very traditional Palayamkottai community, he was a breath of fresh air, free to mingle with the different castes and classes within the religious groups. He was outspoken, sincere, and never held a grudge.

He was well-known for his help to many people in need. Even now, people come up to my wife and mention how *Mama* gave good advice or helped them financially or treated them with kindness. He was well versed in Queen's English and often turned a quaint phrase like "Work is Worship." He authored many books including, *The path to Victory*, *For married people only*, etc., in Tamil and English. He lived his faith and showed the love of Jesus with his words and actions. Many people were introduced to the Kingdom of God by his ministry. This book of Noble Reflections is a living testimony even after his earthly journey is over. I am glad to be part of his family and be the beneficiary of the talents and values he has handed over to his daughter, Kamali.

Monica Pritha Srinivasan,
Fifth child of Noble, Stafford, England

"Believing that Jesus died—will save no-body—is simply a matter of history
Believing that Jesus died *for me*—will save anybody—this is an act of faith."

The above quote is taken from our Appa's personal Daily devotional Journal written for the 10 January way back in 1924 when he was still in his teens. It is very clear from that statement that he was already a committed Christian who had fully understood the deep meaning of the Incarnation of Christ, His suffering and saving act for all humanity. There he continues, "He loved me and gave himself for me." It is this personal relationship with the Lord that motivated him to live and work for God all through his life.

In his vocation as a general practitioner, he served the community with care and compassion. In 1953, when Bishop Jebaraj invited professionals to come into God's ministry, Appa readily took up the challenge and offered himself to God's service. He started his ministry with the English-speaking congregation at Christ Church. Soon he extended the church's outreach by additional services in our native language, Tamil. He introduced Tamil liturgy and a choir trained in Tamil *Carnatic* music. That congregation is thriving now. We set up annual Bible Exams in that church in 1997. It is called "Noble and Mary Kantayya Memorial Scripture Examinations." By God's grace, it is conducted with enthusiastic participation of the church members.

Dad had the vision to spread the Gospel by incorporating Indian culture to reach the local community. He even designed his own Cassock in a shade of cream, rather than pure white, with a "Nehru" collar, to suit local conditions. He got the design approved, and he used it in his ministry. He valued history and heritage and was instrumental in renovating Clarinda's tomb in the little church associated with Clarinda. He began early morning midweek Holy Communion services in that church. Dad's busy day would start with him riding to church on his bicycle, wearing his cassock through the crowded streets of South bazaar for his 8 o'clock communion service and then back to work at his busy clinic!

Brighten others' lives . . .

Make the best of life while you do live.

This is what Dad believed as a young man, and he inspired others to do the same. At Christ church, he gathered a group of enthusiastic young people every week and visited the local leper colony near Manakavalam Pillai Nagar and a nearby village Varsapathu for valuable gospel work. Sometime later, the Christian people of Varsapathu wanted to build their own church. They requested Dad to lay the foundation stone. Dad was unwell and frail at that time, but he had the great pleasure and honor of laying the foundation for the church for which he and the church group had sown the good seeds years earlier! It was all due to God's Spirit guiding him wonderfully all the way as he wrote in his journal "Let the Spirit of the Lord be upon you."

Rev. Dr. Stephen Lionel (former priest of Christ Church) who spoke at the Thanksgiving Service of the Birth centenary of Noble and Mary Kantayya (2005) said in his address that Rev. Kantayya served God with dedication and distinction. The following hymn was written by John Bunyan about Christian's pilgrim journey and I believe that our dear Appa showed the same commitment and dedication in serving the Lord throughout his life. He truly was a visionary and an inspiration to one and all.

He who would valiant be 'gainst all disaster,

Let him in constancy follow the Master.

There's no discouragement shall make him once relent

His first avowed intent to be a pilgrim.

Dr. Dharmu Paul Srinivasan,
Husband of daughter Monica Pritha, Stafford, England

My father-in-law Rev. Dr. G. N. Kantayya

Many years ago, I read an anecdote in the *Readers' Digest*. Immediately, I thought of my father-in-law Noble Kantayya. Now, when I sit to write a few lines about my father-in-law, the anecdote came to my mind immediately. This was about two young men who were identical twins. One was a priest and the other was a doctor. People often mistook one for the other. An old lady accosts one and asks, "Are you the one who preaches?" "No, ma'm," he says, "I am the one who practices."

My father-in-law was a brilliant doctor and winner of several gold medals. He was the first person in the district to introduce X-ray and laboratory investigations in medical practice which were high technologies of the day. As a priest, I have heard him preach inspirational sermons. He had mastery over English language, literature, and poetry. All these were attributes that passed away when he died.

What do I remember of him? I remember him as a practitioner—a practitioner of his faith. Faith lived by example does not die with the person. It becomes a heritage and lives on. Fair are the places marked out for me; I have a noble heritage. (Ps. 16:6, Bible in Basic English)

Elizabeth Lavanyakumari (*Pappa*) Edward,
Sixth child of Noble, Alandur, India

Appa was always a gentle, loving, and affectionate father. Since I was the last child in the family of six, he called me very affectionately, "chinthai chell paps" (which means something like little darling baby in Tamil). Even when I was all grown-up, he used to call me that.

Appa knew that I loved dolls, and he bought all the dolls I desired, even buying a walking doll from Singapore which was very rare in those days.

He always insisted on family prayer in the evenings, and everyone must pray when their turn came. On Sunday evenings, *Amma* used to play the piano, and he made us sing hymns around the piano.

He had compassion on the poor and forsaken and helped them to come up in life. During summer holidays, early in the morning, he used to take us all to the river to bathe, before the buffaloes came to the river for their bath! We had an enjoyable time playing in the water and drinking palm fruit juice afterwards.

During his last days, he was sure of his salvation and was ready to go to be with the Lord. He was a role model to many young people. He was a father of noble character just like his name. I miss him and love him dearly.

Rev. Dr. Vasanth Edward,[†]
Husband of daughter Lavanya (*Pappa*), Alandur, India.

I am happy to pen some thoughts on my father-in-law whom I called *Mama*. He was a noble and great man whom I respected and loved very much. Three advices he gave me made great impression in me while I was at the cross roads of my life. I would like to share them with you.

A word aptly spoken is like apples of gold in settings of silver. (Prov. 25:11)

1. I was in the group which had a misunderstanding with the local YMCA secretary while playing a game. I may have been nineteen or twenty years old. *Mama* heard about it and called me over and advised me in a very loving way. He said that we are from a good Christian family and we must set an example to others and that we must be friendly with everyone. I promised him I would do so. I apologized to the secretary. I never had a fight with the secretary again, who later became a very good friend.

2. I got the job in Air India airlines and was about to travel to Chennai. My father asked me to meet with *Mama* before I left my hometown of Palayamkottai. When I went there, he advised me again in a very loving way about three things I should be very careful of in life—love of money, women, and wine. Again I promised him and told him that now I am a child of God and I will follow his advice. He was very happy. He prayed and blessed me.

3. I married *Mama*'s youngest daughter and had our first son. God called me to full-time ministry. We decided to give up the Air India job and go to Andaman Islands near India as missionaries. Many family members opposed the idea. One day, I was sitting in the verandah thinking and praying. *Mama*

---

†   Rev. Dr. Vasanth Edward contributed this article but passed away on Feb. 21, 2012 before the book was published. He was another Noble servant of God who abided in the Vine.

came and put his hands on my shoulder and said, "We are all working for the world and serve only the body. But if you go into the mission field, you will be working for the Almighty God and take care of the spirit and soul of people, which is eternal. So go ahead and do what the Lord tells you to do."

Mama's words of advice are still ringing in my heart. He is great and noble man whom I respected and loved.

The Secret of a Legend
Dr. Shanth Victor,
Oldest grandson, Windsor, Canada

I consider it a great privilege and honor to highlight some of the exemplary characteristics of my illustrious grandfather, Dr. Noble Kantayya. As his oldest grandson, I was blessed to grow up in the same city where he lived. I was able to interact with him almost on a daily basis during most of my childhood.

Many were the accomplishments of Noble *Thatha* (grandfather in Tamil). He was awarded multiple gold medals for his proficiency in studies at the Madras Christian College. He was one of the top-ranking students at the Madras Medical College. He was a pioneer in starting the first X-ray clinic in the Tirunelveli district. He also was the first physician to start a Mobile X-ray clinic to cater to the needs of hard to reach and underprivileged people in the villages. He was the first-ordained Indian minister for the English congregation of the local Anglican church called "Christ church." He served honorarily without salary throughout his lifetime! I believe that the secret to all his successes is based on Mathew 6:33:

"But seek first the Kingdom of God and His righteousness, and all these things shall be added to you."

Kantayya *Thatha*, like Daniel of the Bible, made a determination to seek the Lord and lead a holy life even in his early years, and this devotional testifies to the fact. He had a very disciplined and consistent prayer life. He took great joy in calling himself a "Physician and Priest" and really practiced what he preached! He always had high ideals to serve the fellow human beings irrespective of caste, creed, or religion. He had a plaque in his Consulting room which read, "Work is Worship." He not only catered to the medical needs of his patients, but also offered spiritual help and advice to their various issues in life! He held responsible positions at various charitable organizations including the local Medical society and hosted many meetings.

Let us strive to carry on the legacy of this great legend by emulating his great principles and finish our earthly race well to the glory of God.

Dr. Stephen Vivek Kantayya,
Grandson, Rockford, Illinois, USA

I was deeply impacted and inspired by how *Thatha* served his patients during the week and served as a minister on the weekend! Whenever someone asked me what I was going to be from a very early age, I always said, "A doctor!" There was never a doubt because I saw how *Thatha* helped so many sick folk in his clinic. The amazing thing is that I became a doctor, and I too am very active as an Elder at our church and chair the missions committee and still take teams to Nigeria including our next trip to Egbe in September, 2012!. He truly did impact me in the few years I was privileged to live in the family home *Shanti Alaya*.

Nimalanand Victor,
Grandson, Chennai, India

I remember Kantayya *Thatha* very well in many ways since we lived in the same town. He was interested in us and in our studies and prayed for us. He always remembered our birthdays. Even when he got older and weak, he never failed to come over in a cycle rickshaw or another hired vehicle early in the morning on our birthdays. He will arrive at our house. He will climb the steps to our quarters and instead of ringing the doorbell, he will make the sound like a rooster—Cocka doodle doo! That was his trademark. We all knew who did that sound. So we will rush and open the door and greet our dear *Thatha*. He will wish us Happy Birthday and talk with us. After cake and coffee, he will pray, bless us, and take off. He was an early morning riser all his life. He spread joy wherever he went.

Dr. Larry Prabhakar,
Grandson, Rockford, Illinois, USA

In reading any literature, knowing the author lends some insight into experiences that influence the author and the voice in which he speaks. Although I do remember my grandfather Kantayya *Thatha*, these are the writings of a different man. The time in which my grandfather wrote these devotions predates both my mother's and my life. They are the devotions, reflections, and musings of a young man. He had yet to live through the trials, tribulations, joys, and sorrows that life brings to all of us. My memories of my grandfather are the final chapters of a great story. What intrigues me is to see how it all began. I know the ending, but now I want to read the prequel. The wisdom that came with age began here with the scholarship and enthusiasm of youth. I hope to see the world from the viewpoint of a college student, not a patriarch. I remember a man whose persona and actions were larger than life. But, I also saw personified the humanity and demons that each of us wrestle with in our daily lives. In many ways, he embodied the fallen man that, through faith, God uses for his glory. I hope to get to know him better through this book. I hope you will as well.

Dr. Ernest Prabhakar,
Grandson, Santa Clara, California, USA

My only direct memories of my "Kantayya *Thatha*" are of a quiet, noble gentleman in his large house when we visited over Christmas vacation every few years. Most of what I know about him comes from secondhand stories, which surely could be told better by others.

And yet . . .

As I was putting my "3-and-2/3"-year-old son Rohan to sleep one night, it occurred to me that the way I raise my children reveals much more about how I view God than any book I might write (or have written: i.e., *Growing Church Leaders* from Westbow Press, a nine-month course on practical holiness.) From that perspective, I do have a wealth of stories about my grandfather that paint a fascinating portrait, which deserves to be remembered.

The first set of stories, of course, are those told to me by my parents and relatives. His achievements as a medical doctor and minister of the gospel are no doubt recorded elsewhere. The teenager I was when he died found both his greatness and his flaws utterly unfathomable.

I now appreciate the second set of stories, those told by the lives of those he left behind. His children, grandchildren, and now great-grandchildren are all faithful, hard-working individuals who not only love God, but actually get along with each other! I took this for granted growing up, but have lived long enough to realize how rare and precious an achievement that is; I can only dream of leaving such a legacy to my progeny.

Only a handful of his descendents follow in the ancestral tradition of full-time ministry stretching back to Rev. Aaron at the dawn of the Protestant missionary movement in India. However, it seems most of the rest are actively involved in volunteer ministry of one kind or another, a tradition I pray will continue with the next generation. These testimonies paint a picture of a man who not only loved God, but must have loved his wife and children in a way that equipped and inspired them to follow in his footsteps.

The third set of stories are those told by the books he owned. As an inveterate bookworm lacking other amusements, I voraciously read many of these during my visits to his house. One volume in particular—a collection of short stories, poems, and folk songs that span the English canon—so captivated me that I asked for it as my "inheritance" when he passed away. Lovingly rebound, it now occupies an honored place on my bookshelf, and I look forward to the day I can read from it to my own children. It is filled with humor, wisdom, longing, and joy, and I like to think it paints a picture of a soul that treasured those traits as much as I do.

Which brings us to the final story, the one which you now hold in your hands. I never really knew my grandfather, despite the glimpses I just shared with you. Yet I know what it is like to wrestle with the deep things of God, as I did on a daily basis when I was a teen, and now do publicly (though much less consistently) on my blog *http://2transform.us/*. I look forward to spending 2012 walking in his footsteps, to see a picture of the man he was, a mirror into who I am today, and a window into the God who made both of us. My hope is that this will deepen my understanding of God, my heritage, and myself.

My prayer is that these pages will help you, too, find the strength you need for the challenges you face in the years ahead.

Vineet Kantayya,
Grandson, Fox River Grove, Illinois, USA.

My time with my grandfather was not very long, and I don't recall much about him, but through the words and many accounts of his life I have heard, it is an honor and blessing to have him in our lineage. One thing I do remember about him is his loving and fatherly smile that portrayed a feeling of comfort and grace. His love for the Lord has an impact on all his offsprings, and he has left a spiritual legacy that has impacted countless people through his life and the lives of his bloodline.

Reuben Srinivasan,
Grandson, Nottingham, England

My memories of Noble *Thatha* are:
- one who did so much for his family
- helped the less fortunate
- ministered on a physical and spiritual level
- his clinic was such an interesting place to be, so many jars with gruesome (to a six-year-old anyway) things inside and strange smells to explore!
- one who wanted to spoil the kids, for example, fixing a bicycle so that I could ride it outside even though it was raining!

Daya Durai,
Niece, Burgess Hill, England

I remember uncle Noble, my father's younger brother, as an affectionate, gentle, and fun loving person. He was sort of a quiet person compared to the other two brothers.

The five Kantayyas were a close-knit family, and even after the parents passed away, Nessamma in Narsapur, Andhra, Babu in Poona or Bombay, Sundi in Madras, Noble in Palaymakottai, and Anand in Vizag kept in close touch. They were also a thrifty family and strongly believed in reusing and recycling. These two traits came together in their correspondence. Since all were equally interested in each other's news, when one wrote a post card or inland letter from one to another, it would be perused, a PS added and then sent on to the third. In a corner in tiny letters would be A, N, S, B, N, the initials of each sibling. As the mail was read, a tick would appear by the initial so that when passed on to the next person, they would know who had already seen the note and to whom it should go. Each one would add a postscript with their latest news—round the edges, on the back, between paragraphs, between the lines of the address—writing either upside down or in another color to distinguish it from the original letter! The second person who received the mail would have to pass it on in an envelope, so they would often add a newspaper cutting or someone else's interesting letter to use up the maximum weight allowed for the minimum postage. They were the forerunners of recycling and chain e-mails without realizing it then. I well remember the ladies in the family reusing envelopes by opening them out and turning the flaps inside out and resticking up the sides for a clean frontage! What a wonderful time they lived in when they had the time to do this and to keep up with the family, as against our time when even with phones, mobiles, e-mail, skype, iPads, iPods, and goodness knows what else, we still say we are too busy to remember each others' birthdays.

I only visited Palayamkottai twice. I had a lot of fun with my Tamil-speaking cousins. I remember the excellent meals and snacks Aunty Mary lavished on us. I am sure I will enjoy this book which will acquaint me with my uncle's spiritual side as a young man.

Ratnakumar Kantayya,
Nephew, Chennai, India

I knew *Periappa* (means Father's older brother) very well. He was my Godfather. I have many fond memories of *Periappa*. My father and Noble *Periappa* were very close, being only two years apart and used to play together. That affection lasted a lifetime. He ran the first X-ray clinic in town.

In 1952, his sister Sundi Michaels' family and our family celebrated Christmas together in Palayamkottai. *Periappa* took us to towns with waterfalls like Papanasam and Courtallam. He bought wooden cheppu (toy wooden pots and pans) for my sister Sunita. I was almost bundled off to Palayamkottai to study there as my dad was working in Orissa State in the north.

Mary *Periamma* made many tasty snacks including *Laddu* in her house. I remember enjoying them so much when I visited them. When someone from Palayamkottai visited us, they brought some of those snacks. *Periappa*'s children earned a good name in society.

Dr. Sunitha Razu,
Niece, Singapore

I always remember *Periappa* in the pastor's cassock. I can never forget his gentleness and the kindness he showed to his younger brother's family. I remember his warm extension of his home to us as kids. He established a prayer room so that we, the next generation will grow up in God's image.

Satya Brink,
Niece, Chelsea, Quebec, Canada

My first memories of Noble uncle are of going over from my grandfather's house to Noble uncle's house to play. I may have been four years old or so. It was while my father was away at Harvard, USA. Noble uncle would always have a pleasant greeting though I was so little. Mary Aunty would have an enormous stock of homemade treats. Her "Neii urundaiis" (Indian snack, ghee balls) were legendary. The house was full of children too. So I enjoyed spending time there and I have many pleasant memories.

Much later, my husband Lars, who is of Swedish origin, and I visited Palayamkottai and stayed with Noble Uncle and Mary Aunty. My family wanted Lars to experience Palayamkottai, the town where my great-grandfathers lived. Noble Uncle was full of stories about the two sides of my family. He was so gentle and welcoming to us both and we remember that visit well.

Dr. Prabha Appasamy,
Grand niece, Chennai, India

I remember Noble *Thatha* in a cassock, always smiling, always cracking jokes or making funny statements to tease. During my childhood years in Palayamkottai, where I used to spend a month of my summer holidays with my maternal grandparents, I would spend most of the day with Mary *Achi*'s and Noble *Thatha*'s children—my young "aunts" and "uncles."

I remember he would tease me and ask whom I would like to marry? (This when I was around six or seven years of age!) I would get so mad at him that I'd say I'm going to kill the person I'm going to marry, which would amuse him no end, and he would laugh heartily at my fury.

Thatha always treated my parents as his own nephew and niece. (My father is Mary *Achi*'s sister's son). When my mother was a new bride (all of nineteen years) in Tuticorin, he would visit her every week as he had a medical clinic there. My mother used to say that he loved fresh fish from the sea (Tuticorin is on the coast) and would ask her to fry a whole *Vanjaram* fish every week for him to take back to Palayamkottai. She loved doing it, and he loved eating it, so everyone was happy!

Manohar Devadoss,
Niece Mahema's husband, Chennai, India

My wife Mahema and I respected and loved Noble Mama. I can think of one aspect in which Noble *Mama* played an important role in my life. It was the day of my wedding to his niece Mahema. He came from Palayamkottai to attend the wedding. The bridal chamber, a suite, had to be booked for our wedding night. Early in the morning, Noble *Mama* went with me on the scooter to choose the suite. I thought, instead of a brash-looking young man going to the hotel, a dignified, patrician older man would do the magic and he did and he approved the choice.

P. A. Kirubakaran.
(Husband of Pritha's friend, Griselda.) writing about his memory of Noble Kantayya during his visit to Stafford.
May 29, 2000

It is really satisfying to recollect the memories of my association with Rev. Dr. Kantayya during my college days (1956-1960) when I used to attend Christ church, Palayamkottai. It was he who imbibed in me interest in gospel work and *Carnatic* music. He was very caring toward us and our Grandfather Mr. G. S Gnaniah, who assisted in the Christ church service. I remember how Rev. Kantayya went with me and other youth members into the cemetery in front of Christ church compound, cleared the place, and unearthed the glory of Clarinda church in 1956. We did gospel work among the lepers in Manakavalampillai Nagar near Samanathapuram.

Miss Peel, England
Former missionary and a lecturer in English at Sarah Tucker College, Palayamkottai, India

I was very interested that your father was Rev Dr. Kantayya, whom I admired greatly, knew very well, as he often preached at the English church, Palayamkottai, which I attended.

Photos of Kantayya Children's Families

Sam Nirmal Kantayya's family.
From left to right
Floor: Nithya, Cadence, Isaac, Joelle, Sanjana
Chairs: Vanu, Carol Vidya, Acacia, Pansy, Rekha, Jacob
Standing: Vivek, Jeff, Samuel Nirmal, Vineet

Alina

Mary Suvarna Victor's family
Seated: Priya, Victor Durairaj, Suvarna, Vanitha
Standing first row: Ramya, Karen, Shiny, Davina, Joshua
Standing second row: Danny, Kenneth, Mithran, Nimal

Shanth Victor's family
Debbie, Shanth, Anita, Caleb

Jayasurya Kantayya

Jayasurya Kantayya with Tippu III

Esther Kamali Prabhakar's family
First row: Rohan, Ernie, Sandhya, Anjali
Second row: Larry, Esther, Nicholas, John, Hannah, Lorra,
Lily, Sophie

Monica Pritha Srinivasan's family
Seated: Shalini, Naomi, Pritha, William, Ashok
Standing: Nikhita, Seema, Reuben, Dharmu

Elizabeth Lavanya Edward's family
Divyan, Dayalan, Amy, Haddasah, Vasanth, Lavanya,
Christine, Roja, Susan

Noble Kantayya's Life: Timeline

G. Noble Kantayya (1905-1981)

1905-06 Birth and infancy in Madras.

1907-10 Vijayawada—Brother Anand Rao was born.

1911-24 Masulipatinam—Elementary School/High school Noble College.

1924-26 Madras Christian College, Madras.

1926-31 Madras Medical College, Madras.

1932 House surgeoncy, Vishakapatinam;

Formal engagement to Mary Samuel at Eluru and wedding in Madras.

1933 Settling in Palayamkottai, birth of Samuel Nirmalkumar, starting of the Kantayya clinic and the passing away of Noble's father, Rev. G. Kantayya.

1935 Passing away of Noble's mother Mary Doraichi Kantayya and the birth of Mary Suvarnakumari.

1937 Installation of the first X-ray machine in the district/county.

1938 Passing away of Father-in-law Samuel. Birth of David Jayasurya.

1941 Birth of Esther Kamalakumari.

1943 Birth of Monica Prithakumari.

1946 Birth of Elizabeth Lavanyakumari.

1953 Clinic building gets a face-lift.

1954 EKG service offered (first in town).

Ordination as Deacon—Honorary Minister of Church of South India and First Indian Presbyter of Christ Church, Palayamkottai.

1955 Ordination as Priest.

1955-81 He continued to serve as physician and priest.

1981 He was promoted to Glory on July 26.

Noble the teenager:
Be true to Yourself.
July 13, 1924.

Priestly Heritage

Mother's Side:

Noble's mother Mary's grandfather was Rev. John Cornelius, first pastor of East Gate Church, Madurai, founded by the American Mission in 1842.

Father's Side:

Rev. G. Kantayya (1869-1933): Noble's father. He was ordained in 1911. He served as CMS School teacher and headmaster, tutor in Divinity School, assistant missionary and deanery chairman for the Eluru and Masulipatinam districts till 1933.

Rev. G. Krishnayya (1838-1916): Noble's paternal grandfather. Hindu Brahmin Convert from the "Ganugapati" family of Kolavenu, near Vijayawada. He was baptized in 1855 by his teacher and missionary Rev. R. T. Noble. He married Rev. W. T. Satthianathan's daughter in 1866. Joanna who died in 1869, three months after son Kantayya was born. Krishnayya was ordained in 1871. He translated many Christian books from English and Tamil to Telugu, including the sermons of Sadhu Sundar Singh. In recognition of his literary work, he was appointed as the literary secretary of the Dornakal Diocese. He served CMS for forty-two years mostly in Eluru as school headmaster and pastor of the Church. Both the CMS School in Eluru and the Noble College were closed on the day of his death.

Rev. W. T. Satthianathan (1830-1892): Father of Joanna Krishnayya, Noble's grandmother. At a young age of seventeen,

WTS, known as Thiruvengadam, accepted Christ as his Savior and was baptized in 1847. He married Rev. John Devasagayam's only daughter Anna in 1849. He was ordained in 1859 and brought Zion Church, Madras, to great heights as its pastor from 1862. He was presented to Queen Victoria in 1877 as a candidate for episcopacy but that did not go through. He served Zion Church for fifteen more years before passing away suddenly in Palayamkottai in 1892. His grave and tomb stone are in Christ Church, Palayamkottai, where Noble served as a Presbyter at a later date.

Rev. John Devasagayam (1785-1864): Father of Noble's great grandmother Anna Satthianathan. He left Tranquebar Lutheran Mission and joined CMS in 1810 and was ordained deacon in Madras in 1830 by Bishop Turner of Calcutta and priest in Palayamkottai by Rt. Rev. Corrie, first Bishop of Madras. He married Muthammal, granddaughter of Rev. Aaron of Tranquebar. Devasagayam did pioneering work in several towns including Palayamkottai. He died in 1864, and his last words were "Be diligent in serving God for that alone is happiness."

Rev. Aaron of Tranquebar (1698-1745): Grandfather of Muthammal Devasagayam. Arumugam of Cuddalore upon accepting Christ as Savior was baptized as Aaron in Tranquebar in 1718 by the pioneer Danish Lutheran Missionary Ziegenbalg. He was ordained in 1733 as the first Asian Pastor. He toiled hard doing God's work and died at age forty-seven. His last words were "Jesus! Jesus! My Lord, My Lord, My Savior!"

Priestly tradition continues.
Rev. Dr. Vasanth Edward, Noble Kantayya's son-in-law, Lavanya's husband.
Rev. Dr. Jeff Hubing, Nirmal's son-in-law, Carol Vidya's husband.
Rev. Paul Divyan, Lavanya's eldest son.
Rev. John Dayalan, Lavanya's second son.

Acknowledgments

Thanks be to God who blessed me with *Appa*.

Words cannot express my thanks to my amazing husband John for his countless hours of scanning photos, editing texts, and providing input toward publishing this book. This devotional will not be a reality without his ardent support and tireless assistance. Our sons Larry and Ernie also gave much insight and critique.

Many thanks to my beloved siblings Nirmal, Suvarna, Pritha, and Pappa and their spouses for their contributions of writing and photos. I owe a lot to my brother Nirmal for writing the foreword and all the background, genealogy, and timeline about the family.

A great debt of thanks goes to my niece Rebecca Chellappa who brought these eighty-eight years old writings to the computer age by patiently transcribing from the original manuscript. My talented grandniece Debbie Victor designed graphic design of the vine and branches. I appreciate sharing her talents so freely. I appreciate Dave Welle for taking time to proofread in the midst of his busy schedule.

It was wonderful to receive memories of my father from my cousins, nephews, and nieces from all over the world. They obliged me at short notice. I would like to thank my network of family and friends who supported me in various ways in this venture. Thanks everyone.

Thank you Xlibris publishers. Together we did it!

Glossary of Tamil Words and Abbreviations

Achi—Grandmother

Amma—Mother, Mommy

Appa—Father, Daddy

BA—Bachelor of Arts Degree

BT—Bachelor of Teaching Degree

Carnatic Music—South Indian music based on the minor scale

Cheppu—Wooden toy set of kitchen utensils, pots and pans

CMS—Church Missionary Society of England

CSI—Church of South India

Ganugapati—The name of the Brahmin sect from which his grandfather Rev. Krishnayya came. All his descendents use that as their first initial.

ICC Lodge—Indian Church Council Lodge

Jeba Arai—Prayer room.

Laddu—Indian sweet made of gram flour, ghee, and sugar

Lala Kadai—Famous sweet meet store in Palayamkottai

LT—License in teaching degree.

Madras—Capital city of former Madras Presidency (State), now called Chennai and the state is called Tamilnadu.

Mama—Uncle

MCC—Madras Christian College

MMC—Madras Medical College

Periamma—Mother's older sister; Periappa's wife

Periappa—Father's older brother; Periamma's husband

Shanti Alaya—Temple of peace

STC—Sarah Tucker College, Palayamkottai

Thatha—Grandfather

Chennai, Palayamkottai are cities in the state of Tamilnadu.
Ellore or Elluru, Masulipatnam, Vishakapatinam, are cities in the state of Andhra Pradesh.

Edwards Brothers, Inc.
Thorofare, NJ USA
March 29, 2012